Confessions of a Jewish Wagnerite

Being Gay and Jewish in America

Lawrence D. Mass

Foreword by Dr Gottfried Wagner

CASSELL

Cassell
Villiers House
41/47 Strand
London WC2N 5JE

387 Park Avenue South
New York, NY 10016–8810

First published 1994

British Library Cataloguing-in-Publication Data
A catalogue record for this book is available from the British
Library.

Library of Congress CIP Data available.

ISBN 0–304–33110–4 (hardback)
      0–304–33114–7 (paperback)

Typeset by Fakenham Photosetting Ltd, Fakenham, Norfolk
Printed in Great Britain by Redwood Books', Trowbridge, Wiltshire

Contents

for Arnie Kantrowitz
for my families
— past, present and future

Acknowledgements

THERE are three individuals who were crucial to the development of this book: Thomas E. Steele, the incomparably wise, witty and glamorous editor of *Christopher Street* and *Opera Monthly*, who nurtured this writing from its inception; Larry Kramer, the searing critic and Olympian hero of the AIDS epidemic, who likewise encouraged *Confessions* from its earliest stages, and who taught an entire generation of writers what it can mean to believe in your own work when others don't; and Arnie Kantrowitz, the writer and activist, whose life has been my principal inspiration, and whose humanity and integrity are monuments to communities everywhere.

I wish to express special thanks to my agent Norman Laurila and my publisher Steve Cook, and I am very grateful to Paul Asman for his painstaking editorial advice on the manuscript. I also want to acknowledge the following people for their assistance, information, support or example: David Alexander, David Bergman, Jay Blotcher, Gregg Bordowitz, Chris Bram, Perry Brass, Philip Brett, Michael Bronski, Jack Bulmash, Victor Bumbalo, Dick Bungay, Lindsley Cameron, John Casarino, Robert Caserio, Robert Chesley, Catherine Clément, Douglas Crimp, John De Cecco, Peter G. Davis, Joe De Cola, Nick Deutsch, Lucile Duberman, Martin Duberman, Tom Duane, Richard Dyer, John Elia, Michael Gans, Bruce-Michael Gelbert, Melvin Gilbert, Adrienne and Roger Gilde, Sander L. Gilman, Frances Goldin, Richard Goldstein, Eric A. Gordon, Vivian Gornick, Stephen Greco, Larry Gross, Robert W. Gutman, William M. Hoffman, Joseph Horowitz, Richard Howard, Chester Jakala, Jamie James, Brandon Judell, Angus Killick, David Kirby, Seymour Kleinberg, Wayne Koestenbaum, Nancy Krems-

dorf, George Leigh, Brendan Lemon, Norman J. Levy, Herb and
Heather Liebman, Alex Lockwood, Michael Lutin, Jaime Man-
rique, Ellen Mass, Steve Mass, Daniel Margalioth, Jed Mattes,
Susan McClary, James McCourt, Donna Minkowitz, Helen
Mitsios, Richard Mohr, Joel Moses, Jon David Nalley, Richard
Nathan, Erick Neher, Jim Oleson, Marcia Pally, Pam Parker, Scott
Parris, Felice Picano, Richard Plant, Gabriel Rotello, Ibrahim
Quraishi, Nick Rango, Campion Read, Cynthia Robbins, John
Rockwell, Ned Rorem, Alex Ross, Edward Rothstein, Steve Rubin,
Vito Russo, Douglas Sadownik, James Saslow, Sarah Schulman, K.
Robert Schwarz, Eve Kosofsky Sedgwick, Ellie Segal, Laura Segal,
Michael Shapiro, Michael Shernoff, Michelangelo Signorile, Ed
Sikov, Alisa Solomon, Susan Sontag, Judith Stelboum, Martha
Stevens, Richard Taruskin, Mark Thompson, Bill and Masha
Thorpe, Jonathan Tolins, Rosa von Praunheim, Gottfried Wagner,
Joyce Wallace, Maxine Wolfe, Elizabeth Wood, Ralph Wynn, Eli
Zal and my friends in the rooms.

Earlier versions or excerpts of several chapters appeared in
Christopher Street, as follows: parts of Chapters 2 (issue 119,
1988), 3 (issue 108, 1987), 4 (issue 98, 1985) and 6 (issue 85,
1984).

Confessions about Confessions

WHEN I tell people I've written a book called *Confessions of a Jewish Wagnerite: Being Gay and Jewish in America*, the question I'm most often asked is, 'What does gay have to do with it?' People of all backgrounds and interests understand that being Jewish and 'into Wagner' can involve conflict. (For those who may not know, Richard Wagner, universally revered as among the very greatest of composers, was profoundly anti-Semitic. In fact, he was the only spiritual father acknowledged by Adolf Hitler.) But what does any of that have to do with homosexuality? More specifically, what would homosexuality have to do with facilitating the oxymoronic phenomenon of Jewish Wagnerism?

'Nothing *per se*', I've always answered. 'These are highly personal memoirs of minority identity and experience. They tell of my life, not everyone's.' But I have pondered whether a connection between gay culture and Wagnerism exists on a scale broad enough to generalize about. The question then becomes, to what extent has contemporary thinking about Wagner been shaped by gay sensibilities and subcultures? This line of inquiry is vague, deceptive, dangerous, extremely challenging, and probably unprecedented, but not, I think, inappropriate. Although it is not articulated as such in the text, the question of this relationship is there, as a *leitmotif*, throughout. Ultimately, I now believe, it is one of the questions *Confessions* most wants to ask.

The conclusion I've come to is that the sensibility that has muted discussion of the Wagner problem is the same as that which has muted discussion of the significance of homosexuality in music. The influential gay quarter of the music world that was at first forced to live in the closet but which remained there, passively, well into the era of liberation has held to the separation of art from questions of politics, morality and ethics with a tenacity that bears scrutiny. As I see it, the popular attitude toward Wagner is a logical extension of this purview. Thus the composers, musicians and music critics, no small number of them closeted homosexuals, who believed that Benjamin Britten's homosexuality was of no abiding interest or pertinence are often enough the same arbiters of culture who have been indifferent to Wagner's anti-Semitism.

Conversely, Jewish musicians, composers and critics who are in varying degrees ethnically closeted have taken much comfort from this purview, in which Wagner's anti-Semitism – and their own Jewishness – need only be addressed perfunctorily, if at all. This is not to say that closeted gays set the stage for closetedness among Jews. On the contrary, something like the opposite is a more plausible scenario, at least in the music world, with Wagner himself as the bottom-line culprit: because of his gargantuan importance in music and the extreme anti-Semitism he propounded, most notoriously in his essay 'Jewry in Music', Jewish musicians, composers and critics have been consequently, subsequently and generically reluctant to call attention to themselves as Jews or their work as Jewish.

So the scheme of Jewish and gay closetedness goes something like this: Wagner – because of his unassailability as one of the greatest composers – causes or profoundly aggravates internalized anti-Semitism and Jewish closetedness, which in turn contributes enormously to a purview in which questions of art are rigidly separated from those of politics, ethics and morality, a purview that is embraced by closeted homosexuals in music, as well as other arts. In this unwritten code, Britten's homosexuality can't be used against the composer or for him, just as a critic's own homosexuality can't be used against or for him – i.e., a homophobe can't say that a certain critic is partial to Britten because that critic is homosexual, and a queer activist can't say that a homosexual critic is minimizing the significance of Britten's homosexuality because that critic is a closet case. Likewise, Wagner's anti-Semitism can't be used against the composer or for him, just as the critic's Judaism can't be used against the critic – i.e., an anti-Semite can't say that a

certain critic is against Wagner because that critic is Jewish, and a
Jewish zealot can't say that the critic is for Wagner because s/he is
an internalized anti-Semite. So instead of articulating what people
are all too often really thinking and feeling, the discourse is about
universals that will, it is believed, apply broadly over time – e.g., the
Ring cycle and *Die Meistersinger* aren't about Aryans and Jews,
just as *Peter Grimes, Billy Budd* and *Death in Venice* aren't about
homosexuality; they're about character and humanity, reason and
passion, instinct and intellect, youth and maturity, the individual
and society, and power – personal, social and artistic.

The quintessential reticence of these aesthetics, I'm convinced, has had a huge impact on our lives – as gay people, as Jews,
as minorities, as critics – on the legions among us who are still in
various closets. But it is an opinion that is better appreciated – and,
more important, *felt* – in the context of personal experience than in
the dryness of academic discourse. As the saying goes, the personal
is political, which is another way of saying that the individual is
universal. Whether you agree will be a measure first, of the capacity
of these stories to communicate, but ultimately, of the truth of that
saying.

Lawrence D. Mass
New York City, 1994

Foreword

Redemption from Wagner the redeemer: some
introductory thoughts on Wagner's anti-semitism

THE discovery of his own complex identity happened in a
most dramatic way for Lawrence Mass. The physician, gay activist
and pioneering writer on AIDS was confronted, through the spread
of the epidemic, not only with his identity as a gay man but also
with his own internalized anti-Semitism. Merciless with himself, the
former naive Wagnerite followed up the roots of his anti-Semitism.
In doing so, he underwent, as he explains: 'a metamorphosis from
an unconscious masochism to becoming easily suspicious and never
confident of my impressions in a society that was consistently telling me I was either wrong or overreacting, i.e., paranoid'. The
metamorphosis he was undergoing had evolved from his adoration
of one of the gods of his youth, Richard Wagner, five different
portraits of whom adorned the walls of Dr Mass's apartment until
an anti-Semitic incident, coinciding with his preparation of the first
reports of the AIDS epidemic, launched what became an odyssey of
self-analysis and discovery. The result is an extraordinary docu-
ment of social history: a description of his personal and cultural
experiences as a homosexual, as well as a critical discussion of
contemporary academic discourse on Wagner and anti-Semitism,
all in the context of his new-found awareness of anti-Semitism – his
own as he had internalized it and society's as that internalization
reflected it.

How deeply the author was influenced by the cultural–
political phenomenon of Wagner and his dangerous anti-Semitic
ideology the reader will recognize by reflecting on Dr Mass's complex observation:

In earlier times I'd been the stereotypic, unconsciously anti-Semitic Jewish Wagnerite. I now see how that worked. Worshipping at the shrine of your enemy, however objectively great and gifted that person may be, is otherwise known as masochism. It's a simple, common defense mechanism: if I, the Jew, am anti-Semitic, the real anti-Semite is less likely to feel the need to express his anti-Semitism towards me. My anti-Semitism defuses his. So if I, the Jewish Wagnerite, effusively proclaim my love for Wagner, notwithstanding or in spite of (excusing) the composer's anti-Semitism, the non-Jewish Wagnerite is less likely to feel the need to express any anti-Semitism towards me. Unfortunately, this tactic hasn't worked well, at least not in the case of the two most famous Wagnerites in history: Richard Wagner and Adolf Hitler.

This confession derives from a profound interdisciplinary knowledge and represents a particularly responsible handling of Wagner's anti-Semitism after the Holocaust. For me, this subject includes fundamental questions about repression – 'not talking about it' – and the falsification of real connections between culture and politics inside and outside Germany, where Wagner had a decisive and inglorious role. The writing of 'Judaism in Music' in 1850 saw the beginning of Wagner's anti-Semitism as a cultural and political concept, a process that included the later creation of the Bayreuth Festival as an anti-Semitic cultural meeting-ground in 1876. Wagner repeated the original hypothesis of 'Judaism in Music', nearly unchanged, in his major essay on art, 'Opera as Drama' in 1851. Though he subsequently changed some parts of his revolutionary theory to adapt it to the taste of his aristocratic and bourgeois sponsors, Wagner continued to develop his anti-Semitism in his writings: from 'What Is German?' (1856/78), 'On the State of Religion' (1867), and 'German Art and Politics' (1867), to his last 'Writings of Regeneration' between 1879 and 1881. In his final pieces, e.g., 'Recognize Yourself', Wagner discussed ideas which today read as a horrifying prelude to Hitler's final solution. Here, he wrote on the future Germany, free of Jews, something he considered as the 'great solution' in the spirit of aggressive anti-Semites like E. Dühring and Berhnard Förster:

> This great solution could only be possible for us Germans as soon as we overcome the most intimate shame of our existence on order to 'Recognize Yourself'. This movement could not be conceived by any other nation. By penetrating into our deepest level and overcoming all our false shame, we will have reached a vision of our presentiment.

Any evaluation of Wagner's anti-Semitism cannot be done through a partial use of his anti-Semitic or his opportunistic pro-Semitic statements. One has to confront the issue and its effects up to the present day as a totality that speaks for itself. In doing so, I feel obliged as a Wagner, born in Bayreuth after the Holocaust, to answer my own painful questions as to what extent Wagner himself was co-responsible for the development of anti-Semitism in the nineteenth and twentieth centuries within and outside Germany. The answer is: to a great degree.

In dealing with Wagner's anti-Semitism after his death in 1883, we find two tendencies that mark two distinct periods. First, from 1883 to 1945, we see his anti-Semitism transformed into a pseudo-scientific theory. Then, after World War II, it was repressed to the point of becoming insignificant alongside the view of Wagner as a musical theater genius whose works themselves do not show any explicit anti-Semitism. Actually, Wagner's anti-Semitism in the New Bayreuth Era often served the Festival marketing strategy when it was carefully shifted into a pseudo pro-Semitism. The most scandalous examples of tolerated falsification were the exhibition 'Wagner and the Jews' in the Villa Wahnfried in 1985 and the speech of Walter Jens, one of Germany's leading intellectuals of the left and a flattered Festival Hill guest, during the celebrations this year (1994) of the 800th anniversary of the city of Bayreuth. How efficient the international Bayreuth connections have been in suppressing a democratic discussion of the issue became evident for me in an article published in the *New York Times* of 15 August 1993. I was denounced for promoting a simplistic perspective of Wagner's anti-Semitism. I responded by sending the *Times* my program of five points for a possible humanization of the Bayreuth Festival. In essence, they are as follows:

1. presentations by independent scholars on the impact of the ideological content of Wagner's works within and outside Germany;
2. the institution of a democratic–pluralistic dramaturgy and independent media service;
3. an immediate halt to the sterile Wagner monopoly dedicated to a commercial Wagner market, and the integration into the Festival's programme of all of Wagner's works (including those before *The Flying Dutchman* as well as his chamber music and symphonies) alongside the works of artists who influenced him;
4. the integration of contemporary art and music theater in accordance with Wagner's original artistic intentions;
5. the independence of the Festival from major talent agencies and its transformation into a modern enterprise using all media in a creative way.

My proposal was not published. In the bigger picture, the reasons have ultimately to do with Festival Hill's inability to mourn the past and the Wagner market's connections within and outside Germany, a predicament that pushes inquisitive and critical individuals like Dr Mass into positions of social isolation where they feel, and are indeed labeled as, 'paranoid'. Seeing the sterile, anti-creative Wagner cult and its evasion of any special responsibility to foster an international climate of political tolerance after the Holocaust, as worldwide nationalism, racism, religious and ideological fanaticism spread alongside ecological disasters (the Gulf War, the former Yugoslavia, Somalia, etc.) and AIDS, I have to ask: who here is paranoid? The frightening vision of old and new scapegoats, which includes all minorities and nonconformists, is becoming a daily reality. Lawrence Mass's book presents a vast panorama for a discussion of intolerance, from the viewpoints of being gay and Jewish and in connection with the Wagner case. He makes the independent reader think about the future responsibility of our decadent, occidental, cultural scenario in which Wagner and his dark sides still play their unconsciously dominant role. The question for me today is: In a multiracial, multicultural, global society, based on a belief in tolerant diversity, has Wagner any future? Seeing the reality of the Wagner cult shrine of today, abused by the self-portrayals of *parvenus*, mostly commercial calculation and sold as a worldwide cultural model, I hope not!

Dr Gottfried Wagner
Cerro Maggiore, Italy
April 1994

Gottfried H. Wagner was born in 1947 in Bayreuth. He studied musicology, philosophy, and German philology in Germany and Austria, and received his PhD from the University of Vienna for his study of Kurt Weill and Bertold Brecht. He works internationally as a multi-media director, musicologist and writer and since 1988 has been a member of the Pen Club of Liechtenstein. He has received awards for his artistic and academic activities as well as for his humanitarian involvement. In 1992 he co-founded with Dr Abraham Peck the PostHolocaust Dialogue Group. Since 1983 he has lived in Italy.

Chapter one

The Epidemic and the Volcanoes

BENJAMIN Goodman was a Jewish war baby who was believed by many, especially himself but including me, to be endowed with priestly powers. At forty-one, he was still a child of the 1960s. At a height of scarcely five feet, despite his devastating smile and virile black forests of body hair, he even looked like ... a young Buddha; like a 'petit lutin', as he was affectionately called during the postgraduate year he spent in France doing such things as street-vending oysters and managing a prestigious international art galley. Benjamin, the human chameleon.

Benjamin, the godfather. Benjie, which he loved to be called by those he loved, was godfather to the son of a theater director who wrote a very strange play about the assassination of a European monarch. When the play flopped, the biological father walked out on his infant son to whore it up and peddle his wares in Europe. For the next eleven years Benjie lived the role the boy's biological father had no interest in even trying to play.

Like all gay people, Benjie had to endure a lot of shit, but he was also quite capable of standing up for himself. Commenting on the biological father's homophobic indifference to all that he'd done for the boy over so many years, Benjie calmly observed that he knew a number of the girls Casanova had fucked. 'They all said the same thing. He'd bang furiously for exactly three minutes, whisper "you bitch", and pop.'

Benjie never told Jonathan, the godson, about his homosexuality or his love affair with me until I insisted on it, at which point Jonathan, then in his teens and getting much closer to biological Pop and a new stepfather, suddenly decided to sever all communications with Benjie. 'He's uncomfortable with your homosexuality', said his mother.

'But I raised him as if he were my own son', Benjie wept. 'It's not right. Don't I even get to say goodbye?'

'Well ... uh ... we felt we shouldn't mix in', she explained with a coldness Benjie had never recognized in her before. 'Jonathan has to work these things out for himself.'

Benjie had worshiped at the altar of science fiction. While he may not have been a card-carrying Trekkie, I think he had memorized every line of every episode of *Star Trek*, reruns of which we often watched together in each other's arms. Benjie saw *Close Encounters* three times and *E.T.* twice, as did I. Benjie felt both movies are about the fear and acceptance of death. The way Benjie saw it, the Richard Dreyfus character experiences complete self-surrender in pursuit of his extraterrestrial destiny.

'I'm not afraid to die', Benjie said as the news, 'Live at Five', flashed scenes of an exploding volcano in Central America, the snaps of a cap pistol alongside the cataclysmic blasts of Mount Saint Helens the week before.

'But who', I asked, 'is the Dreyfus character supposed to represent? Is he supposed to be Spielberg? America? Everyman?'

The news returned to the Middle East. 'I'm not sure. Certainly Spielberg's movies are about himself. And children. But they're also about ... Jews. Did you know there's a book that claims Jews are extraterrestrials?'

I laughed. 'What kind of book?'

'I don't remember. Something about how we have special empathic powers and special intelligence.'

'Wait. Are you talking about that anthology of science fiction by Jewish writers? Oh, what's it called? It's from the mid-1960s and has stories by people like Isaac Bashevis Singer, Bernard Malamud, Harlan Ellison and Isaac Asimov.'

'*Wandering Stars*.'

'That's it.' I recalled the cartoon figure of a sixteen-eyed, twelve-legged, antennaed extraterrestrial that is the book's last page and only illustration. The somehow lovable-looking creature is only a few feet tall, has two big hooked noses above a sweet smile and is wearing a little black skull cap and prayer shawl. My thoughts wandered to another of these books, *Diaspora*, a Jewish science fiction novel by W. R. Yates. Its premise is that the Jews head for the stars in a space ship after being bombed out of the Middle East. As usual, I was so into my own thoughts that I didn't even notice Benjie leave the room. No wonder he was always teasing me: 'Earth calling Larry.'

Benjie was big on the vague, mystical, pantheistic, decidedly unscientific connecting principle we were calling synchronicity. Neither of us could remember exactly where, when or why we had begun using this word. Benjie thought he had first heard it years ago and I had first become aware of it in a dream, having perhaps come across it on the radio or in something I'd read during the preceding twenty-four hours. But the really weird thing is that we were using it for months before we even knew what it meant, and we had a hell of a time trying to track it down. It wasn't in any of the ten or fifteen dictionaries we checked, and none of our friends knew anything about it, not even Benjie's friends. There was an album by The Police entitled *Synchronicity*, but the record album and songs themselves ('Synchronicity' 1 and 2) did not in any way define or clarify the term.

Basking in the twinkling of his eyes, I asked Benjie if he thought there could be a relationship between the epidemic and the volcanoes. Benjie, who lamented that my faith in him did not extend to astrology, beamed and then winked. 'I don't know, but I'll bet there's a relationship between the epidemic and Uranus.'

The news flashed scenes of a catastrophic 'flood of the century' in New Hampshire, not far from Witchburn, where Benjie had attended Christ College; where he received growth hormone injections during adolescence – like the writer, gay activist and my life-partner Arnie Kantrowitz and many other short-statured Jewish boys of their generation – in desperate, failed efforts to make him bigger and taller; where he began writing novels with titles like *The Vinyl Solution* and *Six Million and One*; where the Jewish Community Center refused to include or acknowledge homosexuals in its plans for a Holocaust memorial; where serious anti-Semitic incidents had sharply increased in recent months; and where Benjie's old Jewish mother was dying from emphysema, heart disease and who knows what kind of spiritual exhaustion.

I looked at Benjie. Sitting upright on his bed, next to the upright seated Buddha on his night table, which I adorned with prayer beads before giving it to him (how he loved it!) that Christmas, Benjie appeared to be superimposed upon the gigantic wooden crucifix he kept on the otherwise bare white wall behind the bed. 'With all this flooding, I guess there won't be any trains to Witchburn this weekend', Benjie said to Flux, Flo (Florence) and (Santa) Claws, his dogs and cat. 'There's no point in even trying to go home now.'

The Florida Orange Juice commercial on the prime time news was the same for nearly a year. 'Orange you smart' was spelled out during the brief, often repeated spot. But as my cannabis paranoia was the first to observe, what you actually heard was the more phonetical and very sarcastic 'Aren' Jews smart?!' Later, the commercial changed to a jazzy ditty whose only words were frequently repeated during the short, prime time spot: 'Turn on the [Jews]!'

The news switched to astronomy, and Benjie wanted to know if we were experiencing a supernova 'like the one Carl Sagan talked about on *Cosmos*'. There is pain and humiliation in his voice, because he knew how much I admired the *Cosmos* series, in a central episode of which astrology is trashed.

'No', I whispered tenderly as I took him in my arms. 'But I think they said it's the biggest solar flare ever recorded.'

The news continued. The Elvis Presley mansion, Graceland, had begun welcoming (paying) visitors. Memphis, I thought to myself, is part of the southern heartland I was born and raised in. I tried to cheer Benjie (and me) up. 'Aren't you just dying to visit Graceland?'

On the kitchen table, where everything seems to end up, I discovered something Benjie had handwritten with his characteristically outsized, childlike script. Some of its special innocence and dignity are herein sacrificed to the typewriter.

5: The Epidemic and the Volcanoes

Here we are in the garden of Eden.
Luscious gorgeous fruit hangs from every branch.
We are told some of the fruit is probably poisonous.
Question: Is our compulsion to eat the fruit greater than
  our desire to live?

Benjie, who was monogamous when he was with me, used to love the baths. Who didn't? Now, in 1984, even Benjie has stopped going. 'The last time I was there', he said, 'there was nothing but a couple of old skeletons rattling around in the halls.'

I was recently trying to explain to a friend, a lesbian physician who became prominent in the AIDS community, why Benjie and I had broken up. Like so many people, she had felt an instantaneous bond with Benjie the one time she met him. 'Medicine and astrology just weren't mixing', I sighed. 'I believe in Benjie but I don't believe in astrology.' Then I asked her if she could characterize just what it was about Benjie she liked so much.

'We had a lot in common', she said with a cryptic smile. 'We both read charts.'

'What do you mean?' I asked.

'As a physician, I read medical charts, but I also read astrological charts. Didn't Benjie ever read your chart?'

'No', I admitted, realizing at that moment that I was never able to have that kind of suspension of disbelief and open-minded, light-hearted fun with astrology. Feeling ashamed and ridiculous, I asked what her sign was.

'Gemini.'

'Gemini!' I giggled. Our conversation was taking place at a health conference that was just about to start. It was a measure of how drastically AIDS had changed everything that the conference, which overviewed changing patterns of sexually transmitted diseases in the US, included no talks on syphilis or gonorrhea.

'I'm a Gemini too', I confided during a coffee break. 'Let me tell you what Benjie had to say about Geminis. One day we were having one of our increasingly frequent arguments about astrology with me saying the usual things about how because it's not science it can't be taken seriously and Benjie retaliating by pointing out that a true scientist wouldn't condemn something he knew so little about. Our discussion was interrupted by a call from one of Benjie's clients, a pregnant woman whose baby was going to be born a Gemini. When the call was finished, Benjie pretended they were still speaking. For my benefit, his tongue-in-cheek advice to her was 'Get an Abortion!' Benjie, the magical childe.

Alone with my chaotic kitchen table, where I did most of my pre-word-processor writing, my thoughts wandered to the two-headed snake in the movie, *Resurrection*, with Ellen Burstyn. The snake's name was Gemini and the movie was Benjie's special favorite, even more than *Close Encounters* and *E.T.*, and even more than *Star Trek*. It was the summer of 1984 and I finally bit into the overripe plum I'd been holding, simultaneously anticipating its sweetness and dreading the sticky mess I knew it would make. Burstingly sweet, it reminded me of Benjie ... the sweetest I had ever known ...

Chapter two

Wicked Love

ON a beautiful day early in the spring of 1987, there was a message on the answering machine from Damien Martin. Damien and his lover, Emery Hetrick, who had recently died of AIDS, had been close friends of mine for nine years. I met Damien while I was newsletter editor of the fledgling Gay Caucus of the American Psychiatric Association (a name the nervous APA hierarchy instantly made us change to the Gay Caucus of Members of the APA. Later, it became the Association of Gay and Lesbian Psychiatrists). I wasn't a psychiatrist, but I had made it my business to become expert on the subject of homosexuality and psychiatry. As a medical student, intern, resident in anesthesiology and later, as an openly gay applicant for a residency in psychiatry, I had witnessed and personally endured a vast spectrum of homophobic insults, petty victimizations and worse by psychiatrists, even after the APA officially declassified homosexuality as a mental disorder in 1973–4.

The invitation to edit the GCMAPA Newsletter came from my penultimate psychiatrist, Dr Richard Pillard. I was living in Boston and completing my residency in anesthesiology at the legendary MGH (Massachusetts General Hospital). At Sporters, the sleazy, consistently popular gay bar whose windows cruised the entrance to the hospital from across the street, the many staff members who were Happy Hour regulars would compare stories about homophobia and covert homosexuality at 'The Massive Genital' and 'Most Greatest Hospital', as they would refer to it in their only discernible efforts at retaliation. Considering how seldom things change in Boston, I'll bet they still do.

From 1974 to 1976, while my life partner, Arnie Kantrowitz (whom I then had never heard of), was completing his autobiography, *Under the Rainbow: Growing Up Gay*, I was in therapy with a middle-aged, chronically depressed Harvard shrink who fell asleep during sessions. When awake, he responded to my efforts to have a sense of humor, the mainstay of gay defenses, about my painful memories of childhood cross-dressing, with such witticisms as 'I've heard all fourteen homosexual jokes.' During this unhappy time I had the good fortune to be watching television one evening, something I could rarely do in those days of 36-hour shifts at the hospital. Typically, I was nursing my 'one drink' (which even then must have been a triple gin and tonic) and was alone. The phone was disconnected, and the TV was on in the background. Just as typically, it didn't matter what the program was. The noise was all that seemed to count.

Ice and isolation. That's the way I was liking it more and more on my nights off. Suddenly my radar captured 'homosexuality' from a blur of voices. In those days – not so long ago – for a gay person to hear or see that word in the mass media, in any public context, was something very special. Notwithstanding the Stonewall Rebellion in 1969 and the APA declassification in 1974, we were still so invisible that anything acknowledging our existence, even negatively, was welcomed as affirmation. I gazed up from my one drink and began to watch the program, which was nothing less than a panel discussion entirely devoted to homosexuality! Even more startling was that, right before my eyes, sat this handsome, compassionate, intelligent knight in a white suit, who – was I hearing right? – was both a distinguished Boston psychiatrist *and* openly gay.

The next day I had suddenly found the courage to tell the frumpy Harvard shrink exactly what I thought of him. In a calm voice, I explained that in contrast to his inattentiveness, I had been carefully listening to almost everything he had said to me during the preceding three months, that I had concluded that he was prejudiced and ignorant about homosexuality, that I had decided henceforth to terminate our therapy and that I was considering litigation. He needn't have worried. A quarter century later, psychiatrists still aren't being taken to court for this kind of malpractice.

I had begun my career as a gay activist. That same day I began therapy with Dr Pillard who was, in fact, the first openly gay psychiatrist in the United States. Today, he is world-renowned for his work on familial patterns of homosexuality. Richard introduced me to the small handful of other pioneering, openly gay and lesbian psychiatrists, with whom, as GCMAPA Newsletter editor, I worked closely over the next several years: Damien and Emery, Nanette Gartrell, Stu Nichols, Jim Paulsen, Frank Rundle, David Kessler (whom I already knew), Jim Krajeski, Jean Munzer, Bert Schaffner and others. Like me, Damien wasn't a psychiatrist, but he had done landmark work in defining lesbians and gay men as a legitimate minority. Emery was co-founder and secretary of the group. Emery and Damien – or 'Emerald and Diamond', as Stash, a moderately homophobic ex-lover (the subject of a later chapter of these memoirs) who had no real sense of their achievements and who could never remember their names, unwittingly referred to them – are best known to the gay community as co-founders of the Institute for the Protection of Lesbian and Gay Youth (which is now the Hetrick-Martin Institute) and to the public at large as co-founders of the historic Harvey Milk High School, the first officially sanctioned, fully accredited alternative school for lesbian and gay students.

On that beautiful spring morning of 1987, Damien had called to ask Arnie and me if we would be willing to speak to a reporter from the *New York Times* about what it was like to grow up gay in America. The next day we both spoke to her, separately and at length. Much of what I had to say involved comparisons between growing up gay and growing up Jewish in a small southern town where being Jewish was as ignominious as being queer, if not worse, and sometimes synonymous with it. She seemed especially interested in my experience of discovering, much later in life (in fact, mostly in the process of writing this book), how deeply I had repressed my Jewish identity, even while coming to grips with being gay, and what a turning point that

experience has been for me, how critical to whatever self-acceptance, maturity and serenity I might now claim.

As the interview progressed, the specifics of what I was
telling her began hitting so close to home that she broke her neutrality and began confiding the details of her own circumstances.
Suddenly, I was interviewing her. She explained that she was
Episcopalian and had been dating a Jewish man whom she was
planning to marry, but her family was very discouraging. They
kept telling her things like, 'There will be problems later on.'
Meanwhile, she had begun to notice that her boyfriend seemed
surprisingly indifferent to their prejudice or, for that matter, to
anything else having to do with Jews or Judaism. He never clearly
– and certainly never affirmatively – identified himself as Jewish
or talked about what that might mean. He never celebrated Jewish holidays or discussed his relatives. In fact, our discussion
prompted her to see that his feelings about being Jewish were
probably deeply repressed in much the same way I had repressed
mine. Further, my explanation of how crucially important it has
been for me to come to terms with my Jewish identity had made
her understand what her family kept telling her, that there would
indeed be problems later on. I said that if her boyfriend continued to avoid dealing with his *feelings* about being Jewish, I'd
have to agree. As it turns out, our lives had even more parallels,
for I, too, had had a love affair with an Episcopalian aristocrat.

Andrew Stockhaus Bullen (the only acknowledged bastard
son of Edward, the never-married, 'notoriously bisexual' English
Earl) was born near Hartford, Connecticut, in 1929. Although he
never actually met the Earl, who died when Andy was nine, Andy
knew instinctively that the legend about his father's sexuality was
true.

One day, when Andy was barely adolescent, his mother
sat him down, hugged and kissed him, and told him frankly, as if
she were talking to a close friend, that there was nothing wrong
with two boys having sex together, as long as there was love.
Unless it was somehow through her own experience, how could a
middle-class, exclusively heterosexual woman, albeit a striking
beauty and an extremely compassionate human being and nurse,

have acquired such an enlightened attitude toward what was considered, in World-War-II America, such an unutterable sin and crime?

Andy eventually learned that his mother, who was fond of saying that men were so wonderful she couldn't understand what they saw in women, had been deeply in love with the Earl, who would never marry her, simply because, as he may even have confessed to her, he preferred the company of his own sex. And who could blame him, she must have thought, projecting her own feelings about men onto him. Even in her final days, when she crawled around on all fours lapping up the sleeping pills she kept spilling on the floor and on which she finally overdosed, she referred to Andy as 'my special love child'.

Not that Martha spent the rest of her life pining for the Earl. Within a year of Andy's birth she married a distinguished local physician, a German–American internist named Dr Schmidt she had met and briefly dated while she was training to be a nurse. He was Catholic, so Andy was baptized and raised as Catholic. In those days, you'd think, the 'illegitimacy' of Martha's pregnancy would have resulted at least in social ostracism, especially by the middle class to which she belonged, and especially in New England, which even today is easily recognizable as the realm of *The Scarlet Letter*. Instead, the widely circulated fact that her pregnancy was of noble blood easily overrode all other considerations and endowed her with the kind of social prominence that never meant as much to her as it did to everybody else.

Andy never met his real father, but the Earl continued to play a pivotal role in his son's development. When Andy was twelve, although he'd had a decent, even loving relationship with Dr Schmidt, arrangements were made for him to live with 'Uncle George', a reverend canon of the American Anglican Church. Uncle George wasn't directly related to Martha, Dr Schmidt, or the Earl, but through him the Earl had assumed a wardship that involved financial support of Andy's education.

Andy never suspected any intimate connections between Uncle George and the Earl. So it may have been merely coincidental that Uncle George was homosexual. In fact, he was a

shameless, often publicly embarrassing old lush who had a preference for boys Andy's age. Uncle George (and later, for that
matter, Andy) was the personification of William S. Burroughs'
naughty observation in *Queer* that 'to come out flat for private
property and a class society, you marked yourself a stupid lout or
suspected to be a High Episcopalian pederast'.

But nothing sexual ever happened between Andy and
Uncle George. That's because Andy, though quite interested in
mature men, wasn't the least bit interested in Uncle George, who
had never been remotely attractive and who was always besotted,
and because Andy was much more forceful than his foster father,
so much more adept at having things go the way he wanted, even
at age twelve. Thus, throughout most of their stormy, lifelong
relationship, their roles were reversed. Andy was the boss, as he
was in every other relationship he ever had. Except that with the
Earl of Bullen.

In spite of his precocious ability to dominate others, Andy
made no effort to fight Uncle George's recommendations about
his education, which culminated in the selection of an Episcopal
seminary in San Francisco. Actually, the priesthood was a future
Andy had been contemplating since prep school, even though he
realized that that's what his absent (and, at that age, deeply
resented) father had intended for him. Like a convent for an illegitimate daughter or out-of-wedlock mother, the seminary was
considered to be the most appropriate place for a bastard son,
especially if he had noble blood.

Andy liked the idea of becoming a priest. For one thing, it
would allow him to be boss, albeit in the service of Divinity. And
he especially liked the idea of attending the seminary, which
would be an endless source of sexual satisfactions. That was no
small matter for a young man of Andy's manifest need. According to Andy, at least half of the Episcopalian seminarians, in the
San Francisco Bay area if not everywhere else, were actively gay.
Most important, of course, the seminary and the priesthood
would give Andy the opportunity to carry out the spiritual
mission of Christianity.

So Andy became a happy and successful young priest and
military chaplain, and he was able to exploit his penchant for

success in numerous other endeavors, principal among which were pastoral psychology and a breathtakingly aggressive career in real estate.

Secondary pursuits in Andy's life tended to turn over as quickly as properties. He worked as a bit actor in Hollywood and New York, he directed fundraising for New York's ritziest cancer institute, he got married, wrote plays and screenplays, played the piano, painted flowers, went into politics, and fathered and foster-fathered children.

Though his stint as an actor would complement his roles as priest and socialite politician, it never landed him a major part. In Hollywood, he got a real-estate license and with what was left of a $100,000 inheritance the Earl had arranged for him to receive when he graduated from the seminary (the equivalent of more than $1,000,000 today), he bought a modest two-bedroom house with a pool in a prime neighborhood ('location, location and location', he was the first to explain to me, were the three essentials of a good property) and a small building with four rental units whose tenants included a legendary director of westerns and a famous comedian. The comedian, who was 'flauntingly' gay (though, of course, publicly closeted, rather like Liberace), was extremely embittered and vicious and would have tied Andy up forever in petty tenant–landlord litigation had he not died of an overdose of poppers. Even in those days, and even though he tended to purchase in prime locations, Andy had a kind of prescient (unconsciously gay) pride about the impact entrepreneurs like himself were having on the inner cities. 'Gentrification' gives no sense of the crucial role played by lesbians and gay men in this history.

Another house with a pool was bought and sold within the year to an ex-trick named Merrill, a muscular but otherwise Truman-Capote-esque southern queen. Merrill was addicted to one-night stands, sometimes extending into longer arrangements with body builders he subsidized with the profits of a cosmetics business that appealed almost exclusively to middle-aged and elderly gay men, and which did so via advertisements Merrill placed in the back pages of a leading, moderately anti-gay, main-stream glossy, and nowhere else.

Like most of Andy's gay 'friends', Merrill resented Andy's virile good looks and personal dynamism, a presentation – a 'package' as Merrill called it – that was unconsciously facilitated by Andy's bisexuality, even more prized among gay men in those days as an insignia of masculinity. What Merrill most resented was Andy's attractiveness to other men, especially the younger ones they would sometimes competitively court. Every time the competition was based on looks and demeanor rather than a cash offer (something Merrill did routinely but Andy never had to resort to), Merrill lost. All of this on top of financial independence and success, vocational achievement, and noble lineage! No wonder most of Andy's 'friends' hated him.

In these relationships of the conquered with the conquerer, Andy's sometimes substantial acts of generosity were appreciated like salt on a fresh wound. Merrill had purchased his home from Andy for a substandard price with the stipulation that Andy and a guest could stay at the house (which was a small mansion) whenever he/they liked. That really wasn't very often, and even when Andy and I were there, there was still plenty of room for Buddy, the staggeringly beautiful muscle boy from Merrill's home town in rural Kentucky who never wore clothes in the house and who eventually landed an unflatteringly autobiographical part in a major film. And in any case, Merrill's relationship with Buddy was typically short-lived. Right in front of me one morning, Andy sat Buddy down and with characteristic bluntness advised him to 'wisely' invest the $25,000 fee they were paying him 'because you've got no talent, no brains, and there won't be any more offers'. He was right.

I cherished our weekend visits there, despite Merrill's overt envy and resentment of Andy and even despite the confrontation between my hyperaestheticism and the *faux Empire* decor, which was so uniquely pretentious, as only things in Los Angeles could be in those years, that I actually became nauseated and vomited when I first saw it. ('Philistine' that I would have been labeled by today's aesthetes – notwithstanding recent evidence that the real, historical Philistines were highly cultured – I could never have imagined that such Babylonian ostentation would become the stuff of high art and sensibility twenty years later.) It was in Merrill's living room that Andy gave me the Tissot watch I wore until a few years ago and which always reminded me of him. And of the passage of time.

Andy and I were staying with Merrill the night Merrill found out that his mother had died of heart failure at her home in rural Kentucky. If anything convinced Andy of the truth of conservative psychiatric thinking about homosexuals (this was 1968 – five years before the APA declassification), it had been Merrill's Sebastian-and-Mrs-Venable relationship with his mother. Alarmed by the strange moaning and wailing sounds that kept waking us up, Andy finally arose to see what was going on. Outside Merrill's bedroom, the noises were such that Andy couldn't hear his own knocking. Finally, he pushed open the door and discovered Merrill, apparently deeply intoxicated, jerking off as he fucked himself with the biggest dildo Andy had ever seen, and howling 'Oh Mama, Mama, Mama, I'm s-o-o-o-o sorry.'

During his days in Hollywood, Andy had a passionate love affair with Otto, a man Uncle George's age, a character actor of independent means and inordinate social influence who had the fanciest Rolls Royce in town. Though Otto was always on the verge of landing a real part, he kept playing the same walk-on caricature of a Nazi officer, a fate that gave him prestige in some circles. This was Andy's one big love affair with a daddy figure, and it ended disastrously. I never found out the details, but that's when Andy decided he'd had enough of Hollywood's heavy drinking and destructive relationships, of everything in that phony town. Except the properties.

Over the next two and a half years in New York, Andy repeated a lot of what had happened in Hollywood, especially the successful real estate deals and the drinking. Instead of an alcoholic daddy figure, however, Andy fell in love with an alcoholic 'son', a man his own age and of his own aristocratic English background and means, who loved the way Andy tormented him for being such a whimpering, ineffectual sop. Once, when Andy discovered a huge turd in the middle of the bathroom floor, he even became physically abusive. Though they tried to resume their affair twenty years later, it ended abruptly in the same drunken, sadomasochistic brawling. But this time there was a legacy: an expensive resort home that would keep them tied up together – in litigation – for years to come.

Marriage, fatherhood and foster-fatherhood were much more transient developments in Andy's life than the real estate, a passion that lasted thirty years before being displaced by the stock market. He had never had any problem fucking women, or so he claimed. That was an enterprise he seemed to genuinely enjoy, like his occasional dabs at oil painting, but he readily admitted that he had never been able to sustain any deeply amorous interest in a woman. The marriage was probably a panicky reaction to his status as a Navy chaplain. Well before their first anniversary, he discovered that his bride had been fucking every officer on the base. With her parents testifying on his behalf, Andy was able to arrange a speedy annulment. But that wasn't the liaison that made him a father. At the end of the war, when Andy was still in his teens, he traveled to Europe and had a brief but very genuine (he always insisted) love affair with a German girl; they produced a son. Although he never saw her again and never met his son, he provided her with child support and his son with a trust fund. Twenty-five years later, he took another stab at fatherhood, this time with a foster son he summarily dropped when the boy's mother appeared and began asking for money. It never occurred to Andy that each of these relationships reenacted to a greater or lesser degree the circumstances of his own heritage.

Andy's attempts at playwriting consisted of one never-completed work, sentimental nonsense about Cockney children. His painting lasted the first part of one summer. The subjects, none of which he completed, were all still lifes, mostly flowers. His love for the piano never relented, even though he didn't read music, had no musical sense and played only 4½ pieces.

We fell in love the moment we laid eyes on each other. He was my first real lover and I always regarded him, until my relationship with Arnie, as 'the great love of my life'. It was 1966, the *Advocate* had yet to publish its first issue. I was twenty years old, had just transferred to the University of California at Berkeley from the University of Wisconsin, and had just returned from my first trip abroad. Berkeley, I hoped, would give me the personal freedom to be myself, which at that time meant being gay, first and foremost, and emphasizing the arts and humanities over the dreary, mostly irrelevant pre-med curriculum I had grown so tired of.

I immediately began going to San Francisco on weekends and, though not yet twenty-one, I'd found a number of gay bars that would let me in without any questions. Most of them were within walking distance of the East Bay Terminal, which was important because the taxi fares were, as they remain today, among the highest in the country. A favorite was the Gilded Cage, a hole-in-the-wall in the Tenderloin district that featured a terrific female impersonator named Charles Pierce. It was there that I heard my first Bette and Tallulah routines:

> **Tallulah**: Bette, dahhhling, I understand you're pregnant. Can I have one of the puppies?
> **Bette**: Tallulah, dear, I just loved your last picture. You know, the one where they brought you in on a slab, face down for identification purposes.

Though the stage was the size of a puppet theater, Charles managed the most elaborate costume changes, and the show always concluded with his special rendition of Jeanette MacDonald singing 'San Francisco' in a dress that sparkled with electric lights during climactic refrains, as he sailed over the audience on a precarious swing.

It was at the Gilded Cage that I met Waldemar von Bauerinvolk, the man who introduced me to Andy. Waldi was second generation, working-class German–American on both sides of his family, which seemed to consist exclusively of aunts. All of them had been members of the Bund, the pre-World-War-II association of pro-Nazi German–American organizations, Waldi casually mentioned to me many years later. Waldi may not have come from money, but he had refined European tastes, was reasonably good-looking despite a malalignment of his mouth and teeth that made him look like a later Picasso when he smiled, and he seemed to be unwaveringly friendly. As far as I know, I'm the only person who ever saw him lose his temper, but that occurred only once and lasted less than a minute.

Waldi was also extremely intelligent. He had been an undergraduate at Harvard and was well on his way to a serious career in economics and politics when he decided to drop out of his doctoral studies program at Columbia to pursue more passionate interests in theater and dance. By the time we met, those interests had waned and Waldi had become a government translator of Russian and Slavic intelligence materials, an easy job that gave him loads of free time and full mobility. He could complete his translations as easily in Palm Springs, Sagaponack, Wellfleet, Fire Island Pines, Paris, or Gstaad. Again, Waldi was nice-looking, bright, well-traveled, and affable, but in essence his outsized social status and jet-set lifestyle were based on two things: his dick, which was big, and his position as chief pimp for Baron Jean-Claude Colbert, who was one of the world's richest men.

Waldi lived in one of Andy's apartment buildings in San Francisco in the same arrangement Andy had with Merrill: Waldi paid a lower rent in exchange for agreeing to house Andy at the latter's discretion. It was a situation Waldi wasn't very happy about. As he frequently railed about it, Andrew Bullen was simply the cheapest, stingiest landlord he had ever had. These denunciations were usually light-hearted and ostensibly affectionate, but the subject of Andy was clearly among those few things that could get to Waldi. Perhaps they had had an affairette at some point in the past, like Merrill and Andy. Whatever the ingredients, their relationship, like most of Andy's relationships, involved considerable resentment and rivalry.

Despite Waldi's big cock, good looks and popularity, and notwithstanding my youth, lust, and loneliness, our affairette wasn't really going anywhere – not sexually, anyway. At first, it was like having sex with a dildo. Later, with a 'sister'. The fading of sexual interest was rapid and seemed mutual, but I clung to Waldi. He was the only gay man in San Francisco I knew well enough to call my friend, or so I thought; and with all his social connections, he would be my entree to 'gay society', as I tried to conceptualize it then. I never dreamed that this entree would prove to be a one-way passage to the rest of my life.

Waldi had never had a sustained, amorous relationship in his entire life, and he never had any more romantic an interest in me than in any other of his thousands of tricks. Nonetheless, I don't think he took too kindly the overt fading of my sexual interest in him. Awkward, giggly young opera queens were expected to be more impressed by big cocks, for one thing. As self-involved as I was, I could tell that Waldi had contempt for my 'incessant, sophomoric chatter', as he later described it to Andy, about finding 'a real man' and 'falling in love' ('You've *never* been in love?!' I'd keep interrogating and, unwittingly, taunting him). So when Andy announced that he'd be 'visiting' Waldi again on a stopover to Europe, Waldi planned a double-barreled revenge. He simply arranged for the two idealistic romantics to meet each other. Could there be a more perfect match? The gerontophile was a stereotypically cultured, liberal, self-negating Jew; the daddy was a conservative, High Episcopalian pederast. Both were smokers and incipient alcoholics.

Waldi's apartment was lovely. It was spacious and furnished throughout with fine antiques. The walls were a soft primrose-yellow with white wainscoting and it was held together by a grand piano and an elaborately decorated harpsichord. The instruments belonged to Waldi's talented roommate, Henry. Henry had been on the verge of establishing a career as a concert pianist, but like Waldi, facing what promised to be a solid career in economics, he had needed to satisfy more immediate passions. All the antiques belonged to Waldi, whose knowledge of Georgian furniture qualified him to lecture occasionally at the city's museums. Though he eventually became a regular at Christie's and Sotheby's, he never made much money from his expertise. But it proved grandly advantageous socially. Waldi may not have been the only pimp to whom the Baron and his cronies had access, but how many of the others were also working, credentialed authorities on art and antiques, to say nothing of politics and finance? Fashions, trends, tricks and pimps may come and go in the lives of the rich and famous, but Waldi was there to stay.

When I arrived that February 1966 evening for dinner, and to meet this oft-reviled landlord whom Waldi was now telling me I would like, somebody was playing the piano, and it certainly wasn't Henry. Waldi was finishing a phone call, so I went into the living room where I first laid eyes on the man whose extraordinary, craggy handsomeness and bold gestures held my attention far more than his clattery keyboard rendition of Tchaikovsky's *Pathétique*. It was Andy, and he was playing the piano the way he did almost everything in his life. Lacking knowledge, skill, and patience, he would simply force things to happen. I had found my real man!

I remember little else that happened that night, before bedtime. I don't remember where or what we ate or whether Waldi or Henry or anyone else was with us. We just kept gazing at each other, as we sipped our drinks, falling more and more deeply in love. At bedtime, there were two options. I could either sleep with Waldi in his bedroom or with Andy in Henry's room. Since there were only the two bedrooms, Waldi and Henry must have had an agreement about who would sleep where whenever Andy was in town. One of them would have to sleep in the study, on a hide-a-bed or elsewhere, and that night it was apparently Henry's turn to make alternative arrangements.

Waldi seemed a little surprised, and disappointed, that his matchmaking had been so effective. Even though that had been his objective, another part of him wanted me to reject Andy in favor of him. Andy may have had more money and bluster, or whatever it was people always seemed to find so attractive, but Waldi had a *much* bigger cock. No question about that. Could anything *really* be more important, especially to a neurotic young Jewish opera queen, than a big, unclipped German dick? Yes, Waldi had to concede after that night, but he knew exactly what it was. It was the very same hedonism and scheming that had proved to be the overriding priorities in his own life, a fact he would soon find a way to demonstrate.

In the bedroom, I was shaking. At age twenty, even though I was a lot more sexually vigorous than I am these days, in the age of AIDS, I also had a lot more trouble handling sexual feelings, and what was happening was so intense, so unprecedented in my experience, that I felt overwhelmed and frightened. I needed Andy to take charge. He turned out the lights. I told him I was afraid. Couldn't we just snuggle? For warmth? The next twelve hours were like some extremely intense drug trip. I had never dreamed that people were capable of so much surrender and passion. What people eroticize in sadomasochism, the dominance and submission, the surrender, the giving, come so naturally to people who are really in love and really making love and who know it and feel it. By dawn, there was no question of our commitment to each other. We were lovers. And as George Emerson asserts in *A Room with a View*, 'There's only one thing that's impossible. To love and to part.'

But Andy was twice my age and we had such different backgrounds and lives and beliefs and schedules. We lived in different parts of the country. What were we going to do? Because our relationship, which we always called our 'marriage', wasn't a matter of formality or practicality so much as instinct and imperative, that question didn't have to be answered. We were what we already were for each other, like it or not, and we'd simply have to work within the circumstances, however challenging. I consoled myself with the fantasy that it was like being married to a diplomat or traveling salesman. And that's the way we lived, mostly apart but deeply bonded, for the next five years.

Andy had just been assigned to a small parish in Tennessee, which included teaching responsibilities in pastoral psychology at the local seminary and at a junior college. And I had just begun my junior year at Berkeley. For the next three years, we overcame countless hurdles to be with each other as often as we could. From his end, Andy was constantly having to tell elaborate stories, often grossly interconflicting, to his congregation, his superiors at the seminary, and colleagues at the university about the family emergencies that kept requiring his presence on the West Coast. Any less dominant and independent a person than Andy would have been relieved of his duties.

I was a lot less independent, and on several desperate occasions, I arranged for job interviews with leading Southern and Midwestern corporations and agencies that agreed to pay my expenses. I wasn't the least bit interested in these jobs, of course, only the opportunities they gave me to make side trips, usually for no more than a weekend, to be with Andy. Rich as he was, and even though he did pay a portion of my traveling expenses on many occasions, why didn't he also pay for those trips instead of having me lie? Questions like that only alienated Andy, and eventually, me.

When you're in love, you may be aware of your lover's character defects, but they aren't in perspective or focus. They may even become part of the attraction. And so it was with Andy's legendary parsimony. Everybody complained about it. But I was quite powerless under his sexy combination of sophistry and aggression, and was inevitably persuaded that all the people who thought Andy was cheap, including me, were just envious and/or trying to take advantage.

'Money is love', was one of his favorite expressions. I liked the tough-love truth of this phrase, especially during the first two years, when he more freely contributed to our trips and gave me things (which weren't many and the most cherished of which, like a gold ring that had his family seal on it, he asked me to return the first time we had a bad fight). In later years, however, when he'd never remember a birthday or even return a phone call (knowing I'd call back), such maxims as 'Money is love' and 'You've got to have capital if you want to be independent' seemed sadistic and they hurt deeply.

A decade later, when Andy would not return mailed or telephoned requests for donations to GMHC and other AIDS organizations, 'Money is love' would reverberate, as it did at an ACT UP demonstration on Wall Street, where my preconscious directed me to choose a placard that showed a stack of dollars and a skull connected by an equals sign.

As I did with most of Andy's other character defects, I learned to infantilize his penuriousness and avarice. Behavior that routinely offended others seemed simultaneously cute and sexy to me, like boyishly vigorous displays. (In psychoanalytic terms, such generic, feminine infatuations or limerence would be explained as emanating from the homosexual child's primitive incorporation/ introjection of – identification with – his mother.)

During that first week at Waldi's, Andy felt pressured to invite an architect and his business executive wife – 'good friends' (real estate consultants) – for dinner. So he had me run out and buy six frozen fried chicken TV dinners – the cheapest brand – which he took apart, rearranged on fine china, spiced and decorated so that the meal could pass as 'good, basic Southern home cookin'.' I thought this was adorable. And even Andy had to giggle when Henry, who knew nothing about the secret behind the dinner and who was stoned, went into the kitchen and called out: 'Hey, what's with all these TV dinner wrappers?' I don't remember how Andy weaseled himself out of that one, except that he did.

Three years later, I was still so in love with him that I wasn't the least bit fazed when *not one* of the forty people I invited to a surprise 40th birthday party for him showed up. They were all envious and resentful of his masculinity and success and good looks and wealth and outspokenness, I was sure, and that's why they were treating my 'dear-heart' (his favorite term of endearment) so badly. It never occurred to me Andy could really have serious character defects, not even when he gave me a copy of child psychoanalyst Melanie Klein's study, *Envy and Greed*, to help me understand why I had reacted with such 'childish' hurt to his having 'forgotten' to give me a graduation present.

At first, vacations (which Andy would grudgingly subsidize) were extravagant. Andy had an old drinking buddy with whom he'd lost contact, an English writer and pederast who had gone to live in Dominica, the most primitive and inaccessible of the larger Caribbean islands. So off we went to the tropical rain forests, giant boa constrictors, and satiny black sand beaches of Dominica, where we found Winston R. living in a mountain village, surrounded by native boys with English accents who waited on him hand and foot. Winnie hadn't done any writing in years, but he was blissfully happy and had no intention of ever returning to the mainland, or even to the more civilized Canary Islands, where he and Andy had first met. For Christmas, Winnie had the villagers prepare a feast, the highlight of which was the sweet, delicate flesh of an enormous shellfish, some kind of nautilus, sautéed in a mysterious, garlicky oil with 'christophine', a local variety of cabbage. On New Year's Day we were taken to a great colonial estate, where we dined on roast pig, blood pudding and an excruciatingly tart punch that was made by mixing burgundy with grapefruit juice. But my most vivid memory of that trip is of a brief febrile illness that made me languorous, during which Andy kept seducing me; my torpor perversely enhanced our passion. On this trip, like so many of the times we were together during those first three years, it wasn't unusual for us to fuck five times a day.

Another Caribbean jaunt took us to Guadeloupe, where we stayed at an expensive, secluded French hotel whose white sand beaches were the softest and most shell-rich I've seen. There, a middle-aged Jewish man we'd met on the plane, whose sexual identity was probably as unclear to him as it was to us, asked Andy to account for what he saw as the flauntingly pederastical nature of our companionship. Even though the accusation was not made in my presence, Andy was upset by it and needed to discuss it with me. 'You've got a bad case of Jewish guilt', I reassured him.

At the time, I couldn't have agreed more with Andy that there was nothing the least bit exploitative going on between us. In the first place, although Andy was old enough to be my father and was to some degree acting as such, I was twenty-one (just) and legal; in the second, we were deeply in love. Our relationship, for all its inequalities and limitations, certainly seemed to be a matter of free will on my part, to say the least. Deep in my heart, I trusted that we would eventually overcome our troubles and live happily ever after. Fifteen years later, I realized that what the Jewish man perceived in Andy's relationship with me, and what I was never able to consider to be within the realm of possibility, was simply that Andy, however much he may have loved me, was encouraging expectations which he knew had no real possibility of fulfillment.

In addition to the excursions to Dominica and Guadeloupe, over a period of five years there were trips to Europe, Palm Springs, the Virgin Islands, Puerto Rico, Hawaii, Provincetown, Louisville, Lexington, to a large island Andy owned off the coast of Maine and long weekends in Los Angeles and New York. In Florence, the city of romance, we lived the passions E. M. Forster tried to imagine in *A Room with a View*: 'This tremendous thing has happened between us. Everyone must know.' And so we walked arm in arm everywhere. Italian men do this without opprobrium, of course, but everyone knows that such open displays of affection are taboo for

American men, and we were recognizably American because of our American shoes. Beyond that, we kissed in public, sometimes passionately. In the evenings, we made love in the Fiesole hillsides. Our love seemed so brave and defiant at the time. And for the late 1960s, it was.

Though we were identifiably American, Andy and I relished those times when we thought we were passing as Italian. Andy had a widow's peak of black hair, which he darkened with Grecian Formula, giving him a swarthier mien, and I had often been told I looked Italian or Mediterranean. Andy was just having fun, but I took it seriously. I used to boast about the time, on a subsequent trip to Italy, that an Italian businessman on the Settebello, the luxury high-speed train that travels between Milan and Rome, commented on my American shoes and decided I was an Italian who had lived in America. Fifteen years later I began to notice that my pride in looking Italian often involved a preconscious wish not to look Jewish.

Between trips and visits with Andy, I remained in close contact with Waldi. We'd dine out and go to the opera together, and also to parties, bars, and the baths. So much for true love and fidelity, Waldi must have tittered, while he simultaneously procured for Andy on the side. Despite our sleeping around, however, Andy and I remained all too clearly in love and committed to each other, and our pride must have seemed contemptuous of those who didn't have what we had (and in Waldi's case, it was). Waldi realized that our comeuppance would require something more than learning the details of each other's extramarital sex lives. And so Iago pondered his next move.

Years before, Andy had a disastrous fling with the Baron, which concluded with Andy telling the Baron exactly what he thought of him, something few had the temerity to do. The Baron wanted revenge and Waldi knew it, but these things had to be done delicately. The right circumstances hadn't come along, until now.

Waldi had come to think of me as a solidly routine trick/escort, among the dozen or so such that he annually sent abroad to the Baron. Waldi had already tried on numerous occasions to get me to visit the Baron. But on the basis of a photograph Andy had, and what Andy and others had told me about him, the Baron seemed repellent. On the other hand, his private collection of twentieth-century art was considered to be one of the world's finest, he loved opera, and was richer than anyone I'd ever met. It would be interesting, I had to concede, a unique and perhaps important opportunity. But I couldn't have sex with a man that everybody described as so dour and limp, so homely. At twenty-one, I virtually never had sex with people I wasn't attracted to. That was simply out of the question, and I hedged every time Waldi raised the subject.

So Waldi had to figure out a way to get me to visit the Baron that would not reveal itself as a sexual setup. There had to be a *legitimate* reason. During a recent visit to New York, the Baron had attended the Metropolitan Opera's new production of *Die Frau ohne Schatten*. Some weeks later, I received a letter from the Baron saying that he'd heard from Waldi that I collected tapes of live performances and that he'd be ever so grateful if I could find a tape, in stereo, of the performance he had seen. He wanted to feature it at a party to inaugurate his new sound system. That was an easy request to grant, and I sent him the tape. I immediately received a letter of thanks, which seemed inappropriately effusive for an aristocrat of such rank and power. If I became the least bit suspicious, however, I was reassured by Waldi's characterization of the Baron as a lonely man who was always looking for gay friends. They were the only people he was really comfortable with. The Baron's letter ended with a disarmingly friendly invitation to visit the famous Palais Colbert.

I knew how much Andy resented the Baron, who wouldn't lend him the money he needed to buy a small château in southern France. And I knew that my visiting the Baron would wound Andy's pride. But Andy was carrying on with so many others (even if I was too) and was taking more and more trips without me. In fact, that very summer of the Baron's invitation, Andy had arranged to travel to the Middle East. As previously agreed, we'd spend a week at Andy's château (he got the loan elsewhere) in the heart of Burgundy and rendezvous six weeks later in Greece. In between, he wanted to do the Middle East on his own. I don't know whether he took another lover or (more likely) simply didn't want to have to provide the additional money required if I were to accompany him, or whether there may have been Jewish–Christian issues I couldn't see (doubtful, I was sure, because Andy was so hawkishly pro-Israel). But he wouldn't relent, even when I joked about accepting the Baron's invitation.

At the Gare du Nord, I was met by a liveried officer who took my bags and escorted me to a Rolls-Royce limousine. The hour-long trip to the *palais* seemed alternatively precipitate and endless. When we finally arrived, I felt even more discombobu-lated. Much of the interior of a magnificent eighteenth-century palace had been transformed to create a starkly modern ambience. The foyer was a skylit rectangle that was completely empty, except for a startling arrangement of figures by Giaco-metti, Brancusi and Henry Moore. I was shown to my lavishly appointed room, where I immediately noticed an engraved card that looked like a wedding invitation on top of a Louis XVI *bureau plat*. '*Vous êtes instamment prié de ne pas donner de gratification au personnel*' (no tipping), it read. On closer inspec-tion, I realized it was handwritten.

After being informed by one of the eleven servants who resided at the *palais* that luncheon would be served shortly, I was taken to meet Monsieur Le Baron in his relatively unimposing office. He was sitting at a large, modern desk and sighing as he concluded what had apparently been an exasperating telephone conversation. His first words, in slightly accented English, pre-ceded an otherwise warm greeting. 'Those Israelis! You close the doors, they try to come in through the windows. You shut the windows, they jam the phones. They simply will not be put off!'

It came as no great surprise that the Baron was 'anti-Zion-ist'. So was Waldi, my sister and just about everybody else with whom I felt comfortable. Yet the Baron's comments about the Israelis had an unanticipated effect. Instead of being off-putting or sadomasochistically conjoining, they connected us at an even deeper level, for we were both moderately to seriously self-negating as Jews (though Jean-Claude had been raised as Catholic, his father was Jewish), though neither of us realized it then and Jean-Claude never realized it, any more than he ever developed any consciousness about being gay. At a more conscious level, Jean-Claude, as I was presently invited to call him, probably thought his anti-Semitism would augment my psychological vulnerability and render me more seducible. What quickly emerged is that his self-image was so poor he couldn't imagine that anyone could really like, much less desire, him for himself, or even for all his wealth. His psychic fragility and insecurity were such that there always had to be power games. Ultimately, he paid the highest price a human being can possibly pay for such a psyche – he lived out his life completely devoid of the experience of love.

The formal dining room was another huge rectangle, empty except for a bright persimmon rug, a Louis XVI dining table that could seat fifty and often did, and approximately twenty of the most famous and valuable works of contemporary art in Europe. These included giant canvasses by Warhol, Rauschenberg, Indiana, Riley, Lichtenstein, etc. Great wealth and the art that ostensibly satirizes it seem surprisingly comfortable together, I thought to myself, as I completed an all but sexually arousing meal that began with a lobster and Perigord truffle salad and concluded with a kind of Belgian truffle *crème brulée*.

That week there were fewer than ten in Jean-Claude's entourage. There was a beautiful young German Countess, recently divorced, whose father had been a key figure in military efforts to resist Hitler and whose uncle was at the center of a homosexuality-in-the-military scandal that had Dreyfus-affair proportions in the 1920s. The Countess desperately wanted to marry Jean-Claude, even though she knew he was gay. In those days I was so naive I didn't believe people would willingly marry across such circumstances, against love, for what seemed so much less important: money and status. Others in the group included the Countess's very coddled, adolescent son; one of Jean-Claude's curators, who glowered at me knowingly and than asked me point blank how I knew the Baron and why I had been invited to visit him; a former secretary whose husband Jean-Claude had had an affair with, breaking up their marriage; the American financial wizard Rick Gilette (of Samuels, Malkin and Gilette); and a very handsome blond Swiss Banker I couldn't stop ogling. The first night, except for a polite late evening drink in the salon surrounded by Impressionist and post-Impressionist masterpieces, I had no further contact with Jean-Claude.

The next day the chauffeur was at my disposal, and Madeleine, the former secretary, agreed to act as my guide. At her suggestion, we decided on a tour of the countryside, which included a visit to the little known Châteaubleu, a working château complete with moat, drawbridge, and the only real torture chamber I'd ever seen. (In most castles and palaces the torture chambers aren't open to the public. In Amsterdam, there's a torture museum, a large advertisement for which faces the Portuguese Synagogue.) In the vestibule, we passed a huge painting of a man being skinned alive. In an auspicious tone of voice, Madeleine noted the resemblance between the faces in the painting and 'some of their descendants'. Later, I wondered if the trip to Châteaubleu had been prearranged, with Madeleine's passive complicity, as another attempt to enhance seducibility and/or as an even more subtle reminder that the privilege of having the Baron's confidence was just that, confidential.

The remainder of that day passed uneventfully. In the middle of the night, however, I awoke to find myself in the midst of the fantasy I'd just been dreaming about. My head was in the lap of the handsome Swiss banker and he was gently caressing my hair and kissing my face. We made fast and furious love. An hour or so later we were making love again when Jean-Claude, wearing a floor length scarlet robe, suddenly appeared via a connecting balcony. It was all too unsettling and I had to call a halt to the proceedings.

The following evening Jean-Claude summoned me to the study for a nightcap. Suddenly (and rather comically, actually), a not-very-smoothly revolving bookcase, like Baron Scarpia's in the second act of *Tosca*, opened to reveal an antechamber with a *lit de repos*. Taking a deep breath, swallowing hard, and squeezing my eyes closed for extended moments, we had a go at it, but neither of us could get it up. Mercifully, that was it. I didn't even have to try to sleep with Jean-Claude again until nearly two weeks later, on the trip we took together to Insul Sylt.

On Sylt, the German nudist resort isle off the western coast of Jutland, the games had changed. Sharing the four-bedroom house with Jean-Claude, the German Countess, her son, and myself was a newcomer, Perry, a chunky graduate student from Stanford. At first, there was predictable rivalry for Jean-Claude's attentions between Perry and me, even though neither of us could bear the thought of sleeping with Jean-Claude. The Countess, whose matrimonial aspirations for herself and Jean-Claude had nothing to do with sex, felt no such sense of rivalry. In fact, she was glad we were there, glad for the opportunity that Jean-Claude's rather uninhibited arrangements would give her to demonstrate just how open, tolerant and supportive a companion she could be. (Jean-Claude was never to marry or leave an heir, not even via the artificial insemination and surrogate parent options I helped him investigate over the next few years.)

Suddenly, Perry and I realized we were attracted to each other. But that had been Jean-Claude's plan all along. You see, Jean-Claude's primary method of obtaining sexual gratification, it finally became clear, was to try to enter liaisons that were already in progress. And that's exactly what happened one night toward the end of our otherwise congenial and exciting holiday together. Instead of being angry at discovering Perry and me having sex, Jean-Claude had anticipated doing so, and was counting on our mutual guilt as an incentive to include him. This time he had calculated well. We felt very guilty indeed. Neither of us had much money and we were afraid the punishing parent might kick us both out that very night. Though we instantly made the most valiant efforts to include him in a threesome, however, none of us could get off, or even up.

Despite our inability to communicate sexually, Jean-Claude and I did manage to establish a degree of friendship. We corresponded over the years and spent a number of evenings together with Waldi and other mutual friends at Waldi's subsequent homes in Wellfleet and New York (both of which the Baron subsidized). But Jean-Claude, who suffered from a very aristocratic form of what they used to call neurasthenia, became increasingly depressed and isolated. The last time I saw him, on East Hampton Beach, I felt hurt and insulted when he asked me what I was doing. Through letters and via Waldi, several of us, including the writer D. J. Love, had importuned him on a number of occasions during the previous year and a half to become involved in the AIDS crisis, or at least to make a contribution to the fledgling AIDS organization D. J., myself and four others had co-founded.

Five years later, ever more depressed and isolated under the care of a small army of quack doctors and financial advisors, Jean-Claude died under mysterious circumstances. Was it AIDS? Was he poisoned? Waldi, who became a principal trustee of the estate, would only speculate that he may have died 'of a broken heart'. In the last year, there had been a series of colossal financial transactions that included sales of the Palais Colbert and the art collection. This left Jean-Claude unimaginably richer, but without the home that was dearer to him than he realized and the hobby that had really become his sole *raison d'être*.

At a very businesslike memorial service for his 'loved ones' at New York's most aristocratic cathedral, leading AIDS activist D. J. Love and I coincidentally observed D. J.'s birthday by listening politely as Henry Kissinger and David Rockefeller gave very straight eulogies extolling the Baron's astuteness in devoting himself 'to projects that really counted' and quickness in backing 'any organization he felt was legitimate'. Needless to point out, no one even hinted that the Baron was gay. D. J. and I exited civilly during a refrain of 'The Christian Life'.

Several months later, D. J. found out from Waldi, who now lives with an English aristocrat and has AIDS, that Jean-Claude died of AIDS. Three years later, Dreiser, Bernard & Colbert, the mega-conglomerate Jean-Claude had sacrificed his art collection and home to create, became the center of one of the greatest financial scandals in American history.

The remainder of our stay in Sylt went smoothly enough, but I knew the whole experience was going to cost me dearly with Andrew. When I finally reached the château – not an easy telephone call in 1968 – he was livid, despite my reassurances that the Baron and I hadn't *really* slept together and that I had continually and proudly spoken to the Baron about our primary relationship, which was true. I *was* still very deeply in love with Andy and was constantly bragging about it to everybody, including the Baron. He hung up in my face. I called back, which took the rest of the day. Though still very angry, he agreed to meet me in West Berlin.

It was a stormy rendezvous. Andy had me get dressed for dinner and then disappeared for six hours. By the time he showed up, I had downed three of his miltowns. The next thing I knew we were having drinks at a place – I'm not making this up – called the Eva Braun Bar, near a Hilton hotel. (At the time, that's all this bar with its outrageous name seemed to me – a big joke. I didn't take it seriously and therefore felt no real insult.) Except for a waitress, a bartender and one couple at a table, we were alone. Calmly, Andy began telling me about all the affairs he'd been having on the side. After a few minutes, unable to take any more, I got up and slugged him, chipping a front tooth. The chipped tooth made him look even handsomer, though (so much so that he never had it repaired), and jolted a mutual awareness of how much we both cared. We returned to the hotel, where we made the most passionate love yet.

The next day we honeymooned in East Berlin, which neither of us had ever visited. That was our pattern. We'd have terrible fights, sometimes physical (rare), aggravated by distance, separation and the cognitive dissonance of our inability to be more open and honest about our feelings as gay men, to ourselves and each other as well as to the world at large. The reconciliation and love-making that would follow these fights was, of course, sadomasochistically enhanced by them. But we couldn't be ebulliently romantic in East Berlin, to say the least. This wasn't San Francisco or even Florence, our radar informed us at high pitch, and we watched our every move. Even so, we risked all for one long, passionate embrace in a public square when we thought no one was looking. It was the kind of embrace that in most other places, including being on a train or plane or driving a car, would have led, within moments, to lovemaking.

We passed a building that was draped with the largest banner I'd ever seen. It was bright red with gigantic white letters: 'UNSER WEG IST RICHTIG!' (OUR WAY IS RIGHT!). I had to agree with the High Episcopalian, pro-property pederast that what we were observing was totalitarianism. When I discussed these impressions with my socialist sister, however, she countered that our capitalist advertising, whether on large billboards or television, in the newspapers and magazines, is easily the equivalent of the draped building, but is so ubiquitous, extreme and incessant that we no longer notice how blatantly propagandistic it really is.

East Berlin was unremittingly bleak, but I returned there, by myself, to see two performances at the Komische Oper, directed by the famous Walter Felsenstein (who I later discovered was a resident of West Berlin). *La Traviata* in German featured a buxom, shrill and very inebriated Violetta (Melitta Muszely) throwing chairs across the stage as she chugged leftover glasses of champagne. I think I was more convinced by the comparative subtlety of the director's approach to *Die Fledermaus*, which was conventional except that everything was black, white and red.

The two evenings on my own worked out well for Andy, who had other things to do. First, he would visit an elderly German couple who had known Dr Schmidt. That didn't sound very interesting. Why would I want to sit around with a bunch of old people reminiscing about the man who had raised Andy? The second evening, he would accept a military invitation to conduct a marriage at Wannsee, which also sounded boring. I didn't know at the time that Wannsee was the site of the conference Hitler convened in 1941 to concretize plans for the genocide of my people, and if I had, I probably would have reacted with characteristic detachment. I would probably have thought, 'That was then. This is now. The two have nothing to do with each other or with me.'

At some level of intellectual consciousness, I knew that German anti-Semitism was an ongoing phenomenon and that that wasn't good, but I hadn't the faintest inkling of how truly pervasive it was, certainly not on the basis of my own experience. I had been well-treated during prior opera-oriented excursions to Germany and Austria, which had even included a 'pilgrimage' to Bayreuth, where the Festival people arranged for me to stay in a private, very German home. But never, in any of these experiences in Germany or Austria, had I encountered a single instance of anti-Semitism; at least, none that I was aware of. Of course, I was always the perfect Jew on these trips – grovelingly adulatory of German culture, especially Wagner, unquestioning about the past, and utterly obsequious in manner. In any event, what did anti-Semitism *really* have to do with me? Though ethnically Jewish, I was an American citizen and a very contemporary child of the Sixties. I had completely rejected all that garbage about race and religion and denomination and class. Hadn't everybody, or at least everybody who counted?

From Berlin, we proceeded to Munich, where Andy introduced me to two friends, a German of noble blood named Karl von some-dorf-or-other and Pepi, his prissy, much younger Italian lover. Throughout the afternoon we spent together visiting Schloss Linderhof, the least interesting but most accessible of King Ludwig's castles, their behavior seemed unusually reserved and a bit strange. I kept getting the feeling they were observing me, like scientists. Later, Andy told me that Karl's father had been a high-ranking Nazi officer who was killed during the war. Even then, it didn't occur to me as being within the realm of possibility that Karl's sympathies were anti-Semitic and pro-Nazi. Just as it never occurred to me to wonder what the adolescent Andy had been taught to believe about the war he was living through by his German stepfather, and later, by Uncle George, who was a friend of the Duke and Duchess of Windsor during those years. For that matter, I didn't get around to even asking my mother, whose hysterical response to anything political had always been 'Don't get involved', what she was doing during the war until nearly twenty years later. Her answer, incidentally, was a lot more distressing than it would have seemed ten or even five years earlier: 'I was raising babies.'

On to Salzburg, where we saw the famous Festival production of *Der Rosenkavalier* that had been filmed and recorded with Elisabeth Schwarzkopf. This time Christa Ludwig had switched from Octavian to the Marschallin, and the conductor was Karl Böhm. Like his mentor, Richard Strauss, Böhm had been a Nazi collaborationist. As an ardent admirer of both Schwarzkopf and von Karajan, I had loved the film, which I had seen several times. It never occurred to me to attach any political significance to the presence of former Nazi party members in the most touted post-war production of *Rosenkavalier*. (I've never read anything about Ludwig's past, except that she was in her teens during the years her parents worked with Karajan at Aachen, from 1935–41.) At a more recent performance of this opera, however, I did ponder such intangibles. Inspired by my adult knowledge of Schwarzkopf, von Karajan and Austria, and notwithstanding that librettist Hugo von Hofmannsthal was 'Jewish-identified', I wondered whether the Marschallin, had she lived in a later generation, would have become a Nazi.

Suddenly I had a great idea for a sequel. It would be a Brechtian story about the Marschallin's descendants in pre- and post-'annexation' Austria, as seen through the eyes of Mohammed, the Marschallin's cute little black servant boy. In *Der Rosenkavalier*, Mohammed sees everything but, like all good servants, says nothing, not a word, despite several key moments on stage. The sequel would be called *Der Rosenkavalier II* or, as he's referred to in the stage directions, *Der Kleine Neger*.

The following evening we saw a von Karajan *Don Giovanni* that was so grim, so at odds with the opera's quintessential lightheartedness (though it's called a *dramma giocoso* I've always found *Don Giovanni* to be indistinguishable in tone and attitude from *Nozze di Figaro*), that it often struck me as unintentionally comic. Andy, however, fell asleep and vowed never to go to an opera again, even though he had sort of liked 'the one about the old Countess'.

During the days we took excursions through the gorgeous Bavarian countryside. It never occurred to me (or Andy?) that we should visit Berchtesgaden even though we passed it on the highway and had the time to do so. Did Andy realize that at some level, Berchtesgaden had become more shrine than museum? Alternatively, was it my disinterest that determined this omission from our itinerary? In any event, in those years I never connected Hitler's 'Eagle's Nest' with my favorite leather bars, several of which bore the same name. What did the two have to do with each other or with me?

It wasn't that I was totally unconscious. On my own during a previous stay in Munich, I had visited Dachau. But these things were ancient history. Why dwell on them when I could be seeing a composer's birthplace, an art museum or, best and most important, an opera?

Likewise, Andy's anti-Nazism wasn't as equivocal as my paranoia might wish to imply. On the contrary, Andy and I talked a lot about the war, usually at Andy's initiative – e.g., he gave me a trendy psychoanalytic study called *The Mind of Adolf Hitler* by Walter Langer, which he had me read and discuss with him. On the whole, Andy made me feel deeply loved and supported as a Jew. But that's not what I wanted. I wanted to be loved and supported not for my 'difference', but as an equal in every respect. For one thing, for me to acknowledge the importance of my ethnicity would have meant acknowledging the importance of Andy's ethnicity and his membership in a higher social class. I wasn't willing to do that, even though I was willing to take advantage of any benefits of that class, such as his having a lot more money. Just as I wasn't willing to acknowledge the importance of his being twice my age and a father figure, except when I felt like it, which was often, especially during those first few years.

Thus, our discussions about identity, which were convoluted by our primitive, interconflicting notions about what it meant to be gay, often degenerated into arguments. These arguments usually found me attacking Israel and Jews, denouncing them for nationalism, patriotism and racism, and Andy coming to their defense, often with an emphasis on their status as a crucial ally of the United States. When the Israeli Army destroyed the Egyptian Air Force in the Six Day War, Andy was delirious with joy. 'Aren't you proud!?' he beamed. At some deep level of the instinct for survival, I was indeed glad to know that Jews could defend themselves so ferociously. On the other hand, how could I hold values about one group, even if they were my own people, and not another?

With regard to Israel, I felt a lot like my older sister, who was similarly self-negating as a Jew, more politicized than anyone I'd ever known, and whose politics were ardently socialist. Actually, she had lived in Israel, having accompanied her ardently socialist non-Jewish husband there on a university study grant, during the period just after the Six Day War. Though initially impressed with some of the country's socialist policies and the communal lifestyles of the *kibbutzim*, they were horrified by what they perceived to be its ethnocentrism and militarism in alliance with 'imperialist' and 'capitalist' forces. Under my sister's influence I sharpened my feelings about the Jewish homeland: 'Anything at any cost to anyone at any time as long as Israel thrives.' That's what I told Andy I thought of Israel and its Six Day War.

Of course, my attitude towards Jews extended to all religions, which certainly included Christianity. Whatever misgivings I had about Jews were often compounded in the case of Christians. I had it all figured out. The big culprits were nationalism, patriotism and racism, with Judeo-Christianity and all the other patriarchal religions being unacceptably primitive forms of their expression. We needed to find ways to sublimate less destructively, to transcend these dreadful instincts. I tried to be consistent, but it was impossible to reconcile all the different identities and loyalties and creeds and instincts.

When they re-released *Gone with the Wind*, which I had never seen, Andy took me to see it. In an early scene, Scarlett accuses Rhett Butler of being an 'ill-bred, mercenary creature, just like the Yankees!' To which Rhett responds, 'Since I'm not such a fool ... as to subscribe to this folly of fighting, why shouldn't I take the intelligent man's advantage?' At that moment, I leaned over and whispered something to Andy about how at least there was somebody around who understood the truth about 'patriotism'. Later, when Scarlett is fleeing Atlanta and Rhett informs her that he has decided that she had been right after all, that, for the greater good of the South, he should and will 'join up with our brave lads in gray', even thought they're now clearly losing the war (the morality of the institution they're fighting for is never questioned), and even though that's the last thing in the world Scarlett wants him to do at that point, Andy looked straight ahead at the screen and said nothing. Several years later, Andy would put it all in perspective by suggesting that our relationship was indeed like that of Rhett and Scarlett, in that issues such as patriotism and loyalty and identity were really smokescreens for the fact that we couldn't synchronize our love for each other. Having had a kind of Scarlett and Rhett relationship with the film when I saw it with Andy, I had evaded this painful, complex soap opera truth about the vast majority of lovers in the world.

That moment in *Gone with the Wind* helped me to begin to glimpse the 'complexities' of morality and patriotism Andy was always talking about. But there was one situation he was especially sensitive to that I would never acknowledge (to him) to be a comparable instance of individual moral choices being arguably less important than collective interests: the sacrifice of the wives of Henry VIII for the greater good of England. Needless to say, my identification was as steadfastly with the ladies as Andy's was with the Founding Father of the Anglican Church.

Andy's opinions about the Jews during World War II fell into two categories. The first and principal viewpoint was that the Jews were 'the completely innocent victims' of the Nazis. The second, somewhat contradictory perspective was that 'many' Jews could have saved themselves by recognizing the danger surrounding them and leaving for safer havens. At the time, I knew so little of the actual history of the war. (William M. Hoffman, the playwright, says this first postwar generation of American Jews has been 'numb' and is only now just beginning to deal with the true weight of what happened.) I was so ignorant and self-negating that I embraced the opportunity Andy's statement gave me to blame the victim. Of course, there were wealthy Jews who could have gotten out had they more soberly faced what was happening. In retrospect, however, I wish the fact that they represented only the tiniest fraction of Hitler's genocide had been more explicit in what Andy seemed to be saying.

Andy's beliefs about the Holocaust were a little like his religious attitudes. Like most people and even most clerics, he believed simultaneously in principles of free will and predestination. Unlike most clerics, however, he believed a lot more deeply and outspokenly in free will, in the power of self-determination. This could be very exciting when, exactly like D. J. Love, he would exhort the forlorn and defeated not to indulge in self-pity, but to 'pick yourself up by your bootstraps', a favorite expression of both. Not unlike Andy, D. J. still believes that the Holocaust could have been prevented if the Jews had tried harder to get their act together. That's not to say that the Jews *deserved* what happened. He wouldn't put it that way, but . . .

In Andy's case, this approach could be carried to what often seemed to me, even then, to be horrifying extremes. In Tennessee, Andy convinced a young quadriplegic that his reckless plunge into shallow waters from a cliff ledge had in fact been a premeditated attempt to commit suicide, that he had only himself to blame, and that he now *owed* it to himself, to God and other quadriplegics to demonstrate how his defeat could be turned into victory. 'That's blaming the victim!' I screamed at Andy when he told me what he'd done. Whatever it was, it must be pointed out that the quadriplegic, with Andy's exhaustive support and involvement (which included inventive forms of lovemaking), went on to earn advanced and honorary degrees for his achievements as an expert on the care, needs and rights of the handicapped.

By contrast, Andy never talked much about predestination, which was strange for a priest, if less so for an Episcopalian than a Catholic priest, and especially for a Jungian. As a Metropolitan Community Church priest wrote me after reading 'The Housemates Who Got Nailed', the penultimate chapter of *Confessions*, when it was published in an earlier version in *Christopher Street*: 'it seems most strange that your chaplain "ex" would not be familiar with the term "synchronicity", as it is frequently translated into theologese as "God's will' or "Providence" by Christian clerics who are into Jung.'

Andrew really wasn't familiar with the term 'synchronicity'. Nor did he know that a conversation with Carl Jung was among the earliest, pivotal developments of the great spiritual phenomenon that would eventually become known as Alcoholics Anonymous. Andy certainly understood that Jung was fundamentally Christian, that some of his psychology, though devolved from Freud, involved a vaguely 'Christian' rejection of him, and that many things that were called Jungian tacitly invoked Christianity. And he loved Jung's mysticism, his dream psychology, the simple yin-yang anima/animus concepts of gender and sexuality, and the notions of the archetypes and the collective unconscious. But Andy was no more deeply involved with Jung, nor more interested in the small details, than he was with any other of his life's myriad vocations and avocations, except the real-estate and, later, the stock market. There, certain of the small details counted a lot more concretely, and he easily and thoroughly mastered them.

After Salzburg, we returned briefly to Andy's château,

passing through Switzerland. During the next three weeks, while Andy toured the Middle East, I took my second trip to Italy before proceeding to London for ten days of opera and theatre. In Rome I telephoned Jerry Davis, the blond, beautiful, expatriate American historian and pretentious snob who was a regular on Waldi's circuit. Jerry had just emerged from a catastrophic affairette with D. J. Love – another example of Waldi's matchmaking at its wickedest – and was in no mood to meet new tricks, certainly not anybody who was presenting himself as 'a friend of Waldi's'. So when *two* 'friends of Waldi's' – unknown to each other – arrived simultaneously, Jerry introduced us, hoping we'd connect with each other. When that connection happened – so instantly and totally that Jerry could not even get an answer to his inquiries about our drinks – however, our *ospite* got even more upset and very unceremoniously dumped us both at a sleazy pensione in Piazza Navona.

I never fell deeply in love with Bart (Bartolomeo), but within hours we both knew that this was going to be something more than a one-night stand or even affairette. Burly, hairy, with an enormous, unclipped dick, Bart's dark Sicilian body turned me on more, and for more years, than any I've known before or since. We had all kinds of sex, but there were preferences. After having his densely hairy ass eaten out for hours, he loved to get fucked. We rented a Vespa, drove through the Parioli, the 'closed' Borghese gardens at night, to Castelgondolfo, Ostia and Civitavecchia. It was as sexy and adventurous a Roman holiday as anything I could have fantasized.

As I say, I never fell deeply in love with Bart, but our relationship lasted on its own terms for nearly twenty years to become the most enduring sexual relationship of my life. I slept with Bart the night before he got married, the night after, and approximately once a year, every year, for the next two decades. In addition to the AIDS epidemic, there was another development in more recent times that would strain our relationship. Bart, who was a high school football coach, was entrapped by a policeman he had flirted with in the school parking lot. The policeman was a member of a group called Cops For Christ, a number of whom suddenly appeared out of nowhere. They beat Bart severely, though there were no major injuries. Then they charged him with various crimes, threw him in jail, and gave the story to the local paper which ran it as a front-page *exposé*. Bart thereupon lost his job and had to confess everything to his family, who claimed they had never known or suspected anything about his secret life. It was pretty rough going for more than a year, but his wife and four kids stood by him (after Bart agreed to be tested for HIV). The charges were eventually dropped and he even got his job back.

Prior to this crisis, I had always thought of Bart as a perfect example of the kind of natural, genuine bisexuality contemporary psychiatrists were so certain didn't really exist. I do think the shrinks are wrong. There are plenty of genuinely bisexual or ambisexual men and women, and there would be plenty more, probably the great majority of people, if society weren't so sex-negative. But in Bart's case the shrinks were onto something. After the crisis I finally faced the reality that however functionally bisexual, however 'virile', Bart, who had hundreds if not thousands of extramarital adventures with other men but who probably never had a single extramarital heterosexual contact, was preferentially homosexual. In fact, Bart, whose working-class, Catholic upbringing had been rigorous, was (unlike his openly lesbian sister) a closeted, self-negating gay man who was trying to be straight and who was functioning in that capacity, a circumstance he had homophobically exploited and that I had been homophobically attracted to and had homophobically abetted. To a lesser extent, the same was true of Andy. That is, although Andy would be the first to acknowledge his preference for men over women, at least some of his machismo and bisexuality, however superficially successful, were more adaptive and accessory than natural.

Eventually, Bart and I stopped trying to make even the most clandestine arrangements to meet. Just as I could no longer lie about who I really was in the presence of his wife and family, Bart could no longer lie to them about his own life. They knew too much.

In Paris I telephoned one of the Baron's cronies who

invited me to his home for lunch. As his servants fussed about us I was certain he would be as impressed as I always was by my chatter about opera and Shakespeare. He may have been a multi-millionaire but I was, after all, young, beautiful and Phi Beta Kappa at the world's finest university (according to a poll that had been recently conducted by *Time* or *Newsweek*). Although he was a gracious host, I began to sense that he couldn't have cared less about how Shakespeare's plays were romanticized by nineteenth-century composers. Was his boredom in response to my tacit decision, at first glance, that anything sexual between us was out of the question? He was, on the other hand, quite interested in my being an English major. Having ascertained that I was Jewish and that I had been born and reared in Georgia, he then asked me a question that really seemed to intrigue him: 'Have you ever read anything by Margaret Mitchell?' The answer was no. Years later, I would wonder what it meant, what it would look like to others (to anti-Semites), that a Jew from Georgia who was an English major had never read anything by Margaret Mitchell. What did that say about identities? About patriotism? About paranoia?

In London, I took a chance on a new play that had just opened. It was called *The Prime of Miss Jean Brodie* and starred Vanessa Redgrave. I only knew of Ms Redgrave from *Morgan*, a strange political film that was immensely popular with the literati in the 1960s, and from the most glowing reviews of her Rosalind in a British production of *As You Like It*. Two days later, across town, I saw the most impressive performance by an actress in my entire theater-going experience. It was Maggie Smith, whom I'd otherwise never heard of, in the final performance of the famed National Theatre production of *Othello* with Sir Laurence Olivier.

It was a measure of the times and of my own levels of homophobia that less than a year earlier, in 1965, I had written the following line in a review of the film version of the Olivier–Old Vic *Othello*: 'The malevolence of Frank Finlay's Iago was enhanced by a none too subtle hint of homosexuality.' Although this statement had the obligatory negativity that any printed or public discussion of 'perversion' still always had prior to the

Stonewall period, I remember how progressive it felt to even mention the word that dare not speak its name.

At Covent Garden Joan Sutherland was assaying a new role, Marie in *La Fille du Régiment*. It was a gala premiere and the Queen was in attendance. Sutherland was in spectacular voice and the audience was driven to a frenzy by the endless succession of perfect trills and spine-tingling high notes and by the surprise of this otherwise droopy actress's ability to be funny, even if much of the humor was unintentional and based on the incongruity of such a large woman trying to play a soubrette. Sutherland's singing during those years was unwaveringly thrilling, but there was additional excitement that evening. The inspired casting, which included Monica Sinclair's raucously funny Marquise and a guest appearance by Dame Edith Coates as La Duchesse ('Quelle scandale!' she harrumphed in high English), extended to a newcomer. 'Who is that tenor?' I asked a knowledgeable-looking opera queen during the intermission. 'They [Sutherland and her manager-impressario-conductor-bel canto scholar husband, Richard Bonynge] had apparently discovered him when they were scouting for their Australia tour.' The young newcomer, bursting at the seams with stage presence and the most impressive high C's to be heard from a tenor since the young Franco Corelli, was Luciano Pavarotti.

Between performances I called telephone numbers I'd been given by Waldi, the Baron and Andy. Andy's contact, whom he had met through Waldi and may have had an affairette with (they both told me what happened, but I can't remember), was Donald Jeremy (Jeremiah on his birth certificate) Love, the writer and activist. At the time, D. J. was screenwriting and co-producing a murky adaptation of a novel about repressed homosexuality. The film was released the same year as *The Boys in the Band* (which dealt a lot more explicitly with homosexuality) and was enormously successful. Though progressive in the sense of dealing with homosexuality at all and being at least implicitly critical of society at large, both films tended to perpetuate the negative stereotypes against which an entire revolution of consciousness and pride was about to explode.

Of all the contacts from Waldi and the Baron, D. J.

seemed the most considerate and respectful of me as a person, in rather sharp contrast to all the things I'd heard about his 'narcissism', his inability to sustain any kind of relationship – friendship or love affair – and his terrible, 'adolescent' temper tantrums. And he was the only one who really seemed to respect what I regarded as my marriage to Andy.

That evening he was the perfect gentleman as he guided me on an interesting tour of London pubs, which included one or two gay or 'partly gay' private clubs. He made no effort to seduce me. Not finding him physically attractive, notwithstanding Waldi's suggesting that he had a big cock, I was greatly relieved. A decade later I made the unfortunate discovery that he had been attracted to me after all. One evening at the Everard Baths, as I sat posing on my bed with just the right lighting, he kept trying to come into my room. At first, I said 'D. J. This is ridiculous. We're old friends!' When he persisted on subsequent rounds, I kept saying 'No!' with what I thought would be the obviously, disarmingly self-satirizing, tongue-in-cheek tone of a 'daddy' talking to a 'son'. Since that time (into the early years of the epidemic), when D. J. and I disagreed, I would sometimes wonder if the outsized intensity of his anger had less to do with the substance of our argument at the moment than with the old issue of sexual attraction/rejection between us. What my own narcissism prevented me from seeing is that D. J.'s reactions had to do with a lot more than me; that to whatever extent any resentment of me did develop on the basis of sexual rejection, it was merely the reflection of a much more important one, the core of D. J.'s anger and anguish with this world: the old primary resentment of his father for having rejected D. J. for being a sissy.

As noted, I never learned the details of D. J.'s relationship with Andy and was never very curious. I only know that D. J. had been attracted to Andy and that there wasn't much, if any, response. At the time of my sojourn to London, they were 'friends'. Less than a year later, their communications soured and died when D. J. asked Andy if he'd be willing to invest in the play D. J. had just written, which Andy thought was nothing more than a 'juvenile' diatribe and 'transparent' revenge play about people who had deluded themselves into thinking they were D. J.'s friends. What Andy didn't now is that in addition to being a thinly disguised *exposé*, the play utilized material from an earlier Love play called *The Sissy's Revenge*. In retrospect, Andy probably felt insulted and perhaps frightened by the play's exposure of a closeted homosexual. In any event he declined the offer to back the play which turned out to be among the worst disasters in off-Broadway history. In the *New York Times* Clive Barnes described it as 'an ambitiously conceived cliché, with a few bright lines stuck into a morass of inert writing, rather like cloves being stuck into a ham.' It closed after one performance. But D. J. had made an impact on Andy, who once wrote me that he thought D. J. was 'the most intelligent gay man I've met besides you'.

Through Waldi, Andy and D. J. himself, I eventually met most of the 'friends' who were to emerge as caricatures in D. J.'s forthcoming novel, *The Sissy*. For some reason – a real mystery – these friends didn't include Waldi though there *was* a superrich, jetsetting Baron who got edited out (why?). According to legend, the basis of the novel – and according to critics, of every other thought, feeling, action and creation in D. J.'s life – was D. J.'s need to tell on his father for having called him a sissy. There was a lot more and much worse, but that would not be revealed for another fifteen years. Meanwhile, the novel, notwithstanding the extensive psychoanalytic psychotherapy D. J. was still undergoing during those years, introjected the sadistic parent and spent virtually all of its energies telling on everyone else for being 'faggots'.

Much has subsequently been said and written about *The Sissy*, which D. J. had originally entitled *I'll Show Ya Who the Sissy Is Ya Fuckin' FAGGOTS!* One of the most pungent observations, which I had the youthful temerity to actually tell D. J. to his face, was made by a gay acquaintance in Chicago. 'It would be as if James Baldwin had written what was expected to be *the* major novel of emerging black consciousness and affirmation in the early 1960s – a time when the overwhelming majority of portrayals of blacks was still mired in negative stereotypes – and *all* the characters turned out to be petty welfare chiselers, pimps, alcoholics and heroin addicts who do nothing but victimize each other in a "black" comedy that is patently a screenplay entitled *Niggers*.'

Another acquaintance, an English professor from Yale who I introduced to D. J. and who became one of the readers for D. J.'s forthcoming AIDS play, thought *The Sissy* was 'sweet'. Exactly like D. J., Howard had been wallowing in four-days-a-week, thousands-of-dollars-a-year psychoanalysis for years and years and more years yet while a handful of other gay men were attempting to come to grips with themselves and their homosexuality by coming out publicly and getting involved in gay and other civil rights organizations. Finally, and very much with the support of his progressive young analyst (the last of a long list), Howard made the transition to self-acceptance, having endured the ordeal of becoming one of the first openly gay men to adopt a child in the state he was living in. Unfortunately, by the time Howard finally got custody of Juan, he was in a career crisis. The country was in the grip of an ultraconservative shift and there were no jobs for professors of English, even for ones as credentialed as Howard. D. J.'s response to Howard's predicament was predictably tough Love: 'Ya gotta pick yourself up by ya bootstraps, kid.' Thenceforth their communications rapidly deteriorated. Anyway, when I asked Howard what he'd meant when he characterized *The Sissy* as 'sweet', he said: 'The whole book is based on this naive, childlike assumption of the relative maturity and wholesomeness and stability of heterosexual monogamy. The sweetness of the book is its subconscious, unspoken belief in the goodness of straight grownups and traditional marriage.' The very same grownups who believed D. J. was abnormal, who called him a sissy.

Those 'friends' of D. J.'s, like Jerry Davis, who ended up on crucifixes in leather bars or worse in *The Sissy*, really were awful people. And so most of them have remained – those still alive – virtually untouched by time. They're disturbed and amoral and continue to have almost no awareness of themselves as members of an oppressed minority. At the time he wrote *The Sissy*, however, neither did most other gay men, including D. J. Apart from his boiling resentment of them, which in nearly every case seemed to emanate from childlike rage in reaction to their personal (sexual and social) rejections of him, reflecting his father's rejection of him rather than genuine concern for the plight of gay people or real compassion for the cultural sexism and homophobia that had twisted these people into what they were, D. J. could make only qualified claims to gay consciousness. By his own admission, D. J.'s involvement with the fledgling gay community as it was becoming organized in those years was nonexistent. Up until the time of his truly heroic leadership in the AIDS crisis, which at first seemed so patently a labor of revenge against the gay community for its rejection of *The Sissy*, in fact, he had never participated in a gay demonstration or otherwise contributed any of his time or already sizable fortune to any specifically gay organization or cause. Maybe that's why the community was so slow to formally acknowledge its very substantial indebtedness to that leadership.

Like *The Sissy*, D. J.'s AIDS play, originally entitled *Here's What's Happened to the Community That Rejected the Sissy or I'll Show Ya Who the Sissy Is Ya Fucking FAGGOTS!!*, contained passages of raw, gut-wrenching feeling and dazzling incisiveness. And it was the only real alarm being sounded before the public. As such it was 'explosively powerful and uniquely important', as I myself characterized it in *The Advocate*. As history, however, it contained many untruths, the most remarkable of which was D. J.'s fantasy of himself as a lone crusader for relationships. In reality, D. J. had shown little willingness to enter or sustain relationships, in contrast to the many individuals in the community who had repeatedly put themselves on the line for the right to get married, despite what they knew to be the failure and oppression of the patriarchal institution of heterosexual monogamy. As D. J. saw it, however, the culpability for any failure at relationships in his own life lay elsewhere.

The loneliness and isolation, the inability to sustain sexual or platonic intimacy or interpersonal loyalty (at least implicitly but most often explicitly everybody else's fault); the inability to face and come to grips with his own femininity (did he cross-dress during childhood?), his own 'sissyness' (the portrayal of himself in the play was such that traditionally macho actors could comfortably pass in the part); the inability to handle the reality that younger gay men hadn't rallied around him as one of the 'hot' men or as any kind of real leader (the stupid sissies!, the fuckin' FAGGOTS!), that they rarely wanted him to be 'on top' in any sense and when they finally did, he couldn't handle it – these realities were barely hinted at in *The Sissy*, the AIDS play or any of the earlier work.

As D. J. became the loudest to point out, some of our worst enemies are themselves homosexual. Notwithstanding the incredible extent and heavy burden of this truth, there were more primary and important villains. Not until the late 1980s, however, did the principle targets of D. J.'s battles finally change from the community to its biggest and most powerful enemies. D. J. is unquestionably among the most courageous and important heroes in the history of the gay liberation movement and he is, indisputably, the supreme hero of the AIDS epidemic. He is also an exceptionally gifted and powerful writer. Meanwhile, however, the truth about D. J. is that up until recently, despite all the ear-splitting polemics and all those plays and novels and screenplays in which hyperbole was utilized with unprecedented calculation, skill, consistency and art, and all those years and more years of analysis, he was so obsessed with tattling on everybody else – it was apparently so deeply imprinted in childhood and had become such an established *modus* of relating to people, such a compulsion – that he had hardly begun to tell the truth about himself.

In 1992, with the premiere of his new play, *The Truth about Me*, that situation finally and dramatically changed. Here, it is with painful reflection and acceptance rather than anger at others that the D. J. character finally faces one of his life's most devastating truths: that 'people don't fall in love with me'. Now, at long last, we know the truth about Love. Even here, however, the introjection analogy holds. D. J. is otherwise still the sadistic parent he's telling on. 'You were cruel to me, Papa', is what the protagonist asserts when he tries to confront his dying father, who cannot or will not connect and who dies with no apologies. No moment in theater has touched me more. But the same line could still be said by the gay community to D. J. for the way he treated us in a younger time. Like his dying father, the

D. J. character on his own deathbed has mellowed. If there is more truth and compassion between that person and his father at the time of their final encounter, as finally developed between D. J. and his community, however, there are likewise no apologies from D. J. to anybody for past cruelties.

'From London, I flew to Greece, where I had arranged to rendezvous with Andy. Deeply tanned, he was handsomer than ever, and I got hard just watching him come through the gate. Actually, he would have been handsomer yet if he hadn't been so determined to obscure his age with all that Grecian Formula, which so often made his hair look comic-strip blue and, worse, by shaving off all his chest hair because it was turning gray and white. Even though Greece had just been taken over by a fiercely homophobic military junta, we kissed on the mouth, right there in the middle of the airport. William, my pet name for Andy's dick, was hard too. Unfortunately, when we got to the hotel, we discovered sticky yellow stains on my underpants, and it had begun to sting when I peed. I knew what that was, having been treated for clap on three previous occasions. Andy nearly had a convulsion from the combination of anger and frustrated lust, but I sat on his face and he got off. That night, we found a doctor who gave me antibiotics. As always in these situations, I blamed it all on Andy. If he hadn't insisted on going to the Middle East by himself (if he hadn't been so stingy), or with some other lover he wasn't telling me about, this would never have happened.

The drip cleared within twenty-fours hours and we resumed our honeymoon, this time on Mykonos. Andy had selected a new resort hotel that had just opened on the least accessible part of the island. When we finally arrived, an attendant backed a car over Andy's luggage, resulting in the breakage of a camera and some costume jewelry. What was the costume jewelry for? I never found out. Anyway, because the junta wanted at all costs to maintain good relations with the United States, the hotel people made this extraordinary gesture of paying half of our expenses at the hotel to compensate for the damages.

Everywhere we went in Greece, we were treated with excessive deference.

As an English major and liberal arts student at the University of California at Berkeley at the time, I was an outspoken opponent of our involvement in Vietnam and felt a conflict of ethics about being in Greece. If I'd had the courage of my convictions, in fact, we would have gone elsewhere. In those days, however, I had little such courage when matters of personal experience and fulfillment seemed so overridingly important. Although I took my studies seriously, was proud of my liberal politics and participated wholeheartedly in a number of the demonstrations that constantly rocked 'Berserkely' during those years, there was this other me, the opera queen, on my way to the tailor to have the ass of a new pair of pants redone in the midst of what turned out to be the most violent of the infamous People's Park confrontations.

There I was in the center of Sproul Plaza one typically resplendent afternoon. All of a sudden everyone began fleeing, away from me, it seemed, and in all directions. I tried to remember what I had eaten for lunch. Maybe it was something I was wearing. Or not wearing. A moment later I was immobilized by deafening staccato blasts of wind and sound. I looked up and there, just above my head, was one of Governor Ronald Reagan's giant army transport helicopters spraying nerve gas or whatever it was on me and my bag of pants. When I awoke on a stretcher in the Student Union, which was nearby at basement level and one of the few spaces on campus that wasn't suffused with gas, there was a small band of students and what I slowly realized were patients, some of them elderly, who had fled in their pajamas and gowns and less (the helicopters had even sprayed Cowell Hospital!) standing around me, and they began to clap. I was a hero, they said, apparently not noticing the odd way I suddenly draped my leg over the bag of pants. I guess I was a somewhat atypical member of the class of '69, half of which attended the graduation ceremonies wearing gas masks while the other half stayed away in protest. I counted with the second half and felt the protest keenly – for Vietnam and People's Park and Patty Hearst and Ronny and Shirley Temple Black – even though I ended up taking advantage of this unanticipated free time to have those same pants refitted.

The hotel on Mykonos turned out to be so new and inaccessible that we were virtually the only people there. During the day we climbed the steep cliffs that surrounded the resort and had sex in rocky caves overlooking the sea. On one of our climbs, Andy suddenly became very pale, his eyes rolled up and he began to lose his balance, almost falling several hundred feet into the sea. I grabbed him. He opened his eyes and began gasping. Finally he pointed to something behind me. It was a largely decomposed donkey. Something like this had happened once before in Tennessee, when we almost ran over a dead pig. Andy had a phobia about dead animals. How if at all, I've since wondered, did that connect in his brain circuits with his dread of getting older?

Back in Piraeus for an afternoon before returning to Switzerland and the château, we rented a room in a cheap dockside hotel. With the aid of several faded and cracked but wonderfully placed mirrors, we set a new record for orgasms per hour. Despite the easy availability of some of the most handsome sailors I'd ever seen (the junta notwithstanding), I thought only about Andy, whose hands I liked to lick while he fucked me. No matter what we were doing sexually, no matter who was fucking who, we nearly always climaxed looking in each other's eyes, as we whispered or cried 'I love you'. In all our time together, neither of us ever talked about having a three-way or participating in an orgy or going to the baths together. Notwithstanding our promiscuity outside the relationship, we were much too jealous and possessive of each other to even consider such a thing.

At summer's end, in the mountains surrounding the château, not far from the hoary remains of the great monastery of Cluny, Andy and I finally located the very isolated ruins of a fourteenth-century castle that still had gargoyles, columns, a balcony and a magnificent view of the surrounding countryside. With a heavy silver spoon from our picnic basket, I dug up a square of earth, so rich it looked like a piece of chocolate cake with pistachio icing. I savored its moist texture and fecund smell. Mme Desmoulins, Andy's housekeeper, had prepared fresh salads with the subtlest vinaigrette and creamy dressings, and we drank a priceless bottle of pre-war Château Lafitte Rothschild from Andy's cellar. We took off our clothes and fucked in the gentle summer breezes.

Unfortunately, our idyll was not to last. What idyll ever does? As my romance with Andy faded, reality began to take focus. On our final trip together, to Hawaii, our fighting was so bad I left him for several days, during which I had a three-way affair with a couple from Los Angeles. The wife of the dominant of the two men, both of whom were as generous as they were handsome, was trying to prevent him from seeing his children and was telling them and the courts that their father was a pervert who was unfit to be their parent. It was an exceedingly ugly but typical – for the late 1960s and early 1970s – 'gay divorce'.

Despite his flirtation with the pervasive liberalism of the 1960s, reflecting the relative and growing liberalism of his church; despite his having always told me that not only was there nothing shameful or wrong with being gay, it was something to be proud of (a decade before either of us had ever heard of John McNeill or John Boswell, Andy had pointed out to me that there was nothing in the New Testament about homosexuality and that there was dispute about the Old Testament citations); despite his reassurances that 'your gay friends are your family'; despite the cognitive dissonance (a psychological concept Andrew was forever talking about, but only with regard to others) of holding beliefs that are diametrically opposed to how you actually feel; Andrew could not shake the Republican sympathies and class loyalties that were so deeply imprinted. He was, after all, twice my age and in his early forties at the time of the Stonewall Rebellion. With the greatest distress, I had to begin to acknowledge the unbearably painful reality that not only were Andy and I not going to be lovers for the rest of our lives, but that Andy was slowly withdrawing his endorsement of my pride in being gay, the very same gay pride he was the first to teach me to experience.

One day, trying to reach me, to speak to me as an equal, to explain to me why coming out of the closet was something he could neither believe in nor condone, he looked me in the eyes and said: 'Larry, you simply have no idea how terrified the average straight man is of homosexuality.' Years later, when Dan White assassinated Harvey Milk and Charles Moscone, he said: 'You see what happened?' with the implication that White represented a kind of 'inevitable' (providential?) moral imperative that was about to sweep across America and throughout the world. Whatever happened to Andy's usually so overriding belief in free will, I wondered.

There were still moments of struggle, as when his own hope peeped through his prediction, during the Carter presidency, that 'the whole subject of homosexuality is going to open wide up'. But the drift back to the conservative values of the 1940s and 1950s, the era of his youth, was inexorable and, as I would eventually be able to see past the resentments, very sad.

Because I was still so in love with him, for several years after he had fallen out of love with me, I thought he was being sadistic. In 1980, when I boasted about the Gay Pride Day parade I had just marched in (something I'd been doing in New York, San Francisco or Boston since 1975), he began railing about how shameful and disgusting it was that 'those S & M types' and 'drag queens' and, as Andy's contemporary D. J. had also put it, 'lesbians with truck driver hair', and 'boy lovers' were flaunting themselves that way in public. Here was something he and D. J. were in complete agreement about. The gay community as it existed in the 1970s was such an embarrassing, ineffectual mess that no one of any substance or standing would want to have anything to do with it, certainly not publicly. Imagine what an exciting parade it would be, I pleaded in a letter Andy never answered, if more people of stature, people like you and D. J., were to come out and march with us. If Malcolm Boyd can do it, why can't you? How wonderful it was finally to see D. J. marching, for the first time in 1987, after all those years of rejecting us. How I kept longing for Andy to do the same.

But that was not and is never to be. I could handle the 'natural death', as Andy described it, of our love affair, of our sexual relationship. In fact, the waning of my sexual interest in Andy may have preceded and may even have precipitated his loss of feeling for me. But the intensity of the pain of being simultaneously rejected as a son was the worst I have known, as bad as that of the suicidal depression that followed five years later and for which I was hospitalized and placed on anti-depressants (could these events have been related?); for I truly loved Andy as a son loves his father, a love I still feel and will probably die with. But not of. Because of the seeds Andy himself first helped me to recognize and nurture within myself, people (including Andy), places and things no longer have the absolute power to determine my sense of purpose or serenity, my sense of self.

Andy's position as my mentor, as a father in my life, was based on a lot more than sexual fantasy or Jewish masochism, both of which I had some intellectual awareness of, even as they intermittently possessed me. It's true that I was pathologically self-negating as a Jew at the time we met and was consequently far more intellectualized and receptive to Christianity as a religion, while eschewing Judaism to the point that I knew almost nothing about it. But Andy was never evangelical, at least not overtly. Later, with the ongoing erosion of his ability to respond to me in any context and during the sustained attacks of paranoia I would experience whenever I smoked marijuana, which was more and more often, I would wonder if that's what had been going on all along. Had Andy's only real interest in me been the challenge of conversion? Was it some kind of prized achievement among clerics to convert a Jew?

Or worse? On a late winter night, we were sipping bourbon in front of a crackling fire in the Gothic study of Andy's Tennessee mansion. Andy hated marijuana, but had impulsively taken a few tokes from my joint. Suddenly, he glared at me with glazed eyes and whispered with what seemed like the most intense seriousness, 'Maybe you *are* the devil.' Earlier that evening, we had seen *Rosemary's Baby*, a film that exceeded anything either of us had ever experienced in conjuring for the most primitive, childlike fears of evil and the Devil. That same year, Andy had met Roman Polanski at a party given by Brian Epstein, the Beatles' manager who was so savagely caricatured in *Prick Up Your Ears*, the John Lahr/Stephen Frears film about Joe Orton. Everybody had the creeps about the coincidence of *Rosemary's Baby* and the Manson murders, and that certainly included Andy, who was horrified by the additional concurrence of his having met Polanski during that period. There was one other occasion when Andy said or quoted something about how it was necessary to treat the Devil with contempt. Otherwise, I never heard any indication from Andy that he really believed in the Devil or that his concepts of evil were any different from my own.

Even in the midst of the worst of these paranoid episodes, however, I was usually able to locate the certainty that Andy had loved me. The abundance of passionate declarations of love in so many letters, the love-making itself ... these things simply couldn't be faked. However bad things had become, they could not negate what was. Between 1975 and 1981, as our communications deteriorated further, as alcohol became increasingly problematic in both our lives, as Andy's thinking increasingly reflected the intellectual stagnation of rural Tennessee, as I smoked more and more marijuana and packs of Marlboro cigarettes, as we both became ever more grandiose and paranoid, I became episodically obsessed with notions that Andy had probably always been a sadistic anti-Semite and homophobe. At the same time, I became increasingly determined to resolve my conflicting identities as 'Judeo-Christian' (as I labeled myself in those years) and as a gay man, to find some way to be that would be acceptable to everybody and that would restore Andy's love for me.

On a final visit, I took communion, as I had done on a number of occasions since the beginning of our relationship, at a service Andy led at the beautiful little 'nondenominational' mountain church he had worked so hard to restore. When I told him that I'd begun attending Metropolitan Community and Unitarian Church services in Boston, however, he said nothing. Beyond a half-hearted suggestion that I consider 'Jews For Jesus' and giving me a resurrection crucifix I had asked him for, in fact, Andy no longer cared what I did.

The resurrection crucifix, which one sees infrequently,

shows the risen Christ with hands raised in blessing, superimposed against rather than nailed to the cross. As a symbol of Christianity, this cross had always seemed a lot more accessible to me than the standard, the one that has a human (who is Jewish) nailed to it. The more I explored Christianity through my involvement with Andy, especially as our relationship deteriorated, the more apt the standard crucifix seemed as a metaphor for what Christians have always done to Jews. If Jesus Christ, who was genetically Jewish (neo-Nazis claim he wasn't!), had been living in Nazi-occupied territory, he would have been tortured and murdered, a situation that might have been facilitated by a Jewish Kapo, in analogy to the 'Jewish betrayal' of Jesus during the Roman occupation. In this sense, as an ethnic Jew, I identify with Christ a lot more genuinely than most Christians. Bill Hoffman once said he'd like to write a play about Jesus that has him looking very Eastern European Jewish and speaking Yiddish. Considering how commonly Christians seem unable to grasp this fundamental reality, that their Lord – the man and God they get on their knees to worship – was genetically Jewish, I think it's a splendid idea.

One evening Andy responded to my calling him 'Mr Fifty-one percenter' (heckling him for what seemed to me to be his elitist, cowardly tendency to defend the *status quo*) by drunkenly insulting my 'flaming liberal' and 'pinko' values and friends. My response was uncontrolled rage. I hurled every insult I could think of and even some threats. Summarily and very angrily, he declaimed his need 'to be with people from my own class', and hung up on me. I then took the resurrection crucifix, together with the *keffiyeh* Andy strutted about in and eventually gave me as a souvenir of his trip to the Middle East when we rendezvoused in Greece, and wrapped them in a swatch of oriental rug. The section of rug had been given to me by Benjie, the Jewish astrologer. In the midst of my brawling with Andy, I had suddenly noticed that the section of rug, which kept invading my gaze from its place on the wall next to the phone, was subtly interwoven with swastikas. I then threw the little package into the trash compactor. Symbolically, I had accepted and completed the termination of my relationship with Andy, and of the masochistic self-effacement, the people-pleasing, the always trying to be something or someone I wasn't, that relationship had increasingly come to represent. That was Christmas Eve, 1983.

More than anyone else, Andy was responsible for helping me make the critical decisions that would shape the rest of my life. When we met, I had abandoned a pre-med curriculum to pursue studies in the humanities, and I had excelled. But what, exactly, was I going to do with my life, professionally? As an English major, I was groping toward a career as a teacher, but the only thing I really, passionately loved was opera. I'll never forget how upset I was by a letter Andy sent me, gently spelling out the reality that without any real talent or intensive training, as a singer, musician, administrator or critic, there was no basis for a career in opera. It's not that I was *that* naive, that I knew nothing about the real world, but we were living in the 1960s and anything seemed possible. Most important, one should do what one wanted, work with what one loved and cared most about, follow one's heart. At the time, neither of us realized that the actual 'great love of my life' was writing.

Through a lot of diligent, tough, paternal effort on Andy's part, I eventually reoriented my thinking. Instead of just studying and applauding or even writing about what I really loved so much about opera and literature – the conceptualization and dramatization of life's predicaments and peak experiences – I could live them, as a physician. Instead of being a bystander, an observer of the mystery of death, the awesome power of the human will to survive, the suffering, damage and overcoming of unfathomable extremes of pain, the most incredible examples of human pettiness, altruism and courage, I'd be participating in these adventures, as they actually happened.

My biological father, who was dying of cancer, was stunned but extremely gratified by my decision to return to my pre-med studies and pursue a career in medicine. It's the hope he and my mother had always had for me but had long since given up on. Paradoxically, Dad and I had become so close during my years with Andy that I boldly came out to him and told him about my relationship with Andy (a confession Andy regarded as unconscious attempted patricide). Although Dad died two weeks before the notification came of my acceptance to medical school in 1969, I knew he was proud of me and confident that I would make my way and mark as a physician. Appropriately, my other father, Andy, was the guest of honor, four years later, at my graduation from medical school in 1973. There was a lot of love between us that day, the kind of love I suspect human beings are only rarely privileged to know. Even so, it took as much skill as effort to drag him to Marshall Field and the Art Institute the next day, to buy me the graduation presents he should have bought (and spent more on!) in the first place.

Fifteen years later, my mother casually mentioned in passing that my father, who used to write the most elaborate letters and who left some diary fragments in addition to his many medical papers, had dreamed of becoming a professional writer. My father was a closet writer! Despite our apparent closeness during his last years, he had chosen not to aggravate my ambivalence about medicine by confiding this secret of his own youthful ambitions. Around the same time my mother, herself a closet writer (like my sister and brother and a number of my other relatives on both sides of the family!), casually told me this information, with no awareness of its interest or importance to me, I made a single effort to resume communications with Andy. Realizing that we might never speak again, I took the occasion to make amends for past anger and resentments. Cautiously, Andy accepted the apology, but our disengagement had advanced to the point that we had no sense of each other's current lives. 'Have you become a real, full-fledged, pedigreed psychiatrist yet?' drawled the voice of a stranger (referring back to 1979–80, when I had seriously considered and explored the possibility of doing a second residency in psychiatry). He knew nothing of my current work in substance abuse medicine and continued to have no interest in or sympathy for my involvement in gay politics and the AIDS epidemic, and no appreciation or support for my writing. As the voice of the stranger drawled on about a new romance, something else became clear, something so obvious only love could have obscured it for so long: Andy was serially into twenty-year-olds.

Neither of my fathers, who never really or fully knew

themselves (one a closet writer, the other a pre-liberation gay man), ever really knew me. Since I didn't know myself either, how could they have? It was finally clear. I would have to become my own father.

I recently discovered a long-forgotten book, a sweet, sentimental anthology of poems about friendship and love Andy gave me and inscribed as follows: 'When all else has been won, all desires fulfilled, and all things possessed, the happy hours of our friendship will fill a pit of failure and sorrow with joy and happiness.' Andy gave me the little book to commemorate the night we made the most passionate love either of us would ever know in the cool summer grasses of a Florentine hillside. That was 1968 and I was twenty-one years old. That fall, when he visited me in Berkeley, we drove to the top of the Berkeley hills to watch the magnificent San Francisco Bay sunset. I remember thinking to myself: 'I'll never be this happy again. It's not possible.'

On Christmas morning, 1986, the radio was playing Nat King Cole's version of 'Merry Christmas', which he recorded at the time of my birth in June 1946. Unconsciously, I wandered to my bookshelf and picked up *The Seed and the Sower* (1953) by Sir Laurens van der Post, the close friend and disciple of Carl Jung. The copy I have was retitled *Merry Christmas, Mr Lawrence* to coincide with the release of Nagisa Oshima's film of that name in 1982. I read the last few pages of the chapter called 'The Sowing of the Seed', which concludes the book's first section, 'Christmas Morning'. Here, Col. Lawrence comes to an understanding of the unparallelled bravery of his comrade, Lt Celliers, during their captivity together in World War II. As punishment for that bravery, Celliers was ordered to be buried alive by Yonoi, the Japanese officer he had so literally disarmed by daring to love him, to embrace him in front of all the other soldiers and prisoners. In homage to that bravery, Yonoi had saluted the dying Celliers as he would a superior officer, and after the war, he had burned a lock of Celliers' hair in a ceremony of religious tribute. Celliers' extraordinary bravery, Lawrence realizes on the basis of his dying words, had its origins in a religious experience

Celliers had had some years earlier. The experience involved Celliers' acknowledging a boyhood betrayal of his younger brother, for which, many years later, he had taken the only real leave of his military service to travel halfway across the world to make amends.

Lawrence now begins to understand that the seed Celliers had thus planted had blossomed in its impact on their Japanese captors and military comrades, and in a thousand other, unforeseen ways. In an epiphany, Lawrence imagines he can hear Celliers' voice in the various sounds of a sudden storm. 'Wind and spirit, earth and being, rain and doing, lightning and awareness imperative, thunder and the word, seed and sower, all are one: and it is necessary only for man to ask for his seed to be chosen and to pray for the sower within to sow it through the deed and act of himself, and then the harvest for all will be golden and great.'

In mid-June 1987, one of my patients at the alcoholism clinic I work at wanted to read me something from Alcoholics Anonymous, the classic 'Big Book' that is the basic text of the program. With the help of AA, the spiritual recovery movement that was spearheaded by Jung, he had been sober almost three years, and his life had been completely transformed. He had just completed his eighth and ninth 'steps', which he wanted to read me: 'made a list of all persons we had harmed and became willing to make amends to them all', and 'made direct amends to such persons except when to do so would injure them or others'. Then he pointed out that the way the book is written, the fabled 'promises' of the program 'follow' the eighth and ninth steps. He read from 'the promises': 'We are going to know a new freedom and a new happiness. We will not regret the past nor wish to shut the door on it ...'

A few days before Father's Day, 1988, I was in a card store. My biological father had died nearly twenty years earlier, and a decade later, I had finally stopped sending Father's Day cards to Andy. It's an occasion I no longer celebrate. Stimulated by a card specifically for step-fathers, I decided for the first time, to send one to my step-father. I also purchased a card that showed Tony the Tiger wearing a crown and beaming with pride. It said 'Happy Father's Day' on the outside and 'We love you' on the inside. Impulsively, I signed it 'the gay community' and mailed it with a fictitious return address to D. J. Love.

Around the time of the premiere of D.J.'s AIDS play, I had purchased another card, a response to a conversation D. J. and I had had two years earlier. Sharing a cab home from a conference on AIDS, D. J. had quoted Dostoevsky about how one sometimes has to be bad for the greater good. I was going to send the card to D. J., but never did. It shows a white-gloved hand dangling a lavender heart by a string. The hand looks poised to let the heart drop. On the back page, there's a quote attributed to Dostoevsky:

> Love will teach us all things: but we must learn how to win love; it is got with difficulty; it is a possession dearly bought with much labor and in long time; for one must not love sometimes only, for a passing moment, but always. There is no man who doth not sometimes love; even the wicked can do that.

Chapter three

Rachel Teufelsdreck Carves Her Name in the Cathedral of Ulm

AMONG the lovers and affairettes I've had, two were with physicians who would habitually comment on the sophisticated emotions they felt they could discern in the behavior of their dogs. The more recent of these wasn't a lover or even an affairette so much as an entanglement. José Orlovsky was another habitué of the Everard, an MDA- and THC-marinated, familially and filthy rich, Russian–Jewish–Argentine–American who I used to call 'the evil psychiatrist'. That was back in the good old bad old days of my gay youth, when it was compulsively self-deprecating, depersonalizing 'fun' to nickname new tricks, 'disguising' the fact that we couldn't or didn't want to remember or say each other's actual names, even when those names happened to be attached to oceanfront homes in Fire Island Pines. The reason we couldn't remember each other's names, of course, was drugs. The reason we didn't want to remember them or name them to others who might know them was that we were ashamed of what we'd done and/or because the person we'd done it with was too old, ugly or otherwise reprehensible. In José's case, all of the reasons applied.

Anyway, Manners, the evil psychiatrist's sweet-faced Labrador, who I'm convinced died of chronic boredom and depression rather than the vague 'neurological condition' that was alleged to be primary, was, according to José, 'polite'. When you entered the living room, Manners would get up from his usual resting place on the couch, not to greet you – on the contrary, he would sleepily shuffle to an uncontestable area of the rug without even glancing in your direction – but to offer you his place, even if you didn't show the slightest interest in sitting. In these situations, the evil psychiatrist was convinced, Manners was acting out of genuine compassion and thoughtfulness rather than reflexive submission.

Similarly, Hans Kahltzwerg would anthropomorphize the consternation of his dachshund, Franz. With great self-amusement and ostensible good humor, Hans would stand Franz up on his little hind legs, as if the dog were a puppet, and direct his front paws in dance and sing-song. 'We're practicing "dorg" humiliation', he'd tease with an infectious giggle. 'Oh, Franz!' he'd purr as he noted the somewhat overweight, middle-aged dog's motionless tail and unhappy, forebearing demeanor during these episodes, 'we wuuuuuhhhv yooooo ...'

My three-year love affair with Hans Kahltzwerg, which preceded my three-year entanglement with the evil psychiatrist by approximately five years, began in 1971, during the summer that followed my first year of medical school. Though I was still deeply involved with Andy, our disconnection had progressed to the point that I was ready for another major relationship. At the time, Hans, who was thirty-nine and fifteen years older than I (recapitulating the age differential I'd had with Andy), was the boy wonder of Obstetrics and Gynecology, probably the youngest academic department chairman in the country, and the youngest president in the history of ASCUE (irreverently know as Affiliated Societies for the Control of Undesirable Ethnicities), the largest and most powerful of America's proliferating, international 'Family Planning' associations.

Hans was Bavarian–American with (like so many Germans) 'a touch of Jewish blood'. Or was it more than a touch? In fact, it was Hans himself who first avowed to me what I later discovered to be the widely circulated legend that his grandfather on his father's side was Jewish. The question of exactly how much Jewish blood was a recurrent source of interest and Freudian humor if not overt conflict for Hans who, like so many of the intellectual and highly educated Germans who paraconsciously approved of Hitler's politics (i.e., crypto-Nazis), had outspokenly great respect for the German–Jewish culture that produced the likes of Freud, Mahler and Einstein. Not inconsistently, the affirmation that Freud and Kahltzwerg kin had played together as children was among Hans's most tenaciously cherished and frequently embellished evocations.

If Hans was ambivalently and subtly anti-Semitic, he was often overtly racist, sexist and homophobic, however droll or self-satirizing the context of his remarks might appear. Clearly, some of his truest sentiments were being expressed in jest. Among the funniest of these ostensibly oxymoronic attitudes was his hatred of infants, especially newborns. 'They scream and stink', he'd pout. The lovable, naughty little boy charm of such outbursts bewitched a broad range of audiences and was greatly enabled by Hans's short stature, tiny, hairless hands and preadolescently nasal, high-pitched voice. (One of his students vividly suggested that he looked and sounded like Nowhere Man in the movie version of *Yellow Submarine*, as I rather gleefully confided to Hans when I took him to see the movie.) Like true pituitary dwarfs, as they are characterized endocrinologically, or midgets, Hans gave you the impression that he was a cute little adult, an adult-child, like Oskar Matzerath in *The Tin Drum*. This was especially the case in moments of tenderness and intimacy, when he would comfortably regress to become the little Hans of our love-play, a sweet if mischievous five-year-old in short pants who might get a spanking if he didn't behave himself. Except for a few love taps, he never did.

The kind of insouciance with which I became involved with Hans is captured in an otherwise unremarkable French film called *La Triche*. In a subplot of the film, a young woman in her early twenties, approximately the same age as I when I met Hans, is in love with an excruciatingly venomous, small-time hoodlum – a homophobic, latently homosexual bully who casually resorts to the blackmail and murder of a former trick, the gay owner of a sleazy night club. Because she's in love with him, however, she thinks of his callousness and those of his criminal activities she knows about as boyishly naughty, in much the same way that I excused the conservative politics and selfishness of Andy Bullen.

Youthfully naive and in the throes of being in love, she consistently infantilizes him and is completely oblivious to the reality of the man. Like this mindless girl, possessed by passions she couldn't understand or control, I had fallen in love with a beast.

When confronted with his prejudices, Hans usually wouldn't bother to respond. It wasn't just that a man of Hans's professional stature and importance didn't have to respond to criticism from the relatively powerless and unimportant. Clearly, he enjoyed the humiliation, the suffering he knew he was causing. Besides, as Hans saw it, he wasn't *really* prejudiced. Not by any means. And if necessary, as on those increasingly frequent occasions when his radar sensed he might be losing too much credibility, he could always counter with numerous some-of-my-best-friends-are examples, like the childhood memories of playing with his Jewish 'cousins'. But how could someone who seemed to get along so well with black, Hispanic, Jewish and female colleagues be guilty of true prejudice? How could he have been so popular with the shallowly liberal (youthful and sexual) medical students, who voted him the top award for excellence in teaching two years in a row? It just didn't make sense. So I tentatively concluded that the only reason he so often used such obscenities as *nigger*, *spic*, *polack*, *wop*, *chink*, *Jap*, *dyke*, and *faggot* in my presence is that he enjoyed teasing me.

I don't recall him ever using the words *kike* or *cunt* – *twiffy* and *snatch* being preferred epithets for the female genitalia – but he did talk derisively, however subtly or indirectly, about both Jews and women. His attitude toward feminism was succinct (and not so atypical): 'Women want to be treated like men, but only when it's convenient for them.' The flaunting of such attitudes, I continued to believe, was meant to affectionately goad and show up liberals like myself who had so little in the way of actual achievements behind their inflated, boundlessly optimistic, sixtie-sish, peace-and-love statements of belief in equality and fairness for all. The facts were that simply by virtue of the various offices he held, Hans was on record as having done more to help minorities and the underprivileged, regardless of the degree to which he might be undermining them simultaneously, regardless of what I or anyone else might neurotically suspect he *really* believed or didn't believe, than I could ever hope to do. This was manifestly true even though, as a Republican supporter of Nixon, he was about as genuinely sympathetic with the plight of the disadvantaged as Nancy Reagan, whose drug abuse programs have likewise done more to help the underclass than I, in my small role as a medical director of substance abuse treatment programs, could ever hope to do. My status as an alumnus of the Free Speech and People's Park movements in Berserkeley may have been as impressive to other flower children as they were to me. In the real worlds of business, politics and science, however, they were not very negotiable credentials.

What I wanted to explain to Hans but never could, because I didn't understand it then and because my preconscious was finally beginning to assimilate the fact that it wasn't always so wise to declaim one's vulnerabilities in the presence of those who took pleasure in exploiting them, was the sting I've been conditioned to feel whenever I hear a slur directed against any racial, ethnic or other historically stigmatized minority group. This is not to imply that my simply analyzing or even explaining this vulnerability to Hans would have made any difference because he was reacting instinctively to my 'sensitivity', as he called it, from the moment we met and with an awareness that had been sharpened over thousands or years of collective unconsciousness.

On the other hand, it might have made a difference if I had somehow learned, as a young adult, to face and accept, rather than to regress with perpetual, masochistic denial, the pain of belonging to two stigmatized minorities. The first of these identities, that of being gay, was so culturally illegitimate that my sexuality, the core of my composite identity, had to be hidden not only from society, but from family and friends as well. Unlike other minority identities, it had to develop in a state of complete isolation. Ergo, I didn't know any other homos or queers, and when I finally did, in adolescence, the stigma was still such that we couldn't discuss it.

I botched the one opportunity I did have to talk about 'it'. I was thirteen or fourteen years old. We were living in Chicago, where we had moved from Georgia in 1958. Richard Holman was the remarkable young man with whom I had my first, intensely sexual (though never truly amorous) affair, a liaison that began in grammar school and continued, for six years, throughout high school. As so often happened after we 'French-kissed' our Friday or Saturday night doubledates goodnight, Richard and I ended up staying over at his or my home. This particular night – it was 2.00 or 3.00 a.m. – we had already had sex and were raiding the upstairs fridge. That was our usual pattern. We'd have sex, eat, then have sex again. We were whispering, still terrified of being 'caught' by my slumbering parents. Not because there was anything so shameful about having a late-night snack, of course, but because we were afraid they might somehow discover the much bigger secret we were hiding, the constant sex we were having not only whenever we slept over but also in such places as garages, in a maids' closet at the no-longer-existent Sherman Hotel, where we were once caught, and in various bathrooms at the Art Institute, where we both took Saturday classes. Butch Wandel, a friend from my earlier childhood in Macon, now tells me that the slumber parties and sleeping over we did so much of were not as traditional among the boys my age as I had subsequently always told everyone they were and had myself honestly believed. In fact, they were happening, according to Butch, consistently at my initiative! And he's not just being bitchy. As a married heterosexual, Butch claimed, he always thought these overnight stays, during one of which I taught him how to jerk off and have his first orgasm, were odd, but also, he tacitly conceded, lots of fun. Now I understand he's divorced and has 'gone gay'.

So there Richard and I were, sitting at the bar in the basement recreation area where we slept, giggling at the bovine moans of disgruntlement my half-awakened mother made when we dropped the tray of food we were absconding with and it banged and clanked down the stairs. As our eating and laughter subsided, Richard – a basketball star who was voted the most handsome man and the most likely to succeed in our high school class and who went on to graduate first in his class from one of the nation's most prestigious law schools, but who resented my being the first man in our high school class to get an athletic letter – suddenly turned serious and whispered, 'Do you think we're homos?'

'I don't know', I giggled.

We never discussed 'it' again, not even when I duplicitiously and foolishly confided some of our activities to a low-ranking member of our clique and rumors began circulating that we definitely *were* homos. Unlike the protagonists of the contemporaneous melodrama, *The Children's Hour*, however, neither Richard nor I was expelled from school or disowned by our families, and neither contemplated suicide. And because we were popular and perceived to be strong and masculine, no one even threatened to beat us up. In fact, we weren't officially or directly called to account by anyone. But neither did we in any way come to terms with what was happening or even discuss it. It simply passed, as did we. Richard eventually married and had children.

The other major category of shared identity I likewise never really discussed with Richard was that of being Jewish. We were both bar mitzvahed at about the same time, and most of our friends and neighbors were Jewish. But unlike Richard, who in addition to his many other leadership traits, already spoke authoritatively about Jewish history and culture, I had no real sense of what it meant to be Jewish, just as I had no real consciousness of the anti-Semitism I had so deeply internalized. By the time I met Hans, I had made significant progress in beginning to come to grips with my identity as a gay man, but almost none with being Jewish. The source of my still wishing, like a child, to deny my irrevocably ethnic identity was, of course, fear, a fear Hans sensed the way a shark senses blood the first time he ever used the word 'niggers' in my presence; a fear I had learned as a child in the rural south.

When I was a little boy, everybody, especially my classmates and friends in my totally segregated home town of Macon, Georgia, talked about 'niggers' and 'queers'. I was the only Jew in my class and I don't think there were any other categories of ethnic persons in the school. One day, I repeated something my playmates from down the street, Lee and Curtis, said about 'niggers'. The next thing I knew I was reeling from one of the sharpest slaps my mother ever gave me: 'You're forbidden to ever use that word again', she decreed. 'It's the same as saying bad things about Jews.'

I recalled this incident many years later when I returned to Macon, where my mother still lives with my stepfather for part of each year in the house I was raised in. It was in the late 1970s, and I was in a men's room at Mercer College. The graffiti had changed little over the years. Everything was still 'niggers' and 'queers'. In the midst of all this, however, someone had scrawled a rejoinder that may have been a sign of changing times: 'Lassie fucks halfbreeds.'

I remembered my mother's courageous stand against racism during my early teenage years in Chicago. It was the early 1960s and my mother, now surrounded by her Russian and Eastern European Jewish relatives and friends, seemed uncomfortable as she parroted their advice to my sister not to date 'schwartzes'. Her greater fear, that Judith might some day 'intermarry', seemed to betray the values she had inculcated in me as a child in Macon; values, I'm proud to say, she would re-embrace with greater security in later years.

I continued to play with Lee and Curtis – they were my closest boyhood friends – until I had a real fight with Lee. 'Jewish toosh!' was simultaneously the funniest and most challenging of the maledictions he snarled at me that day. It was based, I assume, on 'tooshie' or 'tuchus', among the many 'dirty' words I had picked up during summer visits to Chicago. During the fight, I'll never forget, his mother came out and watched us, silently approving of her son's boys-will-be-boys roughhouse and anti-Semitic goading. I beat the shit out of Lee but fled in fear when he picked up a brick and began screaming hysterically. I didn't have much to do with Lee after that, and winced when I saw his parents again many years later. They had come to pay their respects to my dying father, who was among the most esteemed physicians in Macon's history (the city hospital library is named after him).

Around the same time (I was five or six) Curtis informed me that because I was Jewish, we couldn't play together anymore. It was the early 1950s, and I remember seeing something about the Rosenbergs on our Motorola. It wasn't his decision, he said. He didn't even know what 'Jewish' was, but that's what his mother had told him. Unlike Lee, Curtis had not yet adopted his parents' prejudices, at least not against Jews, so there was no hostility and no fight. Like most of the boys and girls I knew, however, Curtis frequently used the epithet 'niggers', which now made me uncomfortable because of what my mother had said. It was the first time in my life that I can recall feeling heartbroken. Sobbing, I ran home to tell my mommy. With great bravery she called Curtis's mother, who claimed she was simply respecting her husband's wishes. I think my mother already knew what I later found out, that they were Klan members. Even I already knew that like so many Southerners, like Lee's parents, they were still die-hard Confederates. And Americans continue to be surprised that so many Germans and Austrians remain unapologetically loyal to their Nazi heritage.

I don't know what Mom said. Perhaps she reminded Mrs Lynch of my father's status in the community or appealed for compassion, but somehow she convinced her to allow Curtis and me to resume playing together. Though we did so, the friendship was never the same. I became even more afraid of Mrs Lynch, who looked much older than most of my friends' parents (Curtis was the Lynches' only child and was adopted), whose constant railing against 'niggers' was the worst I had ever heard from anyone, and who had the same warty growths on her oversized, pointed and crooked nose as the wicked witch in *The Wizard of Oz*. I didn't have an equivalent fear of Curtis's father, who worked at a gas station, was never around and seemed to leave all the decisions to the Mrs. I still tremble whenever I recall the look of bitter resentment and hatred on her twisted, American Gothic face one day, subsequent to the Jewish episode, as she handed me a Hershey bar.

Curtis and I grew apart, just as several successive, close boyhood friends and I grew apart. Compounding my adolescent confusion and discomfort, my mother discouraged me from seeing two consecutive girlfriends, my first, both of them from Christian working-class families. In both cases, Mom spoke to their mothers and seemed to be saying things that weren't so dissimilar from what Mrs Lynch had said to her about differences in background that suggested it would be better for the children not to be together. Coincidentally, I now recall, some of the later estrangements with boyhood friends followed more tacit confrontations with their parents, who seemed to dislike me – in two cases the dislike abruptly replaced earlier, sugar-coated, Southern-hospitality sweetness – for no apparent reason. Somehow, I figured, they knew what I already suspected about myself, that I was innately bad. Despite what had happened with Lee and Curtis, it didn't occur to me at any level of consciousness that this dislike could have to do with my being Jewish, because my internalization of anti-Semitism was now such that I no longer thought of myself as Jewish. I wasn't Jewish any more than the Susan Kohner character, in the remake of *Imitation of Life* that was soon to be filmed, was black.

Notwithstanding this internalization, the association between racism and anti-Semitism would be permanently branded in my consciousness and I would always feel like an imposter when I sat with the whites in the front of the bus, following a directive that read: 'White People Seat From Front, Colored People Seat From Rear', or used the whites-only water fountains and bathrooms that were standard throughout the fiercely segregated South I once called home. 'Why were things this way?' I asked our maid Jeannie. 'Why do colored people have poorer houses and neighborhoods than white people?' 'Because of the government', she said. At that age I didn't know what 'the guvermint' was. It was all too much to assimilate.

Hans, one of the world's leading obstetrician-gynecologists at the time of our affair, let me remind you, really was ambivalent about children. Perhaps it was because he had no children of his own. As he explained it to me, his wife, Victoria, was infertile. I forget the alleged cause – a congenitally deformed uterus, endometriosis, or fibroids. During the five or six years of their marriage, she had been extensively worked-up and treated for infertility, in the course of which she had undergone a number of surgical procedures, most of them diagnostic and minor (e.g., laparoscopies). Hans himself had operated on her twice, violating the superstition that a surgeon shouldn't operate on a member of his own family. But superstition implies a vulnerability to religious impulses, and Hans had no such vulnerabilities, to say the least, even if he did have feelings that might be, by his own perceptions, misclassified as 'spiritual' (e.g., his ego-dystonic need for people). In any event, Hans held that he had performed the surgery because he didn't trust anyone else. No other gynecologic surgeon, he insisted, was as skilled or trustworthy as he. Unlike most of Hans's boasting, this particular assertion was discernably, grossly false – Hans was a mediocre surgeon – and symptomatic of his increasingly clinical grandiosity. Over the next several years, I discovered that I was not the only one in their circle to consider the possibility that Hans himself might consciously or unconsciously have made a hands-on contribution to their predicament.

In one of his honest moments, which weren't infrequent despite episodes of characteristically alcoholic lying, Hans admitted that he wouldn't want any child, and certainly not a son, to be cursed with a father like himself. Obviously, there was more to their being childless than Victoria's real or alleged infertility, than the fact that Victoria was 'of peasant stock' or any of the other reasons Hans proffered over the years. Otherwise, why didn't they adopt?

All this seemed particularly baffling in the light of the parallel situation of his esteemed colleague and friend, Stan Rubin. Rubin, who was Chief of Pediatrics at State, and his wife, Cynthia, whom Hans said was 'barren' (do we still use that word?), had adopted several children. When I myself finally raised the question of adoption, Hans was evasive. With what appeared to be great empathy, he explained that a woman who had never been able to conceive feels deeply, irrevocably incomplete. Adoption, in other words, would not solve the problem of Victoria's sense of inferiority. What became clear, of course, is that adoption would not solve the problem of Hans's sense of Victoria's inferiority.

There were two other factors (the orthodox psychoanalysts for which Hans had such fearful respect would say they were one and the same) that doubtless influenced the childlessness of the Kahltzwergs: Hans's festeringly unresolved narcissistic conflicts with his father and homophobic self-hate. As Hans's mother lay

dying of breast cancer, his father, a far more successful practitioner if less distinguished academic than Hans, began having an
affair with his wife's live-in nurse. Within weeks of his wife's
death, this Hamlet's father remarried, precipitating a tangle of
Oedipaloid struggles that seemed to be the source of more pain for
Hans than any other development in his life. With dubious logic
and brutal amicability, we used to tease Hans that the love–hate
relationship he had with his father was the very same 'Elektra
complex' analysts believed to be responsible for the 'pathogenesis'
of lesbianism.

Hans was so horrified by what he perceived to be his
father's sadism and slander against his mother that he gave him an
ultimatum: 'Either the slut goes or you lose your son.' So far as I
know, Hans and his father never communicated again. When
Hans finally did get married, in his mid-thirties, to Victoria, it was
without his father's presence or acknowledgment. From the intensity of his feelings about his father, whose apparent lack of love
for his homosexual son Hans could never face, I sometimes had
the feeling that Hans's entire motivation for not having children,
as well as for becoming an obstetrician-gynecologist, was to get
revenge on his father.

With the proud defiance of a tragic hero, Hans attempted
to exact revenge and manipulate fate by adopting a substitute
father. The man he selected, Dr Charles Worthington, was a
world-renowned endocrinologist who, like Hans himself, grandly
outranked Hans's biological father in academic status and
achievement. But that wasn't the only commonality; for as it turns
out, Worthington's relationship with *his* father had been even
more fucked-up, however more maturely Worthington had
appeared to come to terms with it. Thus, Hans not only earned
vastly greater prestige within his father's own profession, he had
replaced him as a symbol of authority and as an object of adolescent hero worship with a man of ostensibly unimpeachable
moral character and integrity, whose professional achievements,
like Hans's own, were precisely the kind Hans believed Kahltzwerg *père* would most envy. This was an adoption, incidentally,
that worked both ways, in a kind of *folie à deux*. That is, Hans
likewise became the filially devoted, internationally recognized

scientist and disciple Worthington's actual teenage son, Thomas, never would be. Thomas, however, went on to become one of our generation's most liberal and determinedly liberated gay activists! Even in the age of AIDS, when his passionate, defiantly brave treatises on the bottom line, no-matter-what importance of fundamental principles of sexual freedom were so often met with apathy and hostility. How the gods must have tittered as they watched Hans attempting to persuade Thomas (who, like Hans, was at the time married and childless) never to come out of the closet.

Instead of children, Hans and Victoria had animals. First there were the two dachshunds, Franz and Albert. Then came Hans, as Hans had named him as a puppy, a very pedigreed great Dane who eventually manifested myriad genetic defects, including a hip dysplasia so severe that the poor creature howled in pain whenever he moved. Inevitably Hans had to be put to sleep. It was the only time anyone had ever seen Hans Kahltzwerg cry. But the precipitating trouble was not the hip disorder. In a territorial dispute at chow time, Hans attacked Franz, instantly and according to Master Hans 'accidentally', snapping the friendly little dog's neck. The dogs, incidentally, didn't eat canned food. They ate whatever their master ate, which was often directly from the table and usually consisted of sirloin steak or giant prawns – the kind that cost dollars apiece.

Completing the family were Nigel and Horace, two cross-eyed and stereotypically vocal Siamese cats. Hans hated cats generally, but especially these, probably because Victoria loved them. 'They're like women and homosexuals', he hissed, 'always wanting to slink up to whoever likes them the least.' Once, in a miniature fit, Hans kicked at them with his little feet. I also loved these cats and, at least on one occasion, came to their defense with an honesty and self-assertiveness that was very uncharacteristic of people-pleasing, masochistic me, especially in my relationship with a man whom I was sometimes still addressing – even in bed! – as Dr Kahltzwerg. 'They can't help the way they are', I piped. 'That's the way God made them.' Hans and Victoria stared at each other in stunned amazement. 'God!?'

Hans shared with Victoria, who mimicked the beliefs and attitudes of her master much as a tomboy tries to imitate her father, a profound distrust of anything having to do with religion, institutionally or even conceptually. In fact, Hans, who never noticed a dichotomy between his contempt for religion and his membership in the Republican party and admiration for Richard Nixon, was the most impressive example in my direct experience of the coexistence of atheism with racism. At the time, it didn't occur to me that the most impressive example in modern history of the coexistence of racism and atheism is Nazism.

Despite my prior love affair with an Episcopalian priest and my respect for the liberal positions and many good works of the Episcopal church, and certainly as a result of our relationship, I was relatively contempuous of all denominational/sectarian/institutional religion. Simultaneously, however, I had always held a kind of sociobiological view of religion itself and had great respect for the awesome forces I knew it to represent. I believed that 'group psychology' (herd instincts and behaviors), as Freud characterized it, manifests itself throughout the human species, as it does throughout all other higher and many lower life forms (e.g., ants); that what we define as 'religion' is simply a primitive way of conceptualizing social forms of aggression – the imperatives of group psychology – principal among which is herd, group or social bonding. Going to church, evangelizing and waging religious wars are the same stuff the ants do when they socialize, conquer and enslave other colonies. So while one may not believe in a specific deity, it's as dysfunctional as it is rare to find human primates evading the imperative of group bonding that occurs, principally and universally, around symbolic deities or their converse, the religions of atheism (Nazism, communism). When someone says 'I'm an atheist', it doesn't mean that they aren't as fiercely and dogmatically 'religious' as any theist or that they don't otherwise group-bond. At the time of our affair, Hans could continue to believe that he was an atheist even while granting some legitimacy, with regard to others, to what I was saying about herd instincts and behaviors because, like all pathological narcissists, Hans thought of himself as completely unique, very much apart from any merely human or mortal herd. Honest to God, there were occasions when little Hans would come right out and actually say, if only in my presence without witnesses, that that's precisely who he thought he was. Yes. Hans, who didn't believe in God, thought he was God! But I suppose it could have been even worse if Hans hadn't thought of himself as an atheist because he was already all too closely linked with a number of overtly fundamentalist Christian individuals, causes and groups, in ultraconservative Republican sympathy if not signature.

Eventually, as if to prove his virility, his ability to be politically conservative, to liberals like me who didn't take him seriously enough, who weren't sufficiently afraid of him, Hans accepted an offer to practice his very academically distinguished, politically liberal (pro-abortion and birth control, especially for the poor and non-white) brand of eugenics in New Johannesberg, Tennessee. The move from State was *very* abrupt, according to Dr Hymen, a recalcitrantly orthodox psychoanalytic psychiatrist *à la* Irving Bieber who believed that Hans (and everybody else, for that matter) was a 'latent homosexual' and who was the most outspoken of the faculty members in condemning the suddenness of Hans's resignation. Sheldon Hymen's bitterness was almost sympathetic, considering how often he had been the punctured, publicly deflated target (if only at faculty meetings) of Hans Kahltzwerg's notoriously rapacious wit.

In any event, the geographic (the self-help group term for the move an addict makes when he tries to change his life by changing his location instead of his attitudes and behaviors) to New Johannesberg was a relatively late episode in Hans's progression as an alcoholic. I had received my medical degree from State three or four years earlier and had not communicated with him since. But I managed to keep abreast of developments through friends and acquaintances. The most consistently informative of these persons was Gene Thoreau, *né* Jean-Jacques Taureau, a Franco–American Jewish physician who just happened to be my oldest and, ostensibly, closest friend. Even more coincidentally and quite unbeknownst to me until well into my affair with Hans, 'Dr Jock', as he was sometimes affectionately characterized, had been having an affair with Hans Kahltzwerg that antedated my own.

Gene Thoreau. There were stories connected with both

names – something to do with the fact that, in English, Gene was more of a boy's name than Jean, and Thoreau was more American than Taureau. We were the same age, eight or nine years old, and were in the same city parks day camp program together in Chicago, where my family spent so many of our summers prior to our moving there. As part of my teasing for him being much more the sissy I was afraid others might think I was, I kept calling him Jane, and whenever he'd protest, I'd declare that if *he* could change the spelling of his name, so could I. This was affectionate, but also retaliatory. I resented that Gene got better grades in everything (except gym). Sometimes I'd be so envious of his superior intelligence and greater self-discipline that I would see his achievements as acts of rivalry or spite. But why would Gene harbor envious feelings for me? Because I was more butch? Better at sports? Better looking? More popular? Yes, all of these. Unfortunately, it would take decades before either of us could even begin to understand that while we may have been jealous of some of each other's endowments and successes, Gene's achievements and path in life were no more primarily motivated by our relationship than were mine. Meanwhile, that relationship, the longest of my life, was troubled at a very fundamental level.

Gene was my best friend in adolescence and high school. In his eyes, however, we were lovers or incipient lovers, even though that level of attraction and involvement simply was not there for me and never would develop. For one thing Gene was thin and 'feminine', and from my earliest memories, I was more attracted to beefiness and 'virility'. Apart from a single adolescent 'experiment', in which Gene persuaded me to let him blow me to stimulate a sperm sample to examine under his microscope, there were no overtly sexual encounters. But I do remember the one episode. It had the clinical detachment of one of our class science projects, the kind Gene, unlike me, always won prizes for.

In *Love and Limerence*, her clinical study of the experience of being in love, Dorothy Tennov characterizes what happens in these relationships where one partner is in love with the other, but the feeling is not reciprocal. Inevitably there is a lot of misunderstanding and pain on both sides. When the limerent partner, the one who's in love, isn't treated like a lover, he becomes resentful and vindictive, as does the nonlimerent partner, who can't understand why his friend, especially once the often short-lived period of limerence fades (two years on the average), has become so spitefully unresponsive in matters of friendship. Just as the beloved hasn't been there as a lover for the one who's in love with him and may have seemed callous with regard to the latter's most tender feelings, the latter retaliates by not being there in friendship or worse. This situation is so predictable and usually causes such damage that the nonlimerent partner, who is less likely to be in an altered state of consciousness (limerence or lovesickness) and more able to perceive rationally, is advised to terminate the relationship as quickly as possible once the asynchronism is ascertained. Although I read Tennov's book in 1980, I'm only now just beginning to see my nearly forty-year relationship with Gene, and its slow miserable death, with perspective. I guess this means that friendships, like other nonsexual relationships (e.g., the cur who keeps returning to the master who abuses him, relationships between siblings or between parents and children), can be just as irrationally binding as those that are founded in limerence.

It was Gene who first introduced me to opera, to Richard Wagner and to Hans Kahltzwerg. As with most of our shared pursuits of the mind, Gene was the first to become interested in opera. Initially, we became familiar with a few popular works through recordings we both owned: *Carmen* (Stevens, Reiner), *Turandot* (Nilsson, Bjoerling), *Don Giovanni* (Siepi, Price, Nilsson, Leinsdorf) and *The Barber of Seville* (Merrill, Meters, Leinsdorf). Gene, already way ahead of me as usual, had others such as the Callas *Aida*, the Callas *Butterfly*, '*La Forenza del Destano*', as he called it, and a brand-new stereophonic recording of *La Bohème* with Tebaldi and Bergonzi. I eventually bought most of the operas Gene had, but I drew the line with two of his favorites: *Gianni Schicchi* and *Elektra*. I hated the former because I associated it with Miss Goldstein, our junior high school music teacher, who taught it in our class and who, we were certain, grew potatoes under her tits and behind her ears. And to this day, much as I eventually came to love Strauss (is there any real opera lover besides Joseph Kerman, I used to wonder, who doesn't?), I still sometimes think what I told Gene when I first heard his recording of *Elektra* (Böhm, Borkh): that too much of Strauss's music (especially the prelude to the third act of *Rosenkavalier*, as I told D. J. Love at a Met performance of that opera fifteen years later) sounds like the actualization of Strauss's boast that he could orchestrate anything, in this case flatulence.

Then came the brand new Solti/Nilsson recording of *Tristan und Isolde*, the first in stereo. We were both instantly and utterly seduced. We knew what we had read in the libretto notes and in some standard history and opera books of the time (the late 1950s and early 1960s) about the Nazi reverence for Wagner. And our researches into this area were not always superficial. We read biographies of such artists as Flagstad, Furtwängler, and Lotte Lehmann, and admired the politically conscious and responsible heroism of great human beings like Lehmann and Toscanini, artists who risked their very lives, to say nothing of their careers to oppose fascism. But we had absolutely no real sense of just how pivotal Wagner's anti-Semitism was to the Nazi phenomenon in Germany and throughout Europe. And in any event, we accepted as gospel the dispassionate, unengaged and unengaging party line of nearly all contemporary American and European arts critics, especially the music critics we had already begun to parrot with such reverence: that 'true art' always transcends politics; that politics is therefore and quite simply irrelevant to 'true' artistic appreciation.

So deeply accepting were we of these givens that we would buy recordings of infamous Nazi singers and conductors, of live performances from Nazi Germany, without batting an eyelash. Many of these artists became beloved favorites: Roswaenge, Gigli, von Karajan, Schwarzkopf, Lubin, etc. – all unrepentant Nazi collaborationists, party members or sympathizers. (The postwar career of both von Karajan and Schwarzkopf were resurrected by the latter's husband, British recording czar Walter Legge, who, incidentally, was Jewish and rumored, like Richard Bonynge, to be a closeted homosexual. The rumors about who was or wasn't gay turned out to be wrong at least as often as they proved true. In any case, the constant speculating about leaders in music, whose ranks included virtually none who were openly gay, was a cardinal feature of the vernacular of operaqueenspeak.)

But Schwarzkopf and von Karajan were great artists. The bottom line seemed to be just that simple. There seemed to be nothing more to say and so nothing ever was. We could continue to worship at the shrine of *heilige Kunst* without feeling anything but 'objective appreciation'. It was a little like jerking off to fantasies of attractive men in SS uniforms. Why let the trappings interfere with objective appreciation of male beauty? I wasn't to realize until early midlife that all we were doing was projecting our emotional detachment onto the rest of the world. We didn't comprehend that – notwithstanding the legions of Jewish Wagnerites, from the Hermann Levis of Wagner's time to the Daniel Barenboims of today – Wagner's anti-Semitic politics are not nearly so irrelevant to the rest of the world's appreciation of Wagner, then or today, as the worlds of music and culture would so cavalierly have us Jews believe and as we so masochistically convinced ourselves it was. Conversely, we were not nearly so unrelated to the Jews of history or their fate under Hitler as our childish denial of unpleasant realities wanted us to believe. In *these* kinds of pursuits of the mind, the kind that involve intellectual and political consciousness, it was I who, as the years passed, seemed always to be ahead of Gene.

I don't know when or even if, frankly, Gene finally began to *feel* any such concerns, but I vividly recall one of the incidents that triggered my own awareness. I was attending a particularly miserable performance of *Siegfried* at the Met, somnolently conducted by Erich Leinsdorf, the most consistently overrated of the leading Wagner conductors of our time. It was not a performance any self-respecting opera lover or even Wagnerite would have paid money to see. *Siegfried* is rarely performed, however (I had seen it only once), and I was invited by a well-known music critic who had his usual choice reviewer's tickets. My friendship with this critic, who is English–American, had been deteriorating from a peak of some intensity. He was a relatively conservative, closeted, career-oriented homosexual, an apolitical casualty of the 1950s, and I was a bombastically optimistic, ostentatiously politically conscious and politically correct gay activist product of the 1960s. What kept us friends, however unconsciously, was a power struggle composed of diverse elements – my relative youth, sanguinity, good looks and authority as a physician during the sexual 1970s, versus his influence and prestige as the music critic of a politically amoral, homophobic, yuppie glossy (a job I helped him get!) in the aristocratic, Republican 1980s.

During the first intermission we pecked at one another. I bored him, yet again, with my complaints about his not dealing with gay issues. 'It's a job', he sighed in a voice so characteristically softspoken you'd never imagine its secret: that at normal volume it sounded, as his close friend and fellow critic put it with characteristic acuity, like Darrell Fancourt in *The Mikado*. 'Did you know that I've begun investigating retirement options?' he continued with slightly more volume. The implication, of course, was that his priorities were sensible and practical for a professional of his age and rank; and furthermore, his hastily readjusted Marschallin's serenity seemed to be saying, time was passing a lot more rapidly than I might imagine. If I didn't want to wander aimlessly and unfulfilled for the rest of my life the way I seemed to be doing then, or worse, I'd better start to develop some sensible, professional priorities of my own. He was right on target. I *was* floundering professionally, and I *was* the one who was most noticeably unhappy and insecure. Like the child I still was at thirty, I attempted to retaliate by saying something bitchy about his sounding like a tired old woman. The music critic, who was the most passively aggressive person I've ever known, said nothing. As usual, I assumed he didn't want to dignify my acting out with a response.

We returned to the theater for the second half of *Siegfried*. Then, right in the middle of the performance, the strangest thing happened. During the scene that concludes with Siegfried's murder of Mime, the critic turned his head a full ninety degrees away from the stage toward me and silently glowered for what seemed like several minutes. As he did so, Siegfried (who had been raised by Mime), having tasted the blood of the dragon he had slain in an earlier scene, and thus enabled to understand the unspoken intentions of others, was discerning the treachery and hatred behind his foster-father's feigned protestations of caring and love. I was so confounded, so primevally frightened, by my friend's gesture that I initially convinced myself it was marijuana-induced paranoia (that whatever happened was my fault) and never mentioned it to another soul, not even my former psychiatrist. It wasn't until several years later, when the metaphorization of the Nibelungs as Jews in the Chéreau *Ring* would forever shatter the Wotan's sword my denial had become, that I was able to understand just how seriously hostile the music critic's gesture was. With my confession of this incident, I was finally able to begin to see, to glimpse, just how very deeply I had repressed, intellectualized and otherwise defended against my childhood fears and resentments of being Jewish. It wasn't until then that I was able to add this piece of the puzzle to others and resume the agonizing, wandering journey towards self-awareness and acceptance we call maturity.

Gene Thoreau was similarly denied and repressed, with regard to being Jewish but even more with regard to his homosexuality. To this day he remains in the closet both professionally and with his family. As a private practitioner with a very successful and mostly non-gay practice, his circumspection in the workplace is more comprehensible than his secrecy within a family that includes two relatively worldly though utterly materialistic parents, an older, married-with-children brother with whom he had sexual relations into their early adulthood and, believe it or not, a likewise closeted lesbian twin sister who, like Gene, lives with a lover. What doesn't anyone in his family or his colleagues at the hospital already know about Dr Jock? It's just this kind of empress's-new-clothes closetedness that provides the basis for what happened at the medical center where Gene is based. At the annual bash for outgoing house officers, the residents and interns staged a skit in which the hospital's quest for a new intensive care unit was likened to the search for the Wizard of Oz. And guess which housestaff doctor turned out to be the (crucifyingly effeminate) 'good fairy'? At the urging and in the company of his closest friend and colleague at the hospital, to whom he has yet to acknowledge his homosexuality or his ten-year relationship with his live-in lover (correction: technically, the lover lives in an adjoining apartment), Gene left the auditorium during a pause in the skit.

But he never did confront or even discuss what happened with any of his non-gay colleagues or friends, or with his parents, who never included Gene's lover in invitations, a situation both Gene and his lover accepted.

Not that Gene is happy about being in the closet or that he endorses the persecution of gay people, any more than he endorses the ever-worsening, profit-oriented abuses of the medical system that has made him so rich and of which he is so emblematic, notwithstanding his deservedly excellent reputation as a hard-working, first-rate professional with impeccable credentials. But at forty, very much like the music critic when he reached that age, Gene was no longer pretending, not to himself nor even to his rapidly dwindling coterie of more politically conscious friends, that there were any extraprofessional interests that had more priority than his own 'creature comforts', as he liked to refer to the luxury to which he had become so accustomed, with precisely the same character of denial as a drug addict. No. Gene and the music critic were merely solid, eminently sensible, hardworking achievers who were doing what others of their 'station' (their class) did when they reached midlife. They were giving appropriate priority to their own security, however avaricious that might seem to the bleeding hearts and ne'er-do-wells. As mature, responsible, successful professionals with hard-earned status, reputation and entrée into society, neither Gene nor the music critic wanted to be bothered ever again with things that 'aren't important', like tatter-demalion street marches for civil rights.

'Nothing's quite so motivating as money', Gene frankly concluded over Sachertorte at the Plaza Hotel's faded Palm Court. The purpose of the early 1985 trip to New York was fivefold: to complete negotiations for a $64,000 Mercedes Benz (Gene seemed less uncomfortable when I reminded him that his father likewise believed it was important to get a new car every year than when I mentioned a forthcoming book about the enthusiastic collaboration of Daimler-Benz with the Nazis); to attend a two-day seminar on current trends in medical malpractice litigation; to catch up with his always so overbooked, jetsetting hairdresser (whose Minoxidil-enhanced transformations of Gene's receding hairline into a 'Jewfro', as Gene and his German lover liked to refer to them on others, were indeed considerable achievements); to try out a new four-star French restaurant (Gene had little affinity for languages and he never even attempted to learn that of the culture he most revered, the native language of one of his grandparents, though he was conversationally comfortable with a few, select French words and expressions, 'dayclassay' most prominent among them. Instead, he became fluent in the exclusivity and ritual of *haute cuisine* and in gossip about the first class hotels and inns of France's *châteaux* country); and to meet with an expert on the greatest passion of his adult life, which had evolved from his adolescent love-affair with Richard Wagner to the acquisition of Islamic art.

The purpose of the Sachertorte was to commemorate the Vienna 1900 exposition we had just seen at the Museum of Modern Art. Gene wasn't *entirely* oblivious to the parallels between Vienna then and the United States today, just as he wasn't entirely oblivious to the Waldheim scandal that was stewing around him when he scoffed at my notion that that might be a reason to consider postponing a trip to Vienna earlier that year to bid on a piece. Predictably, however, he just wasn't very interested in ruing such things, and if confronted (which he wasn't, at least not directly), he could tell you why: because, quite frankly, that's a perspective he's heard enough times already, especially from the have-nots, would-bes, malcontents and do-gooders who, just coincidentally, so often turned out to be the same people! Gene found it difficult not to feel defensive. Everything about our little Viennese experience that morning seemed to be accusing him personally. But of what? Of being bourgeois? Of being selfish? Of being politically unconscious and uninvolved? To imply that Gene, who often worked twice as many hours each week as I did, who was on call most nights and weekends, who had comparatively little vacation, who was constantly being beeped at concerts and performances, was any of those things seemed the height of effrontery. But just in case there might be a scintilla of truth to the latter accusations of conscience, Gene, who had never attended a gay event, bought a gay magazine or newspaper or made a real contribution to a gay rights organization or for that matter to any other political organization or cause in his life, telephoned me a week after the Sachertorte to report, with startlingly uncharacteristic and sudden concern, on the defeat of his city's gay civil rights bill. Gene's telephone call reminded me of a performance of the Verdi *Requiem* that *Boston Globe* music critic Richard Dyer and I attended together in Providence, Rhode Island, that featured Marguerite Ruffino, the vocally gifted but artistically uncouth diva of the town's provincial little opera company. Every so often in the course of a performance, Richard observed, she'd remember to add an interpretive touch.

Maybe, at some level, Gene really does care. There are few gay people, even among the many who voted for Reagan and Bush, who are still entertaining the delusion that money alone can protect them from the gigantic social upheavals that have erupted throughout history and threaten to recur at every turn. But as research endocrinologist Dr Maude Slater, a similarly professionally dedicated, closeted and apolitical but aggressively antimaterialistic lesbian and former mentor of Gene's had said more than a decade ago, when Gene asked her advice about career options: 'Ya pays ya money and ya takes ya choice.' Gene had paid his choice and taken his money. A bit like the Kevin Klein character in the Movie, *The Big Chill*, he was now 'dug-in'. There was no turning back.

On the penultimate of his annual trips to the New York Antiques Fair, Gene presided over dinner at La Grenouille, alternatively considering a visit to Umbria during white truffle season versus another trek to Istanbul to bid on carpets, and boasting of the day's two bargains – a pair of eighteenth-century Japanese chairs for $200,000 and a pair of $10 reading spectacles from the local drug store: 'Why throw money away?' he asked with such conviction and sincerity that I dropped my planned word-in-edgewise about the successful benefit for the inauguration of the first university based Center for Lesbian and Gay Studies (at CUNY). We had sent him an invitation, but as with all the other invitations to gay and lesbian organizations and AIDS fundraisers, without exception, there was no response. I did boast about one thing on that occasion, however – the tie I was wearing. Glowing with hand-painted pink triangles, it was a treasured inheritance from Vito Russo.

By the time Gene introduced me to Hans during my first year of medical school, I was not exactly out of the closet, but most of my friends knew I was gay and I had already come out to my father. Gene, by contrast, had not yet admitted his homosexual preferences to himself, let alone to me, his closest friend and would-be lover, to his lesbian sister or to anyone else except, as I was later to discover, Hans.

Gene introduced me to Hans during the spring of my first year in medical school. Although we were exactly the same age, Gene was so smart and had worked so diligently through optional summer quarters that he was a full two years ahead of me. Suddenly, Gene began effervescing about this extraordinary doctor he had met during his clinical clerkship in Ob–Gyn. Not since his discovery of Wagner had I heard Gene wax so ecstatic about anything. The man was described as a genius who knew more about medicine, opera and sex than anyone he had ever met. I simply *had* to meet him. Gene was certain we would adore each other. Even though I was gay? Gene reassured me that Hans was extremely liberal and wise and outrageously funny about anything having to do with sex, and though happily married, may even have had a touch of you-know-what himself. To this day, closeted, homophobic Gene credits closeted, homophobic Hans (who used to tell me he thought Gene 'looks like a lesbian'), the first lover of his adult life, with being the person who most helped him to face and accept his homosexuality!

However malignant his shortcomings and defects of character would eventually prove to be, Hans really did seem to be the extraordinarily charming, vivacious, witty, wise and brave human being Gene had described, at least in those days when he was riding a crest of personal and professional successes and, of course, when I fell in love with him. And however homophobic, Hans was nonetheless among the most intellectually if not self-assertingly homosexual adults I had ever met. Although he was startlingly unattractive, unequivocally the ugliest man I've ever had sex with, I eventually found him so sexy that he entered my fantasies. That usually happens only when you fall in love with someone and it usually happens quickly, often at first sight. I did fall in love with Hans, but gradually and in fits.

We didn't have sex until nearly three months after Gene introduced us. And what an awkward, inauspicious milestone that was. Or wasn't. We were on a two-day trip to a satellite medical center. Bloated and inebriated following a greasy steak dinner at the local bar and grill, we checked into a tawdry little motel whose clients were mostly prostitutes and their johns, a place that seemed to happen by accident. I was so upset when Hans put the make on me – a development I neither wanted nor expected, at least not consciously – that I wasn't able to respond. The debacle that ensued was apparently so counter to the suave, easy seduction Don Juan had anticipated that he had a full-blown ulcer attack. In red flashes from the neon sign of the whores' motel and to the rhythmic accompaniment of little explosions of involuntary flatulence, little Hans disappeared into the bathroom, where he remained for nearly two hours. Nuptial bliss was not to be, at least not that night.

Several days later, in the guest bedroom/office of Hans's high rise, water-view condominium, it happened. As we diddled each other, Victoria watched *Little House on the Prairie* in the living room. There was no need to worry, Hans reassured me. Unlike Elsa von Brabandt in *Lohengrin*, Victoria of Liverpool did not question her master's wishes, among which were that he never be disturbed when the door to his office was closed. Not locked, mind you, but merely closed. With my precociously activist pride in being gay (this was 1970), I felt cheapened and resentful, and was very concerned about Victoria. But Victoria seemed so unflinchingly content to be doing her master's bidding that I was seduced by Hans's Freudian viewpoint that, by virtue of being a normal woman, she was innately masochistic and therefore 'immune' (since masochists 'enjoy' suffering) to the kind of humiliation that might seem to be implicit in the literal circumstances of our affair, among the many comparable situations to which he habitually subjected his wife. Furthermore, Hans somehow deduced, I was similarly masochistic for questioning his will and her obedience. If Victoria and I are masochists, I then wondered, what did this say about Hans? In making love to others in all but the actual presence of his wife, he was, yet again and without realizing it, reenacting what he believed was his father's sadistic behavior towards his mother and towards himself.

Doubtless the attraction of my libidinous unconscious to such patriarchally twisted behavior reflected my adolescent attraction to my own father. Dad did not have extramarital affairs, certainly none that we know of (he did have pornography, which I'd discover in a hiding place from time to time), but his contemptuous, infantilizing sense of women as immature, helpless and intellectually inferior, which reflected the misogyny of the Russian and Russian Jewish societies from which he came as well as that of the American society in which he lived, was debasing to me as well as to my mother and sister. Unlike Victoria, however, the women in the Mass household, which tended to include me, reflected another stereotype of Jewish people: we were aggressively outspoken (we complained loudly, we wailed) about any perceived injustice, especially if directed against us. On the other hand, that we were more active than passive retaliators conflicts with yet another stereotype – that of the Jews who were so widely perceived to have gone, *en masse* and 'silently', like lambs, to their own slaughter in the Holocaust and throughout history.

Surpassing all the friction and dysfunction, the real story of Dad's relationship with Mom – of so many of the Jewish men of his ilk with their women – came out in an incident I now vividly recall from childhood. There was a costume party at the breathtakingly beautiful and formerly restricted Idle Hour Golf and Country Club in Macon. The handful of Jewish men who were members decided to dress as cowboy prospectors and their wives, in then-fashionable chemise dresses of gold satin, became their figurative sacks of gold. I remember my mother telling me of one response she overhead: 'Leave it to the Jews to think of something like that!'

Among the many other humiliating situations to which Hans was subjecting his wife (and me) was the affair Hans had been having with Gene. Since I knew nothing about this, however, I had no qualms about accompanying Gene (a senior medical student doing research in Hans's department at the time), Victoria (a first-rate computer technologist and co-author of many of

Hans's papers), and Hans on a tour of guest lectureships in the British Isles.

Despite the complexity of relationships among the four travelers, there were few confrontations. Although Hans would have been happy enough to see his two male mistresses wrangling with each other and with his wife for his attentions, this didn't happen because of the ways we were divvied up by the British, Irish and Scots class systems. Our first stop, Belfast, was the most rigid and offensive of these priggish environments. To begin with, Hans had disobeyed the very explicit request of the Obstetrics Chief not, repeat not, to bring any students with him. Such mixings of full professors with ordinary medical students was simply unheard of there, it was claimed, and would create a scandal. When Hans nevertheless arrived with us, Gene and I were instantly and very unceremoniously shuttled off to the dingiest quarters imaginable – medical student housing in the basement of the hospital for the poor – without so much as a handshake from our host. Over the next four days, we didn't get a call or note from anyone. We were left entirely to our own devices in a city we knew nothing about, where we knew no one, and that was in the midst of a bloody civil war. As it turned out, we had what I at least thought was a wonderful time, driving up the magnificent northern Irish coast to Londonderry, touring friendly cosmopolitan Dublin and stopping at castles along the way. As with most things requiring 'butchness', as Gene would say, I assumed the responsibilities for guide and did all the driving, our first time on the left. At one of the castles, we were advised by an old caretaker not to look behind us as we proceeded through the courtyard, lest we arouse the ire of a ram that grazed there with his flock. As we approached the far wall, of course, we both turned to look and sure enough there was the ram, charging us at full speed. We narrowly escaped. Years later, I would sometimes wonder if the caretaker gave different directions about how to see the castle and its grounds to different visitors, depending on her fancy. What I was really wondering, of course, was whether or not the ancient, custodial spirit of Isolde's castle somehow knew we were Jewish and/or gay.

And Gene, what was he wondering? Probably why I was treating him so badly again. It was the most time we had ever spent together in closed quarters and there was still, after so many years, this asynchrony of his being in love with me, while I, who had never been in love with him, kept trying to relate as his closest friend. Thus, when I'd go on and on like a lovestruck teenager about my latest infatuation, a straight Irish medical student I kept cruising in the dorms, Gene thought I was purposely torturing him, as he likewise did when I brought him to meet Andy Bullen. Years later, apparently in retaliation for these and other love injuries, Gene never called or sent a card when I was hospitalized for depression. That was the most memorable of many of what were or seemed to be such *petites vengeances*, the most despicable of which were his refusals to contribute to any of the various AIDS organizations that so desperately needed money in the first years of the epidemic; the most recent of which was his failure to call my mother on the occasion of her seventy-fifth birthday after he'd promised to do so and I'd prepared her for the call (perhaps this would upset the balance of my not having had any contact with his mother – a former interior designer who used to quip to Gene and me about all the 'frou-frous' in her work – in many years, a situation Gene rigidly controlled, lest I let slip the truth about my homosexuality and, directly or indirectly, his); and the most novel of which was the women's wristwatch he gave me on the single occasion in all the years since the hospitalization that he acknowledged my birthday; all for the crime of not being in love with him. And the worse crime of sometimes exploiting that fact, consciously or unconsciously, during years when I was too young, too self-centered and, later, too intoxicated to know better.

After four days of foraging for ourselves in Belfast, we received a whispered invitation to join Hans and Victoria at the home of one of the younger associate professors who asked us not to say anything to anyone at the student quarters, lest he be reprimanded by his superiors. The invitation could not have been more sincerely appreciated since, to put it bluntly, we were starving to death. There is probably no place outside of Siberia that has less palatable food than Ireland, a situation we found to be so dire that, apart from one Chinese restaurant dinner in Dublin, we simply stopped eating. The only problem with the invitational chicken dinner (our first home-cooked meal since arriving in

Ireland), which we didn't realize until we had already vacuumed up large portions of it, was that it was prepared with an excess of extremely spicy curries our host and his wife had brought back from India.

The following morning, our heads still pounding from the gallons of beer we had to drink to douse the curries (in those days, before the sovereignty of *haute cuisine* in Gene's life, he hated alcohol), we bade farewell to Belfast and headed, next, to Glasgow. In appearance, the principal difference between these two unremittingly bleak cities seemed to be that the former was surrounded and interlaced with barbed wire. Although we were treated with less overt hostility by our Scots hosts, we were startled by the prejudices that were being flaunted. Responding to Hans's complaints about the provincialism he had encountered in Belfast, Professor McGregor, Chief of Obstetrics at the medical center in Glasgow, commiserated that 'the Irish have become for us what your Puerto Ricans are to America'. The classism and racism were subtler in Edinburgh, Sussex, Newcastle-Upon-Tyne and London.

The tour concluded in the environs of Bordeaux, where we spent nearly a week at a magnificent chateau affiliated with one of the scientific institutes. Our host was a French Jewish researcher whose imagined personal 'filthiness' Hans kept obsessing about. Although he wasn't able to get Gene and me to participate overtly in his incessant games of humiliation, we did so passively. We may not have been convinced that Professor Bonheur was (implicitly) a 'dirty Jew', but we were flattered by the implication that neither of us was.

Hans Kahltzwerg was the only true genius I ever knew intimately. In addition to his mastery of numerous scientific disciplines, Hans lectured in three languages and was literate in several others, including classical Greek and Latin. He was a proficient if not very gainly pianist, could spontaneously plunk and embellish just about any tune on the harp and cello, and had even conducted Gilbert and Sullivan, all of whose soporettas he knew by heart, in prep school and preppy college. His knowledge of opera was as profound as it was vast, and he enriched my knowledge and experience immeasurably. He was always dropping (or casting) pearls. For example, as we listened to a famous live performance of *Anna Bolena* from La Scala with Callas, he pointed out something very important I'd somehow never noticed. The principal melody of the Queen's great aria as she awaits her beheading (her 'mad scene'), is the melody of 'Be it ever so humble, there's no place like home.'

Among the few superior endowments Hans didn't seem to possess was what might be called good taste – in food, clothes, furniture, sculpture, painting and non-classical music. Clearly, only some of what was essentially a Biedermeier sensibility could be attributed to Hans's congenital color-blindness. But he knew more about opera than anyone I had ever met. This was crucial because nothing seemed more important to me at the time than opera. Not even medicine.

One of the ways Hans reassured me, as well as himself, that the Nazi phenomenon had nothing whatsoever to do with him was in his distaste for Wagner. Very much in disagreement with Gene and me – ardently perfect Wagnerites at the time (we believed that with the possible exception of Mozart, Wagner was the greatest composer who ever lived, period), Hans would sincerely argue that Wagner was a grandiloquent aberrancy of German cultural history. With visionary objectivity, he emphasized that much of what the composer wrote – the political and philosophical diatribes and large amounts of his music – were assaultingly aggressive, ponderous, and empty-headed. Worse, Hans asserted, some of Wagner's greatest ideas regarding the integration of music and drama were stolen from Meyerbeer, a Jew! I remember thinking how ironic it would be if the Alberich of Wagner's imagination really did turn out to be Wagner himself stealing the key ideas to the evolution of music from his contragenic rival, Meyerbeer. ('Contragenic' is the Nazi conceptualization Richard Plant often cites in his book, *The Pink Triangle: The Nazi War Against Homosexuals*, that was used to characterize genetic deviation.) Hans's observations about Wagner and Meyerbeer weren't very novel. I had heard them before. Far more interesting and new to me were his explanations of the sexual *doubles entendres* throughout Wagner's poetry, especially in the *Ring* cycle (e.g.,

Siegmund's 'Heraus aus *der Scheide* zu mir' that consummates the motives of Act 1 in *Die Walküre*. In German, 'die Scheide' means vagina as well as scabbard).

Unlike me, Hans simply didn't trust the 'new' Wagner of the 'new' Bayreuth. That is, he didn't believe that the so-called neo-Bayreuth style of Wieland Wagner could successfully transform Wagner's oeuvre into something that could genuinely transcend the composer's politics and German history. As was quite often the case in discussions of politics and culture, Hans was searingly incisive, prophetic and absolutely correct. Among the things that didn't seem congruent with such sincere concern about Wagner and his legacy, however, were Hans's frequent jokes about a certain black soprano. After seeing her in a revival of *Lohengrin* at the Met, he kept referring to her as 'Elsa von Baboon'. We opera queens (and this included some of the country's best-known music critics) were notorious for our shameless, boisterous, usually affectionate jokes and vulgar but not intentionally cruel and sexist nicknames for opera stars (e.g., Mary Curtis-Vermin, Disgrace Bumbry, Theresa Screech-Scandal, Katia Screecharelli, Helluva Nerve, Latrine Amara, Vagina Resnik, Angina Silja, Monsterfat Cowbelly, Beverly Shrills, Evelyn Drear, Phallus Cuntin, Dyerea, etc. If there were comparable names for the men, I never heard them. Not one. Correction: I do remember one – Ego the Wart). But 'Elsa von Baboon' was explicitly racist and exceeded anything I had ever heard from any other opera person before or since in crossing the line from outrageous to genuinely shocking. Somehow, I was once again persuaded to think of such 'humor' as self-deprecating and more of a putdown of Wagner, of me and of Hans than of the black soprano. Nevertheless, I couldn't help but begin to wonder about the real meaning of all those times little Hans joked about 'niggers', whom he also frequently characterized as 'baboons'. This seemed especially chilling whenever I thought about the real, live baboons Hans, under the guidance of Worthington and like thousands of other medical researchers around the world, vivisected in hideous but important – at least sometimes, I must *very* ambivalently concede – medical experiments.

Hans's racism was too blatant to ignore, but as I had done

with most unpleasant things in my life and like most immature people, I could look away from things I didn't like by employing defense mechanisms, especially denial and intellectualization. Utilizing the latter, I would see Hans as the victim of a medical establishment that still described the facial deformities of black persons with sickle cell disease as 'prototypical rat *facies*' (as in *facialis*). Besides, the racist anger Hans privately vented about the rising rates of ectopic pregnancy among the indigent black women his department was so aggressively fitting with Dalkon shields (the now notoriously hazardous IUDs that were subsequently withdrawn from the market) didn't seem consistent with the graciousness and humanity he demonstrated in the filmed interview with a shy, infertile black woman patient that so impressed each new crop of medical students.

Similarly, his denigration of lesbians didn't seem very consistent with his willingness to befriend and defend them. Once, at a departmental meeting to discuss the qualifications of a prospective research gynecologist, a lesbian who eventually established a Manhattan practice catering to well-known feminists, someone volunteered that he or she had heard that the candidate was 'a heavy drinker'. 'Not only that', seconded the chief resident, a whoremongering antisexual authoritarian and alcoholic. 'I've also heard that she's ... a ... a ... a ... hom-o-sex-u-al.' 'So what?' Hans casually rejoindered in front of everyone and without missing a beat. 'So are you.'

That was the *man* I had fallen in love with. But it's the human being with the infinitely greater, the *real* courage to say 'So what? So am *I*!' that my soul was seeking. I wouldn't connect with a representative of that rare breed until more than a decade later, when I met the true love of my life, Arnie Kantrowitz.

Again, despite his use of racial and ethnic putdowns, Hans seemed to get along famously with representatives of each of the minorities he so regularly slurred – Blacks (whom he savaged more often than the others), Chinese, Japanese, Indians, Pakistanis, Italians, the French, Puerto Ricans, Poles, the English, Jews, etc. One of Hans's typical jokes: 'How can you tell if a town has Jews? Answer: If it has a baths and an opera house, it has Jews.' I don't recall him ever telling a joke about Germans, but I do remember him very seriously observing that he didn't like most German *lied* as a genre because it was 'too introspective'. That's why Hans didn't care much for the great German *lieder* specialist (and former *Hitlerjugend*) Dietrich Fischer-Dieskau. Like the repertory he sang, Hans thought, Fischer-Dieskau was altogether 'too serious'. Hans habitually told jokes at my expense and then, catching me with my tail between my legs, he'd tease me for being too serious, for not laughing enough. 'It's the ones who don't laugh very much who put other people into ovens. You don't have to worry about people who can laugh at themselves.'

Like Hans? At least some of this kind of black and gallows humor was simply repartee between lovers. At a performance of *Der Rosenkavalier* in Munich, I kidded that it was good to see that his favorite singer, the short-statured but stentorian tenor, Mario del Monaco, the leading dramatic Italian tenor of the preceding generation (I was a fan of del Monaco's greater-voiced successor, Franco Corelli), was still able to find suitable employment – as Valzacchi, the sleazy Sicilian intriguer whose tiny character role in *Rosenkavalier* includes some of opera's least flattering music. In retaliation at the following evening's performance of *Don Pasquale* (in German), Hans bemoaned the inept staging and pathetic choreography: 'It looks like the Dachau ballet', he whispered. It wasn't until fifteen years later that I first began to wonder whether he was alluding to some very provincial corps de ballet that might exist in the town of Dachau or to the concentration camp inmates (the first of whom were homosexual, something neither of us knew at the time). Like Hans's joke about how you can tell if a town has Jews, this, I now realize, was vintage German humor. At the time, I think I appreciated the ambiguity and found it just as amusing as Hans, a response that is explained with depth and integrity in Sander Gilman's study, *Jewish Self-Hatred*.

I understand that after all these years – which have included a bout with an unusual cancer of the endocrine system, acute and chronic alcoholism, periodic flareups of a bleeding gastric ulcer associated with his drinking and multiple geographics – the only person besides Charles Worthington who will have anything to do with Hans personally anymore is his Puerto Rican secretary, Carmen. Victoria finally had enough, demanded a divorce, fled two thousand miles to resume an affair with a Chinese–American technocrat and subsequently told Gene when they bumped into each other in San Francisco that the lies in Hans's life were greater than anything we could imagine and included falsification of some of the biographical information he so carefully distributed.

It was no secret that Carmen, among plenty of other 'contragenic' women (and men) admired Hans, and maybe even fell a little bit in love with him. You could sense the affection when she'd joke that the reason Hans was bald was because he had so much brains there wasn't room for his hair follicles. Hans's jokes about Carmen were also affectionate, it seemed, but they played less on Carmen as a real person, as an individual, than on standard ethnic stereotypes of preferences for bright colors (in fact, Carmen preferred dark earth tones) and hypersexuality. Then again, the ridiculing of Carmen as a genetic retardate who spent every nonworking moment getting fucked when she wasn't 'stuffing' her face (in Liverpoolese, getting stuffed meant getting fucked) wasn't really different, in essence, from his ridiculing of Dr Goodall, a WASPy attending physician Hans had imported from Georgia. For the benefit of select audiences – which usually included Gene, Carmen, Elva (a black secretary who was similarly enamored of Hans), and me – Hans would imitate Goodall, often in the latter's presence, as follows: he would stick the pinky of one hand through the fist of the other so that only a small nubbin of finger protruded, which he would then wiggle while contorting his face into a defiant sneer of utter contempt. The wiggling nubbin, Hans had explained after the first such display, was supposed to be Goodall's penis, which Hans insisted really was that small. As we dissolved with laughter, Hans swore that it was true. He had seen it when they shared a room together at a convention. Harlan Goodall was a more hard-working than brilliant southern gentleman of English and German extraction, the happily married father of four children, who so far as I know never said or did anything beyond being naturally, comfortably masculine (he had the physical presence of a quarterback) to elicit such unbridled aggression. Hans's resentment of this man was the 'motiveless' hatred of an Iago (which is not the same as saying that Iago was a homosexual whose envy of Othello's virility is the primary source of his hatred, an erroneous interpretation I believe I successfully laid to rest in my senior honors thesis at Berkeley on the subject of Verdi's *Otello* as the exemplar of operatic romantifications of Shakespeare's plays). Clearly, Hans's need to ridicule, to humiliate others, was more primary than the racial, ethnic, sexual and class prejudices it fueled. *Any* human vulnerability, any weakness would suffice that could be exploited to compensate for the short stature, homeliness, homosexuality, German ethnicity and other sources of insecurity he believed so inequitably empowered others in their dealings with him. For that matter, the object of this need to dominate needn't even be human, as in the case of his little 'dorg' Franz.

These humiliations were truly vicious, but the most damaged of Hans's professional associates was not Dr Goodall. On the contrary, Goodall knew that Hans was disturbed, and he knew that we knew it, despite our laughter. Goodall's feathers may have been ruffled, but he was hardly destroyed. Unfortunately, the same could not be said about Vern Matthews, the young resident Hans had increasingly come to regard, fatefully if not fatally, 'like my own son'. It must immediately be said that what happened to Vern is not directly attributable to Hans, and it's perhaps most unfair for me to imply otherwise, however obliquely, without more facts. But here's what happened. Vernon Joseph Matthews was the very handsome, blond son of a fundamentalist preacher from the Bible Belt, not far from St Louis, and one of the nicest persons I had ever met. Hans, like everyone else (without a single exception that Gene, Hans, Victoria, Carmen, Elva or I knew of), felt that way about Vern. I suppose part of his appeal was a certain vulnerability, a certain tendency to people-please that, in retrospect, may have been a symptom of his illness.

As Vern prepared to marry a beautiful Italian girl he had been dating for several years, Hans persuaded him to do a residency in his department, in preparation for a career Hans would personally shape. Several years into the residency and marriage, things seemed to be going less well for Vern. His wife began consulting Hans for what she was told were problems of infertility. It was at approximately this time that she began speaking vaguely to Gene and me of her growing distrust of Hans. Vern, meanwhile, began drinking on the job. His descent was relatively short. Within two years he developed cirrhosis of the liver and hemmorrhagic pancreatitis. After an incomplete recovery, he disappeared and was later found dead in a national park, apparently a suicide. Like Hans himself, his protégé/son had become an alcoholic whose wife was diagnosed, in both cases by Hans, as infertile.

I caught Hans completely off guard only once. We were in Hamburg, Germany. Upon walking into the bathroom of our small hotel room, I was overcome by the most disgusting stink I had ever encountered. With mock seriousness, I scolded him: 'Didn't anyone ever teach you to light matches after you take a shit to burn off the stench?' Well, it was as if I had called Jerry Falwell a sissy. It was the angriest I had ever seen him (so much for Hans's ability to laugh at himself), though his incoherent rage on that occasion didn't upset me nearly as much as something he said later, on the same trip. I don't remember what instigated it, but I'll never forget his response. With the coolest detachment, he simply stated that 'it' could happen again. The if-you-don't-behave-yourself, like the Nazism, was implicit. 'I don't think that's very funny', I said with identical cool.

That I was never really afraid of Hans had more to do, I think, with my youthful naiveté and 'masochism' than with any conscious perception of absolute dangerousness. In the first year of our relationship, Hans told me an inebriated story about his having killed another man with his bare hands. At the time, I was incredulous because of his already manifestly alcoholic tendency to confabulate, but mostly because Hans weighed no more than 120 pounds, had no muscle tone, had the tiniest, most delicate hands I had ever seen on an adult male, and was no taller than Napoleon.

Hamburg was our first stop on another of Hans's working trips to Germany and Austria. Tours to museums and castles, operas, concerts and formal dining were arranged with and around meetings with publishers and researchers. This time, Hans bluntly disinvited Victoria.

Gene was also out of the picture. He had become so disgusted with Hans, had been so badly hurt by him so often and had consequently become so convinced of the urgency of disentangling his own very nearly signed-on-the-dotted-line career plans from Hans's clutches that he actively and successfully sought to be inducted into the army and sent to Vietnam! His enlistment became the turning point in our relationship, not because of the political chasm it reflected (like all liberals, and everyone at Berkeley, I was anti-war), but because of a more personal development: I chose to seize what I knew would be a last opportunity to rendezvous with Andy Bullen, with whom I was still so in love and whom I hadn't seen in months, instead of sacrificing that trip to be with Gene on the eve of his departure for a war zone from which he might never return. Henceforth, Gene would regard me as the significant other who failed to be there in his moment of need. So deep was this hurt, on top of the preexisting hurt of being the limerent partner for so many years in an unreciprocated relationship, that another twenty years of retaliating, notwithstanding my repeated apologies, would not heal it.

Or so it seemed. Back in New York for this year's antiques fair, Gene and I met, alone, for coffee, an occasion I took to make amends, as we say in the language of 12-step recovery, for past anger, resentments, and injuries. In the course of our discussion, I told Gene my theory of the asynchrony and dysfunction of our love for each other. 'If you divide the forty years of our relationship up into two halves', I proposed, 'the first half would be characterized by you being disappointed as a lover and the second half by my being disappointed as a friend.' He could not disagree, and he likewise quietly apologized for whatever hurt he'd caused, but there was another facet to all this he needed to point out. What I was interpreting as retaliation was not all so personally directed as my narcissism had perceived. The greater truth is that he was generally unable to show up for friends and relatives in moments of need, a pattern that had been consistent throughout his life. Recent examples included an uncle and cousin with whom he had virtually no contact when they were hospitalized with serious illnesses, a close friend with AIDS whom he likewise abandoned on his deathbed, and his own lover during a severe flu. In each of these cases he was able to offer some medical advice, but he wasn't able to be there emotionally.

So it was just the two of us, little Hans and I, visiting such citadels of western civilization as Kaiserslautern, Heidelberg and Ulm, in addition to the aforementioned stays in Munich and Hamburg. The trip concluded in Vienna, where we were alone together longer, nearly a week without professional obligations or interruptions, than at any other time in our now rapidly deteriorating relationship.

The largest hotel bathroom I have ever seen and a provincial performance of Strauss's pretty but maudlin *Arabella* are my principal memories of Linz, in the region where Hitler was born and raised, a fact I didn't know and that Hans didn't tell me at the time. Was it the same opera house where Hitler saw his first performance of a Wagner opera (*Lohengrin*)? Linz was an overnight stopover on our way to Vienna, where we spent nearly a week seeing operas, eating real Sachertorte at the Hotel Sacher, dining at Hungarian restaurants that gave Hans ulcer attacks and sniping at each other. Since Hans was paying for everything, as he always did (such generosity proved he was a *mensch*, didn't it?), I was, you might say, in the 'underdorg' position.

Like the hoary Staatsoper's position as the geographic and cultural center of the city, the heart of our experience in Vienna was a series of opulently cast if characteristically ill-rehearsed Vienna Opera Festival performances. Despite our quarreling, we were able to share our enjoyment of a highly charged *Der Rosenkavalier* (our second production of this saccharide in less than a week), conducted by Leonard Bernstein, oh-so-beloved by still pervasively anti-Semitic Vienna, and featuring Sena Jurinac, resplendent in a rare appearance as the Marschallin, and Christa Ludwig in her last performance anywhere as Octavian. Several evenings later we were similarly transformed by a budgety-looking *Macbeth* with Christa Ludwig in her most voluptuous voice and Kostas Paskalis in a star performance of one of the greatest roles ever composed for the baritone voice.

By midweek, however, our ability to share anything, even the continuing moments of real excitement afforded by these simultaneously slovenly performances, became increasingly effortful. Two days prior to our return, Hans irritably and abruptly changed his decision to go with me to a performance of Nicolai's operetta, *Die Lustigen Weiber von Windsor*. Why? 'Because I'm not into garbage.' Not yet having the courage or maturity to face, let alone to directly address the reality of our deteriorating communications, I dealt with this situation as I did with so many other sources of pain in my life. I intellectualized it. Instead of consciously *feeling* and *then* analyzing what Hans had said and what was happening to me and to us, I immediately launched into a kind of frantically reasoned discussion, with myself as well as Hans, about the operetta. The process went something like this: I began by agreeing that unlike Verdi's *Falstaff*, which is probably the only example of an opera based on a Shakespeare play that is dramatically, qualitatively superior to its source – the trivial *Merry Wives of Windsor*, Nicolai's adaptation of this comedy, can hardly be called a masterpiece. Even so, I reasoned, Frau Fluth (Alice Ford) was one of Lotte Lehmann's favorite parts and I was most interested in the whole business of operatic romantifications of Shakespeare (which include, without exception, all of the Shakespeare operas of Verdi). Furthermore, I had never seen the Nicolai work, which is rarely done outside of Vienna. Nor had I ever been to the Volksoper. And so on.

I thus convinced myself that what was happening between Hans and me had nothing to do with whether or not I would enjoy seeing the performance. Life had taught me that the best decisions, the ones that are truly important, are not made on the basis of emotions. This, I thought, is what it meant to be grown up, when one faced the reality, unencumbered by messy, effeminate *feelings*, that the young Elisabeth Schwarzkopf had an absolutely beautiful, silvery voice. Did the fact that she was a *Hitlerjugend* and Nazi party member mean that the voice *wasn't* beautiful? (Hans, incidentally, disliked Schwarzkopf not because of her early career opportunism, but because her singing was 'so mannered'.) Did the fact that I was heartbroken mean that I shouldn't enjoy the operetta? Of course not! So I went alone and didn't even think about Hans. Instead, I savored the performance, but with the same artificial, intellectual enjoyment with which I lived so much of my life. On the way home, I entertained my unconscious with romantic fantasies about the pre-war Viennese world that revelled in such works as *Lustigen Weiber*, *Wiener Blut*, *Die Lustige Witwe*, *Dollarprinzessin* and of course, *Die Fledermaus*.

At this point, the fact that our shared sentiments included a consistently outspoken distaste for Vienna, the birthplace of a number of Hans's relatives, didn't seem to help our communications. We agreed that the city exuded an asphyxiating atmosphere of sadness and gloom. It haunts the senses, like Klemperer's slow-motion version of Mahler's *Song of the Earth* (my most cherished recording of music whose sensibility – of joy overwhelmed by pain, of hope overwhelmed by, but titanically struggling to transcend, pessimism – has haunted me throughout the writing of these memoirs). Of course, every large city, especially if it is or has been one of the great international capitals of Europe, conveys a powerful sense of a past that has faded. Unlike Paris, London or even Munich, though, Vienna seemed to have only this past. Not solely because so many young men of the postwar generation left Vienna to seek their fortunes elsewhere, there seems to be no sense of future, of youth or vitality. No soul. Like the illustrious Freud and Arthur Schnitzler, the doctor/writers who diagnosed the sensibility of Vienna and its people at the beginning of this century, we could sense the pervasive persistence of incurable mental and spiritual illness, the presentiment of history repeating itself, at its conclusion.

During the last two days of the trip we were simply marking time. We both knew that our relationship, like Vienna's romance with history, was dead, even though repercussions of it would continue well into the future. On our last evening together, we saw the great Viennese soprano, Leonie Rysanek, whom we both adored, in a role I believe she sang only for a few Festival performances: Cherubini's *Medea*. This intensely melodramatic work has not exactly been a twentieth-century favorite, but it reentered the repertoire in our time as a *tour de force* for the magisterial arts of Maria Callas. Hans, incidentally, was dead serious in his instinctive certainty that Callas had a preference for 'taking it up the ass' – Callas, whom Hans revered as much as I, and about whose later years he had the most poignant observation: 'it was like Heifetz trying to play on a broken fiddle.'

The production (Svoboda? Everding?) was the crudest and most bizarre staging of an opera either of us had ever seen. The unit set consisted of a giant kewpie doll-like structure with a man-sized hole in its pelvis. The doll – a deity? Medea? – was also supposed to function as a Greek temple with the hole as a gangway. Depending on what the director thought was psychologically coloring the events onstage, a variety of anatomical human parts would appear and disappear in the mid-air background. During the first act duet between Medea and Jason, for example, there was a suspended phallus with testicles. Translation: Medea's problem is that she's still horny for Jason. Later, in the scene with the children, a pair of breasts and a uterus with ovaries appeared. Hans's racist reaction to the production was to suggest that the kewpie doll, which had dark skin and wild black hair when a skrim was lowered during the overtures (was the director implying that Medea was a contragenic?), looked 'more like Elsa von Baboon' than Medea. In comparably racist repartee, I observed that the reason so many of the Germans and Austrians in our audience had slobber dribbling out of the sides of their mouths was not just because they were all over eighty, which they were, but because they espied so many good things to eat in the production onstage (this was the latest in a long series of smirks about such not uncommon delicacies of Teutonic cuisine as lungs, placenta and other viscera). In the title role, Rysanek was more maternal, more emotional and impulsive than Callas. When she raised her dagger to murder the children, I really thought she was going to do it, but less as an act of calculated retribution for past betrayals than as a last, paroxysmal stab at bringing her amoral husband to consciousness and feeling. In either interpretation, of course, the only surviving offspring of their marriage is the carving of an immortal story of love infused with hate – what Hans Kahltzwerg, quoting Richard Wagner, called *hassliebe* (hatelove) – on the surface of a contemptuously faithless lover's petrified heart.

At the bitter conclusion of what was left of our relationship some months later, Hans gave Carmen a pen and ink drawing I had done for him of a leafless winter tree (a subject I drew frequently, usually with an early spring sun in the background). In a final gesture of contempt he knew I would hear about, Hans gave the drawing, which had been hanging in his office, to Carmen. Knowing how lovingly I had worked on it, Carmen, with whom I had remained in contact, returned the drawing to me, though I subsequently gave it, without any consciousness as to why, to the yuppie music critic with whom I attended that performance of *Siegfried*.

The afternoon of the *Medea* performance, our last in Vienna, Hans offered to buy me a gift, a souvenir of my own choosing. As I recall, he was delighted by my selection of an antique map of Europe, hand painted in rich colors on a burnished parchment. It wasn't until nearly a decade later, in fact, that I myself suddenly noticed that the map, which was hanging on my dining room wall alongside drawings and engravings of Richard Wagner, showed Germany occupying something like half the continent, including Austria. Livid with an epiphanic realization of the extent of my own masochism (and, coincidentally, in the late stages of bottoming-out on alcohol, marijuana and cigarettes), I telephoned Hans, whom I had not seen or spoken with in eight or nine years. His latest geographic had brought him to the Southwest where he must have been relatively happy with so many contragenics (Indians, Chicanos, Hispanics and combinations thereof) to sterilize. Following the briefest exchange of pleasantries in history, I asked him if he remembered the map he had bought me in Vienna. 'What about it?' he answered with the honky quack that the alcoholism and endocrine cancer had made of his boy's voice. 'Well, I just wiped my ass with it', I said, and then slammed down the phone.

Though I never spoke to Hans again, I did see him once subsequently. He was on national television debating a far more sober and informed authority than himself on, of all things, circumcision. There, of all people, was little Hans, world authority on babies, women and motherhood, who had been circumcised in infancy and who was so homoerotophobic that even the thought of a foreskin made him nauseated, shouting fire and brimstone not against, but unreservedly *in favor of*, the arbitrary practice of routine neonatal circumcision!

In all honesty, I must reemphasize that Hans often spoke with great respect and affection for the Jewish people. In Munich on the Germany–Austria trip, he went out of his way to introduce me to another of the world's leading gynecologists, a middle-aged but still strikingly handsome German blueblood whose contrastingly homely but imposingly intelligent and gracious wife, Hans kept pointing out, was a 'Jewess'. 'That degree of culture', he explained, 'you find only among Jewish women.'

Which brings us, at last, to the ordeal of Rachel Teufelsdreck. Moderately stoned on grass and alcohol and in bed with Hans in our Ulm hotel room, I entered into the fantasy of being a woman, subservient and submissive but proud and very grand ... I was some sort of classical tragedienne ... I was ... 'Rachel' ... in a hypothetical play by ... Racine. I don't know where I got the name from. Subconsciously, perhaps I was thinking about Halévy's rarely performed masterwork, *La Juive*. Hans seemed especially playful and eager to help the fantasy along. 'Rachel ... yes ... Rachel ... Teufelsdreck.' 'Teufelsdreck!?' Instantly comprehending the compound word's meaning but not understanding the context, and finding *that* reflexively funny, I squealed with laughter. 'Why Teufelsdreck?!' I insisted, when my giggling finally subsided. According to Hans, Teufelsdreck, which literally means 'shit of the devil,' was a Viennese-Jewish family, many generations old, that for reasons of pride had never given up its medievally assigned name. Fifteen years later I learned that Teufelsdroeck from Weissnichtwo (I-know-not-where) is the central figure in *Sartor Resartus* by Thomas Carlyle, a work revered by the Nazis. What had happened to me at that moment was what happened to the maid in *Les Liaisons dangereuses* when the aristocrat who has seduced her casually lets her know, as he's fucking her, that he likewise seduced her mother. It's also what happens to Alwa in the Wedekind/Berg opera *Lulu* when Lulu casually observes that the ottoman she and Alwa are making love on is the one on which his father – having been shot by Lulu, who was his father's lover at the time – bled to death.

Down the ancient, cobbled streets of Ulm, where the conductor Herbert von Karajan began his career as an enthusiastic member of the Nazi party, Verdi's *Nabucco* was alternating with *Hallo Dolly*, both in German, at the local opera house. Also nearby was the famous Gothic cathedral whose spire, among the world's tallest, I climbed one afternoon while Hans met with a leading German publisher to discuss the translation of a book he had written about babies. As I wandered up what seemed like an endless helix of stairs, I was inspired to commemorate my journey on the wall of that edifice, among thousands of other names and messages, some of them hundreds of years old. With the tip of my ballpoint pen and with such determination that I repeatedly cut my fingers, I carved the following epitaph: 'Rachel Teufelsdreck loves Hans Kahltzwerg.'

Chapter four

Confessions of a Jewish Wagnerite

WHO knows when another Jew will come along to set the entire cycle in motion again? Watching this question emerge from the mouth of one of Richard Wagner's closest living relatives, who bore a striking resemblance to the composer, would be enough to scare the daylights out of even the most masochistic Jewish Wagnerite. I had to replay my videotape of the Bayreuth Festival centennial production of *Die Götterdämmerung* to be sure I wasn't being paranoid. Was that really what Friedelind Wagner, the only prominent Wagner family member to publicly renounce rather than embrace Hitler during the Nazi era, had concluded during the cycle's final intermission feature? I located the spot on the videotape. Sure enough, there it was. Summing up her grandfather's intentions with a powerful endorsement of Patrice Chéreau's staging, there was the genetic legacy and voice of the German race (however unwittingly or reluctantly so) looking me straight in the eyes as she warned the world:

I suppose we should feel that mankind has learned his lesson, that now all will be right with the world, that the balance of nature has been restored, and that justice has prevailed over greed and the lust for power. Yet some of us are left with the nagging sensation that just around the corner lurks another Alberich, ready to set the entire cycle in motion again. Those who reject the past are condemned to repeat it, we are told. Surely, Chéreau understood this to be Wagner's intention.

The reason these remarks seemed so disturbing – the reason I heard 'Jew' instead of 'Alberich' – is that they were taking place in the context of what may have been the first production of the *Ring* cycle in history in which the Nibelungs Alberich and Mime, the archvillains of the *Ring* dramas, were being portrayed as Jews.

For the benefit of non-Wagnerites, the scheme of the composer's twenty-hour tetralogy may be distilled as follows. In the opening scene of *Der Ring des Nibelungen*, the hateful dwarf Alberich, whose tribe, the Nibelungs, inhabits the underworld, steals the precious Rhine gold from its careless, flirtatious guardians, the Rhine maidens. (In the Chéreau production, the Rhine maidens are depicted as common prostitutes.) Alberich then fashions this gold into the magical all-powerful ring of the saga's title, with which he would enslave the gods, giants, and humans as well as his own people. At the conclusion of the cycle, the Rhine maidens and Alberich (so far as we know) remain alive while most of the others – including all of the gods (even Loge, the god of fire?) – have been destroyed by the power struggles that were 'set in motion' (accelerated but not, in fact, originated) by Alberich's theft of the Rhine gold, the price he had to pay for it (the renunciation of love), and the curse he put on the ring when the gods stole it from him: death to all who possess it, envy to those who don't.

Some weeks following the telecast of the Chéreau production, I was at a farewell gathering for John D'Emilio, the gay socialist historian. The party, which followed by several months the party Arnie and I co-hosted with the University of Chicago Press to celebrate the publication of John's book, *Sexual Politics, Sexual Communities*, was being given by John's close friend and colleague, Jonathan Ned Katz (*Gay American History*). John and his lover of several years, Jim Oleson, were about to move to Greensboro, where John had been given a professorship at the University of North Carolina. Jim and I had been fellow opera queens and friends for more than a decade. (Robert Jacobson, the closety former Editor of *Opera News*, thought the term 'opera queen' was pejorative.) Also invited were music critics Richard Dyer of the *Boston Globe* and Peter G. Davis, who is currently with *New York* magazine. Jim and I counted Dick and Peter among our closest friends throughout the 1970s. Jim's friendship with Dick went back to their Iowa City days a decade earlier.

The interrelationships among these four friends were the principal ones of my life during the period from 1973 to 1979. They followed the death of my affair with Hans Kahltzwerg, accompanied the much slower and prolonged death of my union with Andy Bullen, preceded and accompanied the first years of my next big affair (the subject of 'Children in Love'), and witnessed my 'entanglement' with José Orlovsky ('the evil psychiatrist') and my involvement with Bill Jones, an alcoholic from a blue-collar, Catholic family – first generation Portuguese on both sides – in rural Massachusetts, who sincerely believed that he would pay for his homosexuality by burning in hell for eternity and who precipitously quit his excellent job at Mass General Hospital, where I was training, and did a geographic to San Francisco, where he quickly drank himself to death. But the aggregate relationships among the four friends represented another love affair, one that had begun to wither even as it reached full bloom – that with the world of romantic opera and its greatest exponent, Richard Wagner.

In the early eighties Peter, Dick, Jim and I grew apart. Time had passed, and we had each moved on to new friends and new lives. But some of this estrangement, I was sure, was the result of an acerbic piece I had written for *Christopher Street* entitled 'Confessions of an Opera Queen'. In part, the piece was an ambitious indictment of the closetedly gay quarter (half? more than half?) of the music establishment for obfuscating gay and lesbian contributions to the worlds of music and opera. I summarized my complaints in a letter to David Denby, with whom I'd been in communication when *New York* was hoping to snare Dick Dyer to replace Alan Rich as music critic. The occasion for the letter was the worst of the serial John Simon *New York* scandals, this one ignited by Simon's indictment of a play as 'faggot nonsense'. I believed that Simon wasn't the only culprit at *New York*. 'With the spectacular exception of Ned Rorem', I wrote, the burgeoning phenomena of gay issues, gay artists, and gay themes in the worlds of music and opera continue to be almost completely ignored outside the gay press.' Although I did not mention it in my letters to him, I was also disappointed with Denby for authoring a rambling, uncritical piece about the Chéreau *Ring* for the *New Republic* that didn't even mention that the Nibelungs were being portrayed as Jews.

I remember how Jac Venza, the executive producer of most of WNET's 'Great Performances', including the Chéreau *Ring*, reacted when I told him about the 'Opera Queen' piece in *Christopher Street*. We had met at the Everard Baths and were having dinner on the first night of a flaccid and very short-lived affairette. 'You can't expect to be taken seriously writing for a publication like *that*!' he sneered. Incidentally, Robert Jacobson, who subsequently died of AIDS, never came out in print. I guess he assumed that appearing in public in his trademark mink coat, accompanied by his lover, was the equivalent. Not surprisingly, neither of these great facts of his life and death – that he was gay and had AIDS – were acknowledged in his obituary in *Opera News*. Only slightly less not surprisingly, this is the kind of blunt information you won't find in Wayne Koestenbaum's richly poetic ode to the opera queen, *The Queen's Throat: Opera, Homosexuality and the Mystery of Desire*, with its stellar endorsement from closety Susan Sontag. Like those B-list types who had already written about opera, homosexuality and opera queens from within the gay community – e.g., Michael Bronski, Bruce-Michael Gelbert, George Heymont, James Saslow and myself – Jacobson's existence is not therein acknowledged.

I knew that Peter and Dick would not acknowledge 'Confessions of an Opera Queen'. In reality, they probably hadn't read it. Neither followed the gay press. In fact, if Peter had ever read an issue of *Christopher Street*, the *Native* or the *Advocate*, even three years into the AIDS epidemic, he never said so. So I didn't have to worry about defending myself. We could just pretend it hadn't been written and that there were no problems of any kind between us. Instead, we could talk about tacitly unrestricted things like our diets, how expensive everything had become, even my recent hospitalization for depression, so long as it didn't get too ... uh ... personal.

Sensing that I might not have many more opportunities to

speak directly or comfortably with Peter, my unconscious selected what it considered to be the most important question that it felt, at the time, needed to be directed to a leading music critic: 'Is it my imagination or were the Nibelungs in the Chéreau *Ring* cycle being portrayed as Jews?'

Peter acknowledged that this was in fact true, especially so in the case of Mime, Alberich's treacherous brother, in *Siegfried*. As Peter understood it, Chéreau's motivation was to 'expose' Wagner's anti-Semitism.

I became uneasy. Not yet making much sense to Peter or even to myself, I asked him about Friedelind Wagner and her politics. As I recalled, she had fled Germany and worked in New York City during the war years. Throughout this period, she was known to have been an outspoken critic of Hitler and the Nazis. What seemed so incongruous and what was making me so uncomfortable was her very personal endorsement of a production that, perhaps unwittingly, gave credibility to Wagnerian anti-Semitism. I was particularly alarmed by her concluding remarks in that final *Götterdämmerung* intermission feature. I tried to explicate my concern. If Friedelind is even indirectly implying that Wagner's bottom-line conclusion about the *Ring* cycle is that future repeats of such titanic power struggles can be circumvented by eliminating any Alberichs that might still be lurking about, and if Alberich is still alive at the end of the cycle, and if Wagner conceptualized the Nibelungs as metaphors for Jews, and if Alberich and his brethren are being portrayed as Jews in the production Friedelind is talking about, and, finally, if everybody connected with this production keeps emphasizing that the *Ring* cycle is a drama of *today* ...

This sounded paranoid to Peter, even to me, and he had difficulty finding anything to say. When I pressed the subject in a subsequent telephone conversation, he suggested that I contact John Ardoin. Ardoin had written the intermission features for the teletaping and had, Peter suspected, probably written the lines Friedelind spoke.

So I wrote John Ardoin, music critic of the *Dallas Morning News* and author of *The Callas Legacy*, a dignified, musically-oriented guide to the great soprano's studio recordings and recorded live performances. The response I got seemed honest and forthright, but was not very reassuring: 'The words Friedelind Wagner spoke on the Chéreau telecast were written by me but discussed in detail with her and agreed upon by her.' As the Chéreau *Ring* (which she was enormously enthusiastic about as one way and a valid way to approach the cycle) dealt primarily with man's corruption of nature, thus Alberich became a symbol of this corruption – a sort of Napoleon or Hitler or Perón. That led us to the line, used symbolically, 'Who knows when another Alberich will come along to set the entire cycle in motion again?' The cycle referred to was not Wagner's *Ring* per se, but the cycle of corruption that brought us to our over-mechanized and under-humanized state.'

I was now even more uneasy. The obvious problem with Ardoin's response, as I subsequently wrote him, was that in the Chéreau production, there wasn't the slightest suggestion that Alberich was a Hitler, a Perón, or even a Napoleon. On the other hand, there was a lot to suggest that he was a Jew. 'Now write me back', I challenged, 'and tell me that the thought that Alberich was a Jew never crossed Wagner's, Friedelind's, Chéreau's, or your mind!' I got no response. Several weeks later, I picked up a copy of *The Opera Quarterly* (autumn, 1983), in which John Ardoin had written a piece called 'A *Ring* Diary' describing his impressions of the Chéreau production. Here, he wrote the following: 'Mime, masterfully realized by tenor Heinz Zednik, is a Jewish busybody, bustling about the stage and occupied in a center pit area with a panoply of pots and cooking utensils.'

The other matter I had asked Ardoin about had to do with Callas. It's intriguing that several of her closest involvements were with gay men who were outspokenly socialist, like Pier Paolo Pasolini and Luchino Visconti. Some deeper exploration of these associations, I implied, would be of interest to those of us who are trying to understand the phenomenon of Maria Callas in broader socio-cultural perspective.

'As for the Callas–homosexual connection', he wrote back, 'I don't believe there is much or rather anything to be made of this. She was not unique among singers in her associations with homosexual men. It is a fact of life in the world of the arts. Callas, in fact, when confronted with the question of homosexuality was very anti-gay. This might well have stemmed from her infatuation with Visconti and her shock on learning he was homosexual. In fact, I wonder if she had ever come face-to-face with the question before.' Did Ardoin, a gay man and one of Callas's closest friends during her last years, ever *attempt* to discuss the subject of sexual preference – his own or anyone else's – with her?

'The only association that I know of with a homosexual', he continued, 'that she went into with her eyes fully open and completely aware of the fact was with Pasolini. I never saw the two of them together, but she said and others told me it was a sort of brother–sister relationship and that she felt very close to him as a human being, much as she did with the late Lawrence Kelly [the gay impresario under whose auspices Callas made her American debut and sang some of her most memorable performances in Chicago and Dallas]. But to see any broader "sociopolitical" meaning in any of this, I believe, would be to belabor the point.'

As I see it, the fallout from portraying the Nibelungs as Jewish capitalists in the Bayreuth Festival's centennial *Ring* cycle production will be different from what was intended, or said to be. It's true, on the one hand, that Chéreau's interpretation exposes Wagner's anti-Semitism. The gods' constant references to ugly, loathsome dwarfs seem at least intermittently vicious and victimizing in view of the Nibelungs' more human appearances on stage. Thus, Jane Boutwell wrote in her article, 'A Controversial *Ring*' for WNET's *The Dial* (January 1983): 'Political conservatives, some of whom recalled the Nazi era with a certain nostalgia, were stunned to find that Chéreau had turned two of the *Ring*'s villains (Alberich, the Nibelung capitalist who renounces love in exchange for a chance to rule the world and Mime, his demonic brother, who first raises the hero, Siegfried, and then tries to kill him) into desperate, displaced, nineteenth-century Jews, forced into antisocial actions by a world that constantly tries to humiliate them.'

On the other hand, Boutwell, like Ardoin and Friedelind Wagner, did not question the anti-Semitic prejudice that Jews were behaving 'antisocially' in Germany before Hitler. Although many viewers will be reminded that Wagner was anti-Semitic, I suspect that many, perhaps the majority, also will be subliminally *seduced* by the 'socialist' Wagner's *Weltanschauung*, in which the great industrial revolutionary rise and decline of capitalism is seen to be epitomized in the struggle of the godlike Germans against the treacherous, physically degenerate Jews who corrupted them. In fact the production itself, the first complete *Ring* cycle ever shown on international television, tells its unprecedentedly gigantic audience (an audience that is probably already greater than the combined size of all previous *Ring* cycle audiences) that the Jews, however abused, are nonetheless fully culpable, bottom-line criminals who must be stopped before they initiate another cycle that could destroy the entire world, as they almost succeeded in doing in the period that culminated in World War II.

'The *Ring* ... is a drama of today, and not of a remote and fabulous antiquity', wrote G. B. Shaw in *The Perfect Wagnerite*, the socialist interpretation of the cycle from which Chéreau drew many of his ideas. 'These words', begins the press release for the WNET broadcast of the *Ring*, 'might well have hung above the doors of the festival theater in Bayreuth in 1976' (the first year of the Chéreau staging). The *Ring* cycle, everyone seemed to be at great pains to point out, is a drama of *today*. During a time when the future of the Jewish people (Israel) is once again providing an outlet for world tensions, as anti-Semitism reemerges throughout the world, fueled by Arab–Israeli conflicts, here was the closest blood kin of the man Adolf Hitler claimed as his only spiritual father, concluding to the world, in the context of a production in which Alberich is portrayed as a Jew: 'Some of us are left with the nagging sensation that just around the corner lurks another Alberich, ready to set the entire cycle in motion again. Those who forget the past are condemned to repeat it.'

No wonder ultraconservative Bayreuth, under the directorship of Friedelind's brother, Wolfgang, nurtured the Chéreau production, whatever the more superficial misgivings and protests. Like their other sibling, Wieland Wagner, who ran Bayreuth after the war until his death in 1966, Wolfgang had been coddled by Hitler. Unlike Wieland, however, Wolfgang has made little effort to distance Bayreuth from – to directly address – its Nazi past. (A biography of Wolfgang Wagner, whose close associations with James Levine and Daniel Barenboim are characterized by Gottfried Wagner, Wolfgang's son, as examples of his father's 'pro-Semitic anti-Semitism', will be published by Weidenfeld/London, which is also Barenboim's publisher.)

Did the Chéreau production, like an earlier *Tannhäuser* directed by Götz Friedrich, constitute such an effort, or was something else going on? Were at least some conservatives secretly or even unconsciously pleased with the broader implications of Chéreau's revolutionary conception? Showing the Nibelungs as Jews is a little like Madonna's crosses. At the superficial level, she's sending up religion and prudery. At another, probably much broader level, however, she's encouraging Christian bonding. Many among the numbers of people wearing crucifixes today, in no small measure a result of the incessant media images of Madonna, are wearing them not to be fashionable so much as to signal their Christianity. Today, the talk about the Chéreau *Ring* is about how it exposes Wagner's anti-Semitism. Eventually, however, viewers will begin to ponder the other implications of rendering explicit Wagner's metaphors.

Here, at last, was an interpretation Winifred Wagner, Friedelind's mother, could approve of, if only unconsciously. Winifred, the English wife of Wagner's only son Siegfried, single-handedly ran Bayreuth during the Nazi years (Siegfried died in 1930), and was a fervent supporter and among the closest confidantes of Adolf Hitler. One of the most disturbing features of the *Ring* telecast was its gloss on Wagner's anti-Semitism and the Nazi history of Bayreuth under Winifred's directorship. The coldly analytical, self-confident and articulate Winifred Wagner is, however, well-captured in Hans-Jürgen Syberberg's lengthy, uncritical, sometimes (unwittingly?) affectionate and nostalgic documentary interview with her from the late 1970s. In an unqualified endorsement of Chéreau's concepts during one of the broadcast's intermission features, Friedelind affectionately tells the story of how her mother, who is said to have been highly disapproving of everything that went on at Bayreuth after the war – including the Chéreau *Ring*, which she publicly denounced – finally met and warmed up to Chéreau, and even hinted at respect for his conception ('Better to be furious than bored', she said, according to Friedelind).

Nowhere in the Bayreuth Festival videotape, however, did Friedelind say anything about her mother's pro-Hitler, pro-Nazi remarks in Syberberg's film (which I saw in the reticent company of

Richard Dyer) and nothing about the fact that Winifred was officially forbidden to participate in the running of Bayreuth after the war because of her Nazi allegiances. Winifred's links with Hitler and the Nazis were perfunctorily acknowledged – she was deNazified with little more than a wrist tap because she was able to prove that she had helped a number of artists escape persecution – but her *ongoing* pro-Hitler and Nazi ravings were not. In the telecast, Winifred comes across as a naughty girl rather than as the principal architect of Bayreuth's transformation into the Nazi shrine and spiritual home of Adolf Hitler. Likewise, nothing was said in the intermission features about the fact that Wieland and Wolfgang Wagner, who, consecutively, ran Bayreuth after the war, had both been in favor with Hitler.

What Winifred had so disapproved of was the Wagner I was seduced into believing in throughout the 1960s and 1970s – the 'apolitical' Wagner, as reinterpreted by her son, Wieland. Wieland, who dominated the world of Wagner that introduced me to the composer in the early 1960s, and his followers greatly deemphasized Wagner as we knew him. Instead, we were diverted into these very abstract, psychoanalytical ('Freudian') interpretations that removed Wagner from any temporal or historical context. So great was the diversion of attention away from the composer's politics and history that I scarcely knew they existed. Although I was a committed Wagnerite long before I ever met Dick and Peter, with whom I later attended a number of performances of Wagner's operas, and although we did talk frankly about the problem of Wagner's racism and other character defects (Peter knew more about Wagner and was more involved with the composer than was Dick), I didn't realize until much later that Wagner's anti-Semitism had any more absolute significance than his hatred of the French. I thought of it, reflecting what I had been encouraged to continue to believe by Peter (who kept a signed Wagner postcard as the sole adornment on the wall above his bed), who was in turn reflecting the attitude of the majority of contemporary music critics, as something outside the immediate realm of Wagner's art and therefore relatively unimportant. What had been obscured by the music critics and what I unconsciously and masochistically denied and ignored throughout my years of involvement in the worlds of music and opera was the fact that Richard Wagner was nothing less than the only spiritual father Hitler acknowledged, that Wagner was a major force in the evolution of Nazism and that Wagner's operas, especially the *Ring* cycle, *Die Meistersinger* and *Parsifal* ooze anti-Semitism and xenophobia. What the music critics kept insisting was that Wagner's politics, like Benjamin Britten's homosexuality, are so irrelevant to a full appreciation of the composer's artistic achievements – which are timeless, universal and apolitical – that they don't merit anything more than a passing mention.

I confided my concerns to my friend Richard Plant, the professor of German and comparative literature who was completing *The Pink Triangle*, his long-awaited book on the Nazi persecutions of homosexuals. 'I know all about Friedelind's supposedly having been so outspokenly anti-Nazi', he said. 'But things are so complicated. Who knows what factors actually played into her decision to come to the U. S. at that time? Actually, I met her when she was in New York and was never very comfortable with her politics. At the time, she used to complain about the homosexuals and their influence in the world of opera.'

I next sought out Robert Gutman, the Wagner expert whose book, *Richard Wagner: The Man, His Mind and His Music* (1968), is unstinting in its exposure of Wagner's anti-Semitism and is still widely regarded as among the finest studies of the composer. Over two lunches several weeks apart, he did not say anything very reassuring. While he had respect for Peter G. Davis and felt certain that his friend, Friedelind, would never consciously participate in anything anti-Semitic, he could not say much about her endorsement of the Chéreau *Ring*, which he had only seen in bits and pieces, even though a lecture he gave at Yale was one of the intermission features of the telecast and contained observations about the production. As for Wagner's anti-Semitism, he had nothing mitigating to say. It was all too true. Like Peter, however, he couldn't understand why I had so much trouble separating issues of artistic greatness from those of political background and subtext. When I next ran into him, he had just seen the Met's new *Tannhäuser*, which he recommended. He was especially impressed with Richard Cassilly's singing of the murderously difficult title role.

At the opening of Terrence McNally's play, *The Lisbon*

Traviata, I ran into Bill Hoffman and John Corigliano. We all admired the play, which seemed to me uniquely successful in exposing the sensibilities and value systems of two stereotypical opera queens. Everyone laughed when one of the protagonists – a Callas fanatic who would probably sell his own mother to the Nazis to hear La Divina in a live performance of *La Traviata*, pirated from Lisbon – suggests that Renata Scotto causes AIDS. I couldn't suppress my own laughter which, however, suddenly choked with rage when I thought of how relatively few leading figures in the worlds of music and opera, to say nothing of their fans, had publicly committed themselves (as of mid-1985, four years into the AIDS epidemic), to ameliorating a crisis that was decimating their own ranks. In a development that would make a good epilogue to the subsequently rewritten *dramma giocoso*, which could never quite reconcile its anger with its love for the opera world, McNally wrote an introduction to a reprinting of Ardoin's *The Callas Legacy*.

Bill, who was writing *The Ghosts of Versailles* (in those days they were calling it *A Figaro for Antonia*), had begun working on a play that will probably assimilate the Nazi decimation of his biological family with the kind of wisdom and serenity that characterize his coming to terms, in *As Is*, with what AIDS is doing to his gay family. Or will it? Will there be as little rage at the Nazis in the new work as there is at AIDS in *As Is*? Will the forgiveness that is a theme of so much of Bill's major work likewise extend to the Nazis? The answer to these last two questions, at least on the basis of a student reading of a still very rough first act of what is presently being called *Riga*, are already in: emphatically no. As Arnie suggested to me – a suggestion I conveyed to Bill, who would seem to agree – the people from whom forgiveness would count most can't forgive, even if they were willing, because they're dead.

Unlike me, I discovered, Bill and John were never Wagnerites. At the time, before I got to know him better, I wondered if Bill had always been as uncomfortable as I had suddenly become with the fact that countless Jewish artists and intellectuals remain dedicated Wagnerites. I wondered to what extent Bill has been bothered the way I am today by the celebrations of Wagner that are routinely cycled, without qualification, but so often with Jewish participation and support, throughout Europe and the United States. But then, what sort of conflict would exist when the sponsor and conductor and overseer of your opera, the biggest and most important event in your life, is one of the apolitical stars of the festival that became the holiest shrine of the people who murdered most of your family?

Why didn't Leonard Bernstein ever conduct at Bayreuth? His many fine Wagner performances and recordings notwithstanding, how did he really feel about Wagner? Was there any part of him that was in sympathy with the Israeli citizens who didn't want Wagner's music to be performed in their presence? '[The reason Lenny didn't conduct at Bayreuth is] obvious. He was very uncomfortable there', said Gottfried Wagner, when I interviewed him in 1992, nearly a decade after the telecast of the Chéreau production, on which Dr Wagner had assisted in its later years.

Are James Levine, Daniel Barenboim, Lorin Maazel and Georg Solti the token Jews of Bayreuth? Do they actually abet the problem of Bayreuth's not facing its past? Yes, was more or less Dr Wagner's answer. (He received his doctorate in musicology for his dissertation on Kurt Weill, which was subsequently published.) Dr Wagner was in New York to lecture on the controversies surrounding the performance of Wagner in Israel, which he felt Barenboim had handled vainly and insensitively, and to encourage German–Jewish dialogue. He was also working with painter and scenic designer Toby Heifetz on a series of projects inspired by the art and artists of Terezin (Theresienstadt, the so-called 'paradise' Nazi concentration camp in Czechoslovakia), the most intriguing of which was a production of Viktor Ullman's political opera *The Emperor of Atlantis*. They were also looking at another of this composer's works, *The Anti-Christ* (after Nietzsche), which apparently has never been performed. Ullman, a pupil of Schoenberg, was an inmate at Terezin who eventually died in the gas chambers at Auschwitz. His uncompleted opera, about a tyrannical monarch who outlaws death, had its first performance in Amsterdam in 1975.

A fiercely uninhibited critic of Bayreuth's inability to acknowledge and mourn its past, Dr Wagner is every bit as much a pariah at Bayreuth today as the recently deceased Friedelind, the only Wagner to encourage him, was for most of her adult life. At the time of our interview, neither Dr Wagner nor his nine-year-old son had had any communication with Wolfgang Wagner for more than a decade. Even letters were returned unopened. As for Friedelind, Dr Wagner had mostly praise, but was concerned about her inability to come to grips with the anti-Semitism, which was incontestable, of her beloved father, Siegfried, who Dr Wagner believes was preferentially homosexual. The fact that Siegfried Wagner was surrounded by domineering women, principally his mother Cosima and wife Winifred, was also maintained by Dr Wagner, notwithstanding his respect for my being assertively gay and my rejoinder that contemporary thinking no longer gives credibility to the domineering mother theory of the etiology of homosexuality. What other Wagners were/are homosexual?

In his critique of *Kiss of the Spider Woman* (*New York*, 5 August 1985), David Denby noted that Molina, the old movies queen played by William Hurt, 'cannot criticize; he adores even the viciously anti-Semitic Nazi films, for he sees them as throbbing with passion and self-sacrifice, and he takes every movie the way it wants to be taken. He's the ultimate fan.' Denby's adoration of the Chéreau *Ring* cycle in the *New Republic* was, as I recall, without qualification. Like many of our most esteemed music critics, Denby didn't mention that Chéreau had depicted the Nibelungs as Jews. Perhaps the Chéreau *Ring* was an example of what Denby had in mind when he concluded in his review of *Spider Woman* that Hector Babenco, the film's director, unintentionally ridicules Molina's taste in films. 'Surely Puig's point wasn't simply that gay movie rhapsodists have terrible taste. We need to see, or at least guess, what Molina sees in these movies.' Could it be that what Denby so admired, without qualification, about the *Ring* cycle and Chéreau's production of it is exactly what Molina so adored, without qualification, in the old Nazi propaganda films? Should we be as unconcerned as Molina – as Denby? – with political subtext in our arts and entertainments?

Likening me to 'Reagan looking for Commies under every cabbage leaf', dear Ned Rorem blasted me for presuming to tell music and opera people that they should come out of the closet, that they should be dealing more regularly and substantively with gay issues in print, and that they should have been doing much more about the AIDS crisis than they had done to date (mid-1985).

Privately, Rorem told me that he admired Larry Kramer's *The Normal Heart* (a play that is mostly about the evils of the closet) 'without qualification', but who was I, Larry Mass, to be telling leading music critics, musicians, and other artists what their priorities should be? It's through Ned that I first heard the wonderful if too long-awaited news that a series of AIDS benefits involving Metropolitan Opera artists was being planned by, among others, Robert Jacobson – who proposed in an interview for the *Advocate* during that time (1985) that Leonard Bernstein and James Levine were becoming more publicly open about themselves, while slyly failing to come out himself in this or any other interview (like Jacobson, Bernstein and Levine may have been 'becoming more publicly open about themselves' everywhere except in print) – and Matthew Epstein, who never responded to my repeated requests to interview him but who unequivocally came out in an earlier *Advocate* interview and who recently came out in *Newsday* and the *New York Times* as a person with AIDS. It was around this time that Rodger McFarlane confirmed the plans for the first big Music For Life benefit at the Met. I remember my reaction: '*Finalmente!*'

'Would a portrayal of Shylock as a "Jewish busybody" be objectionable to you for the same reasons?' asked *New York Review of Books* editor Jonathon Lieberson in a six-page response to a rough draft of this piece. 'Is it because such portrayals encourage anti-Semitism?'

It's true, of course, that Shylock is a negative stereotype, albeit among the most dramatic ones in all theater. It's also true that Shylock is Shakespeare's only leading, explicitly Jewish character and that Shakespeare was doubtless anti-Semitic, reflecting as well as exposing the anti-Semitism of his time. Unlike Wagner, however, Shakespeare did not write major treatises on the pernicious influence of the Jews in the arts and society. Nor did he call for their conversion, and much worse, in public tirades. Unlike Wagner, Shakespeare was not widely revered as the forefather of the greatest wave of aggression against humanity in the history of the human race. Without too much personal conflict, I can continue to love and revere Shakespeare, if not *The Merchant of Venice*, which is so unquestionably and seriously anti-Semitic. (Like Richard Wagner and his operas, Shakespeare and his play became emblematic in Nazi Germany, where, however, *Othello* and *Antony and Cleopatra* were barred.) But my love for Wagner – deeply, permanently, ineradicably imprinted in the pleasure circuits of my brain – will henceforth be experienced with considerable pain.

The morning papers were filled with Reagan's visit to Bitburg. I went to Videoworld to look for a good movie, preferably one Arnie and I hadn't already seen. No luck. As I was leaving, however, my unconscious suddenly remembered Ken Russell's *Lisztomania*. Although I consider Russell to be one of the great filmmakers of our time, every bit as brilliant a surrealist and noble a humanitarian as Fellini, I never saw *Lisztomania* because of the trouncing it got from the critics, especially from Peter G. Davis, at that time writing for the *New York Times*. In those days I had a lot of respect for Peter's politically and socially unconscious opinions, so against my better judgment I decided to skip the film when it was first released, and hadn't heard or thought about it since. Unlike other Ken Russell films on the shelves at Videoworld, the *Lisztomania* box didn't have an 'OUT' sticker. I rushed home with the videotape and was amazed, not so much by the film's vitality, which even Russell's detractors would acknowledge, as by the sophistication of its perspectives.

Lisztomania contains many heresies. It suggests that Cosima von Bülow's involvement with Wagner was primarily motivated by revenge against her father, composer Franz Liszt (profoundly anti-Semitic Cosima, herself part-Jewish, was Liszt's illegitimate daughter). Even more perspicacious, however, is Russell's depiction of Wagner as a blood-sucking vampire, the figurative embodiment of diabolical evil, an archvillain who was obsessed with Jews, who coincidentally stole some of his best ideas from Jews, and who was accordingly determined to rid the world of Jews. In one scene, a parody of the *Ring*, a Frankenstein-like Alberich wears a Jewish star on his forehead and chases naked Rhine maidens. In *Lisztomania*, as in the *Spiels* of Hans-Jürgen Syberberg, Richard Wagner is attributed with nothing less than full responsibility for Adolf Hitler and the Holocaust. The difference between the two filmmakers' points of view is simply that Russell has rejected Wagner while Syberberg has been seduced by him.

'Will we ever be free of the oppressive curse of guilt if we do not get at the center of it?' Syberberg asks in the introduction of his eight-hour romance, *Hitler: A Film from Germany*. In *Reflections of Nazism: An Essay on Kitsch and Death* (Harper and Row, 1984), Saul Friedlander expresses his concern that Syberberg, among too many other contemporary artists and intellectuals, sets out to expose the romance of Nazism but ends up revelling in it. Has Patrice Chéreau been similarly corrupted? Have his collaborators? Has his audience? Has Susan Sontag (who called *Hitler* 'possibly the greatest film ever made' and 'one of the great works of art of the twentieth century')?

A decade later (March 1993), Syberberg told *Harper's*:

> Instead of being worried about making our neighbors nervous, we should be taking a look at ourselves. We are afraid to sing our grandfathers' songs; we are afraid to appreciate Wagner; we are afraid even to mourn history's theft of our myths and fairytales.

What Sontag thought was 'an act of mourning', of expiation, turns out to be just what Syberberg's art appears to be on the surface – an act of longing, of nostalgia. Just as the racist intentions of Wagner, as the Nazis understood, turned out to be just what they appear to be on the surface of Wagner's art.

In my files I came across some clippings about the Claus von Bülow affair. Why, I wondered, didn't anybody clarify how Claus is or is not related to Hans von Bülow, the close friend, colleague, and disciple of Wagner, the conductor with whose wife, Cosima, Wagner had an affair that produced children while Cosima and Hans were still married? Did Claus have any second thoughts about naming his daughter, Cosima, after such a notorious anti-Semite?

In the *New York Times* (4 June 1985) there were two stories about the frenzy in San Francisco surrounding the city's first Wagner Festival of *Ring* cycle performances. One of the articles was a review of *Das Rheingold*, the first opera of the tetralogy, in which Alberich steals the omnipotential gold from its natural home at the bottom of Germany's Rhine river. The second article told of a Miss Bardoff, who planned to see all three of the scheduled four-opera cycles, and to attend the eleven-hour film biography of Wagner with Richard Burton and Vanessa Redgrave. Considering the controversies in which she has been entangled in recent years, I wondered if 'the greatest actress of our time', as I described her in the never-answered letter I sent Richard Dyer when Ms Redgrave was in Boston for her political censorship court battle with the Boston Symphony, had any second thoughts about portraying rabidly anti-Semitic Cosima in a major film at that time.

'I'm a masochist, I guess', Miss Bardoff mused in the *Times article*. 'It's taken me quite some time to accept Wagner', she says. 'I'm Jewish and it's taken time to deal with the anti-Semitism. My family, the cantor for my temple, have given me a hard time. I try to ignore his philosophy and look at him solely as a composer. I love his music.'

I thought back to my days as an undergraduate at Berkeley, where I reviewed San Francisco Opera performances for the University newspaper, where I saw my first staged performances of the *Ring* cycle, and where I first met John Rockwell, the *New York Times* music critic. John was completing his Ph.D. thesis in comparative literature on the subject of opera in the Weimar Republic. At the time, he was a very serious Wagnerian and Germanophile with the largest personal collection of German language, German artist, and German opera tapes I had ever seen. In his apartment one evening he played, at my request, excerpts from several different live performances of *Otello* in German with tenor Wolfgang Windgassen. Other goodies in this collection included numerous live *Walküres* and *Holländers* with Leonie Rysanek. It was in the *New York Times*, of all places, that John Rockwell, without qualification, described Syberberg's *Parsifal*, in which overt Nazism is concretized as being within Wagner's purview, as the greatest film of an opera ever made. Years later, Rockwell did another piece admiring Syberberg's ongoing creativity while simultaneously reporting, with characteristic neutrality, that Syberberg (who is now overtly right-wing) was being accused of having made anti-Semitic statements. Likewise in the *New York Times*, Rockwell suggested that America should establish its own Bayreuth. To be directly linked?

As music critic of the *New York Times*, Rockwell, who has been perhaps the least (morally) qualified of Karajan admirers among New York's leading music critics, also had high praise for the DC Comics version of *The Ring*. Here, as Philip Kennicott observes in *Opera News*, 'racial overtones are emphasized' and 'masculine sexuality is glorified to an embarrassing degree'. Rockwell's endorsement, which adorns the book's cover, reads as follows:

> This comics version treats [Wagner's] operatic texts with faithfulness and intelligent care ... [It's] more faithful to the composer's vision than a genteel, gravity-bound stage production could ever be.

When I asked a representative at DC Comics to verify the Rockwell quote for me, he asked me why I wanted this information. 'It's for a project about Wagner.' 'What's the project?' he persisted. So I told him the title of my book. 'Very interesting', he said, 'but don't you have to be something of a masochist to be a Jewish Wagnerite?'

Back in New York in November 1992 for another lecture tour and more meetings with Heifetz, Gottfried Wagner discussed the skyrocketing violence in Germany and Italy, where he lives in a suburb of Milan. The hot spots included Bayreuth, where neo-Nazi rallies specifically incorporated the symbolism of Wagner, and where Daniel Barenboim remains a regular visitor, often with complimentary – never with critical or confrontational – things to say about the town and its people. 'Why doesn't he tell Bayreuth that he won't return unless he sees more action taken against the hooligans?' Gottfried (as I now feel free to call him) asks. He was still lecturing in Germany, and was even planning to speak in Rostock, where so much of the worst violence was centered, but the danger was such that he was persuaded not to travel with his wife or son. The lectures and meetings in America had gone well. Following his presentation in Cincinnati, James Levine's mother asked him what he thought her son should do *vis à vis* Bayreuth. Gottfried sensed that his response, 'Your son has to answer your question with his conscience', troubled her deeply.

In Toby Heifetz's living room we watched a tape on Gottfried that had been shown on Austrian television. With us was Hannah Busoni, the eighty-six-year-old daughter of one of the most important Jewish liberal judges in the Weimar Republic and daughter-in-law of Ferruccio Busoni, the anti-Wagner composer and mentor of Kurt Weill, with whom Gottfried has been staying on his New York sojourns. 'She has been a mother to me', he said, as he glanced lovingly at Mrs Busoni. Gottfried frankly acknowledges that he wrote his study of Kurt Weill as 'a protest against the Wagner family's racist past'.

When our talk returned to Bayreuth, Gottfried reiterated his concerns. As he notes in his lectures, he was particularly upset about Bayreuth's exhibition on Wagner and the Jews in 1985. He felt it was a complete whitewash, at the level of showing Wagner together with Hermann Levi, who conducted the world premiere of *Parsifal* (at Ludwig's insistence), and not saying anything about how profoundly troubled that relationship was. There are two issues here. The first, of course, is Germany's inability to acknowledge its history, to apologize and mourn. The second is that of Jewish complicity. Elaine Brody summed it up best in her essay, 'The Jewish Wagnerites', in that same issue of *The Opera Quarterly* that contained Ardoin's 'A *Ring* Diary':

> That many of [Wagner's] followers, indeed many of his close associates, were Jews may well be. The curious love–hate relationship of the Jewish Wagnerites with their savior/ redeemer seemed to me to warrant investigation. Many, in addition to those listed above [e.g., Levi and Angelo Neummann, Wagner's agent], paid special tribute to Wagner. If, however, we examine the nature of these members of the Jewish faith who became so enthralled with the composer that they threw aside their dignity, their heritage and their families to work for him, we would find that all suffered the curse of self-hate, *Selbsthass*.

Like *hassliebe*, the word *selbsthass* was introduced to me by Hans Kahltzwerg.

After rereading Brody's essay in 1985, I telephoned Richard Plant, who was about to leave for a summer vacation in Switzerland. I asked him if I could use the aforementioned quotes about Friedelind Wagner in 'that piece we talked about months ago. I'm ready to publish it. I think I'm going to entitle it 'Who Knows When Another Wagner Will Come Along to Set the Entire Cycle in Motion Again?'

Richard, who always found Wagner's philosophical ravings to be lunatic and who was never seduced by his music, said, 'You can publish the quotes about Friedelind Wagner, all of them.' Then he chided me for not more honestly acknowledging how much of my anger with Wagner – like Alberich's anger with the Rhine Maidens? – is really that of a spurned lover.

Chapter five

Children in Love

IF this were 1975 I'd be able to put the car alarm that woke me up again at three fucking o'clock in the morning in operatic perspective. I'd say something very clever like, 'It sounds like Maria on her farewell tour', which had just taken place the year before. That was the same year (coincidentally?) the shrinks voted us sane. But let's face it, Maria's top was shot *much* earlier. Even in 1960, had a more gaping wobble ever been recorded?

In 1977 I stopped talking and even thinking *'cosi'*, as we used to say in the 1960s vernacular of opera and gay. That was the year I stopped putting everything in the context of a world in which I suddenly began to feel very alien – so suddenly, in fact, that I can trace it all back to a certain night at the opera.

I was thirty-one and had just attended my umpteenth performance of *La Bohème*. In those days keeping count mattered. The production was the one that preceded the current Zeffirelli monstrosity at the Met. I don't remember who the director or designer was. Does anyone? (Are most of the opera queens who would remember such esoterica dead?) What I do remember is the earthshaking insight I had as I witnessed Renata Scotto's vocal and histrionic *agitazione* as Musetta, though that's *not* to say that Renata Scotto causes *agita*. It was her first Musetta. I remember that, but was it her first Musetta that season? In New York? Ever? Such distinctions were very important. Correction. It was the first time 'Madame Scotto' had 'assayed' the role, we would say, unwittingly ridiculing the Francis Robinsons, Edward Downeses, John Culshaws, Mary Ellis Peltzes, Terry McEwens, Tony Randalls and other opera … uh … 'afficionados' who were likewise unwittingly our role models. (As Bill Hoffman puts it 'Opera is fairies' basket-ball'.)

Anyway, the earthshaking insight was simply this. In Act III, as the lovers bade '*addio*' to each other, I became conscious that I too was bidding *addio*, to both of them and not very *senza rancor*. But let me say right now that Scotto, a serious artist who felt she was always getting kicked around by the critics – try to think of her as the Nixon of divas – Scotto didn't cause my defection from opera any more than 'Scotto causes AIDS' in the realms of *The Lisbon Traviata*, though I suppose my story will add to the grievance repertoire of 'the diminutive soprano', as critics characterized her with the same ostensible affection with which they talk about Jessye Norman's 'physical grandeur'. No. What I was going through was even bigger than a question of divas. In a great epiphany, I suddenly realized that it didn't matter who the stars were anymore. I never wanted to see or hear *La Bohème* again, period.

Precious? The insight seemed so to me too at first, but I knew it was serious. In fact, it was so serious that I did something unprecedented. I left the theater after Act III. Now, on principle, I never walked out of an opera mid-performance no matter how terrible or how bad my mood. I'm no longer sure what the principle was. Something sweet, I think, like respect for the artists. Perhaps I fancied myself one of the artists, as committed and important in my role as a member of the audience as they were in their roles on stage. But most likely, it was a discipline I'd learned from attending so many performances with well-known music critics (all of whom happened to be gay). Fancying myself their colleague as well as their friend (since I never slept with any of them, why else were these semi-public figures always inviting me to these public events?), I didn't want to be witnessed or interpreted as walking out on a particular artist, and with her luck, 'that poor little mouse of a Scotto', as one of the certifiably heterosexual critics once referred to her in the *New York Times*, would be certain to overhear some malicious gossip about my deportment *vis-à-vis* her performance. '*La Scottissima*', as Peter G. Davis once noted in *New York* that she was dubbed by a coterie of her most devoted fans (all of whom happened to be gay, a fact Davis of course didn't mention), might hear someone whisper: 'Isn't it terrible! Remember that swarthy doctor we decided was Italian or Spanish and rather sexy but who turned out to be Jewish? You know, the one who's doing that public health study of the medical care of professional singers, the opera ... uh ... aesthete who escorts all those homely [except Trixie], closeted music critics who dubbed him "Maeves" [combining opera ... uh ... maven with the *fantasia assoluta* of James McCourt's Mawrdew Czgowchzw?]? Well, Maeves doesn't just walk those bitches. She spies for them, and Maeves just walked out on Madame Scotto's first assay as Musetta.'

As I meandered toward Times Square, not consciously aware that that's where I was going, I lit a joint, which may or may not have been my first that evening. I must have thought I was going to 'the tubs' – to the St Marks Baths or the 'Everhard' (the 'h' was never theirs and not always mine), as was customary on each of the two or three nights and sometimes days of these periodic sex-and-drugs-and-opera weekend sojourns from Boston. Marijuana always gave me the classic dry mouth, motor dysfunction, paranoia, munchies, giggles, sex enhancement and sopor, in something like that order. As the years passed, the paranoia worsened, as did another symptom, one I'd never really noticed but which eventually put me in the hospital – depression.

On 42nd Street I took another toke of the joint I'd begun at Lincoln Center and became increasingly paranoid as I passed movie marquees with titles like *The Hills Have Eyes* and *Beyond Cannibalism*. I finally realized where my feet were taking me – to The Barracks, a baths in the heart of The Deuce (42nd Street, between 8th and 9th Avenues) that was known as the sleaziest and most dangerous of Gotham's vast array of sex establishments, even though nothing was ever even rumored to have happened there that approached the horrors of the Everard fire, which claimed nine lives on just the sort of beautiful summer night in 1977 I so often spent there before the fire and later, when the Everard reopened and I moved to New York. (The Everard was shut down during the early years of the AIDS epidemic and is now an emporium of clothing accessory wholesalers. On 28th Street just west of Broadway, only the arch of a facade remains to commemorate what fewer and fewer care to remember.)

The Everard was my favorite baths, hands down, but the New St Marks Baths, the largest and busiest of them all, and Beacon Baths, which was known for its chubbies and chubby chasers (both of which I would become), and, very rarely, The Barracks, East Side Sauna (the 'East Side' killed it for me), Club Baths (likewise too prissy) and Wall Street Sauna (much too small, far away and inactive at night) were diversions which became, like an alcoholic's periodic switching of bars and preferred drinks, increasingly necessary to sustain a pleasure that even in 1977 had already begun to acquire the bland, white taste of habit.

As I ascended the staircase to The Barracks, I was watched by a glass door at the top of the stairs that captured and precisely reflected a Picasso-eyed gargoyle with blood-dripping fangs and a necklace of human parts, the beheaded visage of a much larger movie poster outside the entrance. Was it the grass, or did the clerk really leer contemptuously at my opera garb and smirk knowingly (of a secret I wasn't in on) as he handed me the keys to my room? The leer and the smirk were real, I decided, when I arrived at my room, which featured a decorative fraternity paddle on the door. I undressed and cruised the corridors in my towel which in those days wasn't any kind of struggle to keep fastened at the waist.

The Barracks was known for its large black clientele, a real attraction. On the two or three previous occasions I'd been there, however, I guess I hadn't noticed just how predominant that clientele was and never thought about the possibility that the patrons may have preferred it that way. As I passed one handsome man after another, none of whom seemed interested in me on what was after all just the first tour, I began to hear whipping and slapping noises from the rooms, not unlike the same noises one often heard and sometimes even created on other occasions, but which seemed much louder that night, as interpreted by the marijuana.

My paranoia began to waft. What if I'm the only white man here? I began to wonder, as if I were one of the racist, anti-Semitic boys I grew up with in Georgia. My musings moved to another fear of similar etiology and character: 'Are Jews white'? This struck me as funny, and I got an attack of the giggles that seemed to go on forever. Then, 'What if those rumors about people disappearing from this place are really true?' The paranoia began to pass and was replaced by depression about what I determined were indeed the altogether self-hating ratiocinations of my Southern heritage. It didn't occur to me that the character and intensity of my feelings might have something to do with the marijuana.

I retreated back to my room. Whatever the reasons, cruising the halls had been fruitless and scary. Time to try the other approach of dimming the lights and striking the right pose. That worked much better. In fact, in very short order and just at the moment of perfect synchronization of light and posture and mindset, in walked Stanley Kowalski. Actually, Stanley Katkowski, who, I was to learn very quickly, hated the name Stanley, preferring to be called Stash. At six foot one, weighing just over 200 pounds, being naturally rather than artificially muscular and covered with hair, here, in the look-and-smell flesh, at first sight, was the real-live champion-cum-villain of some of my richest fantasies.

As our eyes met and locked in an embrace, I was electrified by the same grand bolus of hormones the body injects in the presence of real danger. Without a word he sat down in the chair. (Unlike most baths' cubicles, which only had slab beds, this one had a table and chair, but otherwise also looked like the generic prison cell that was such a cherished staging of these theaters of sleaze.) Dangling one leg over the armrest, revealing his upper thigh and a soupçon of crotch, he passed a joint to me and spoke with a deep, virile tone that seemed gentle and reassuring, even as it instigated another wave of endocrine secretions. His 'So what are you into?' sounded like Robeson reciting Shakespeare.

Like a cat or Jack Benny, I looked away from him, towards the door and back again, to help me decide whether or not this was all real, and if so what to do about it. I took a toke and answered the stranger very honestly. As in my writing, which likewise embarks on a romance with strangers, I didn't realize or care how much I was exposing myself: 'Oh, the usual garden variety stuff ... cops, prisons, love, football players, sanitation workers, romance ... repair men, soldiers ... And what are you into?'

Stash stretched and yawned in a great display. 'Gladiators.'

I lit a cigarette. 'Gladiators?'

'You know,' he said with what seemed like not altogether mock-seriousness. 'Like the Romans.'

'Oh.' I tapped the ashes of my cigarette into the ashtray, missing it only by about three feet. We passed the joint back and forth again and I began caressing his leg. The grass made the silence seem loud and endless. 'So what happens with these ... uh ... gladiators. What do they do?'

'You know what gladiators do ...' he said with a sexy, menacing, I've-got-the-upper-hand grin that finally dissolved into a broad Cheshire Cat smile. He began petting my crotch with his foot. 'They have combats.'

The whipping and slapping noises suddenly seemed very loud again, like the pounding of my heart. 'And what happens in these combats?' I inquired with the same tone with which I might have asked the time, my voice cracking only twice.

He kissed me gently on the lips. 'What happens?' He began to chuckle with a condescension that emphasized he was stating the obvious. 'What happens is that one of the gladiators wins the combat.'

I lit the wrong end of another cigarette with the first one still going in the ashtray. 'And what happens to the other one?' I persisted, thinking at the time that this was proverbial feline curiosity.

'Well,' he beamed. 'You know that too. The loser gets tortured and killed.'

I experienced this one brief moment of absolute terror and panic, turning porcelain white and still as the cigarettes and joints dropped from my gaping mouth and fingers. Stash roared with laughter and took me in his arms, kissing me tenderly on the face and lips. The brief moment of horror was followed by a much longer moment of exhilaration.

When his jollity finally dissipated, we kissed again. 'That's quite a fantasy', I conceded. 'But Stanley ...' Stash bristled. 'Sorry ... uh ... Stash, there's just one thing that's still not clear.' Assuming command with swelling confidence, I gently squeezed his balls and hardening dick and began working in earnest on his nipples, which I'd guessed correctly at first sight were his most erogenous zones, especially the left nipple which was twice the size of the right. 'What's still not clear', I purred, 'is which of the combatants is you.'

Our repartee melted into some of the hottest sex I ever had.

Sex with authentic communication, with eye contact. Not the usual masturbatory scenario that consists so rigidly of a specific script that a spontaneous giggle will kill it. Sex with the courage and freedom to really explore your fantasies with someone you genuinely care about. Sex with real feelings, with more adrenalin than you could ever hope to share with an ordinary trick. There's nothing hotter. Sure enough, we had fallen in love.

In 1979 my life really seemed to be changing. I had just completed a three-year stint in the private practice of anesthesiology in a working-class Boston suburb and was in the midst of fulfilling a lifelong dream, one that had become increasingly urgent from the moment I set foot in grim, homophobic Boston – moving to New York. So natural and comfortable did I feel in Gotham that whenever anyone asked where I was from, I always said something like, 'I live in Boston now, but I'm planning to move to New York, which I consider my home.' The year 1979 was also the year I wrote my first pieces for the gay press, one of which was a survey of the academic literature on sadomasochism. Entitled 'Coming to Grips with S–M: Psychiatry versus Sex Research', it was published in the *Advocate* on Stash's birthday and was received by Stash as a loving if cockeyed tribute to that occasion.

Unfortunately, Stash lived in Chicago. And there was no job waiting for me in New York. I was not happy in anesthesiology, the boredom and stress of which I would compare to flying an airplane. Being the pilot of a commercial airliner is important, highly skilled work that entails enormous responsibilities. If you're flying day in and day out, however, it can be pretty deadly, even when the routes are varied. The truth is that I had gone into anesthesia in anticipation of being able to work part-time, so I could do the writing that was already dearer to my heart than anything else. But part-time work in anesthesia turned out to be a lot more difficult to obtain than I was led to believe would be the case during my residency at the MGH, and it became even more unobtainable when my colleagues in the Harvard Anesthesia Society discovered that I was a faggot and had written a satire about them for one of the mainstream medical journals.

The satire, an autobiographical comedy of errors, 'Impatient

Inpatient: Notes of a Hospitalized House Officer', was the first piece I had published since writing the opera reviews for the *Daily Californian* at Berkeley. The circumstance was that within days of having completed my internship in Boston and Cambridge, I suddenly developed a high fever and serious diarrhea during a brief vacation to New York, where I was hospitalized at a large, august training hospital and cared for by overworked, disgruntled house officers like myself. My indictment of academic medicine and its exploitation of house officers was incisive. However, I should now add that my illness, shigellosis (aka. 'rim fever'), was probably not acquired, as the piece implied, from a Manhattan restaurant. In fact, the piece never mentioned that I was gay, to say nothing of how much of my rage had to do with my being in the closet and with the homophobia I had encountered in my medical training and throughout my hospitalization.

My first trips with Stash were to Fire Island Pines where we stayed with José Orlovsky. The panoramic view from his ocean-front home was greatly enhanced by the MDA José had shown me research papers about as an incentive to try it. 'The love drug', they called it, and sure enough, I had two peak ('religious') experiences under its influence, experiences I will never forget. The first was on the beach. I was alone with José and feeling very loving when I spotted a small pile of dead shrimps. 'They were bad shrimps', I suggested. 'They made the wrong moral and ethical choices and now they're paying the price.' As our eyes met, we exploded in laughter and tears. It was as profound an exchange as any I've ever known. In that moment, we were at peace with ourselves and each other, and we were bonded with the universe. A similar experience happened the next day. Gustavo, another gay doctor, had stopped in to visit. As we each took some additional MDA, wincing, as always, at its bitter, metallic taste, he told us of his most recent confrontations with his biological family, which had completely rejected him because of his homosexuality. We all began to cry when José said, 'But Gustavolach, *this* (signaling himself, us and Fire Island with a broad, benedictory wave of his hand, which he then joined with ours) ... this is the family.' I've had many moments of feeling bonded with the gay community, but none is more deeply imprinted. Unfortunately for my friendship with José, the love drug stimulated every feeling of bonding in me except sexual arousal, and my inability to respond to him led to repeated rejections, sometimes with contempt.

No sooner had I arrived in New York than I felt pulled away to Chicago, not only to be with Stash but to cover the John Wayne Gacy trial for a piece that eventually appeared in *Christopher Street*. (Like a later piece, 'The Most Important New Public Health Problem in the United States', which would have been the first in-depth feature on the AIDS epidemic to appear in the mainstream press in New York, 'Sanity in Chicago' was at first commissioned and later killed by the *Village Voice*.) The Gacy trial was extremely important, I felt, because of the certainty that Gacy, who had committed the greatest number of serial murders (most of the victims were gay teens) in American history, would be perceived by the public at large to be some kind of gay person, and because of the related certainty that conservative American psychiatrists who still believed that homosexuality *per se* is pathological would be taking this national occasion to abet that perception with discredited neo-Freudian concepts of a cause-and-effect relationship between repressed homosexuality and paranoid schizophrenia. I was convinced that this trial had the potential to unleash a major wave of scapegoating, the holocaust more and more of us in the gay community were already beginning to sense. As I read it, the public would never give a shit about the details of the case, would never care about the overwhelming extent to which Gacy's homophobia mirrored its own ignorance and prejudice. And that's exactly what happened, but the fallout from the Gacy trial was less than feared, thanks to the simultaneity of the Dan White trial during the period, which made American psychiatry look so ridiculous, even in the eyes of a Dickensianly stupid and vicious American public.

Gacy was very homophobic and his homophobia clearly reflected cultural ignorance and prejudice, but the real explanation for Gacy's behavior had little to do with homophobia or sexual orientation. Gacy, who was actively bisexual and who was never convincingly demonstrated to have been psychotic, was a sexual sadist and lust murderer who discovered these pleasures, which he began to crave, almost by accident. Sadists and serial killers are extreme versions of what, in today's language of addiction and recovery, are called 'excitement junkies'. Like Josef Mengele and Gilles de Rais, Gacy had become addicted to aggression, in the form of torture and murder, not unlike the way I became addicted to cigarettes. And the baths.

In New York, I'd taken everything I had and purchased a co-op, then immediately sublet it and lived off a small margin of profit during the months that I covered the Gacy trial and lived with Stash in Chicago. But this was only for the short term. What about the future? How were Stash and I going to work out our lives together? When we lay cuddled in each other's arms watching reruns of *Cosmos* and *The Muppets*, the answers didn't seem so urgent.

Stash appeared to be asking himself the same questions but seemed farther along with answers. A former Jesuit seminarian who had done graduate work in economics and political science at Northwestern, where he felt very ethnic and class-conscious, he became one of the youngest contenders to run for City Council in Chicago's history. After losing, he became an independent marketing consultant and real estate entrepreneur. But unlike so many of the other gay real estate entrepreneurs, the gentrifiers (e.g., Andy Bullen) of this period, Stash placed his bets on the suburbs.

When we met, he was managing a three-hundred-unit apartment building in the kind of picket-fence pretty, Blue-Velvet suburb where Gacy had lived (was it the same?), and which he had purchased with mortgages up the kazoo, and was trying to get national and international contracts for an array of hydroponic plants, notwithstanding the shrinkage of the sample violets on his window sill. Other products included mopeds and fiber-optic lamps, which were briefly fashionable, like the lava lamps that preceded them a decade earlier and were already making a comeback – a false ray of hope, alas, that some of the nicer values of the 1960s would soon be returning.

In the first few months of our affair, we took honeymoons in Fort Lauderdale and Key West. Later, there were trips to Cozumel, San Francisco, Provincetown, Italy, and, of course, New York. In Lauderdale, we stayed at the notorious Marlin Beach and rendez-voused with Pete Wilderman, a suburban Los Angeles friend of

Stash's, a school teacher and guidance counselor who wore baseball hats and a black leather vest just like the ones Stash and I had; who made and sold poppers, which Stash really liked but which always gave me headaches and impotence; who liked to get fist-fucked in private clubs and back-room bars and who once did so in a black-out and later received photos of the event in the mail from anonymous admirers; who died of AIDS; and whom I treated with indifference when he called to ask me for medical advice. This was in passive retaliation for the contempt he'd expressed for my having been a 'gay libber' and 'do gooder'. (Parenthetically, I first heard the latter phrase in the asides of East Hampton real estate broker and Hamptons charity benefit regular Michael Braverman.) When 'the wild man' called for the AIDS advice, the targets of his contempt had just begun the switch from gay libbers, do gooders and screamers (including early AIDS activists), to doctors and medicine. What did the wild man think of Jews? Mercifully, I never found out. Or can't remember.

The affair with Stash was the only long-term relationship I'd had in which sexual jealousy was almost non-existent. Almost. We went to the baths together and had three-ways, several times with an extremely handsome but chronically depressed and floridly paranoid Argentine whose wealthy, Catholic parents had put him, as an adolescent with 'homosexual tendencies', in a mental institution where he was subjected to repeated series of shock treatments for nearly a year. The freedom to be gay was clearly the most serious issue in Franco's life. In fact, it was a matter of life and death to him to remain in the United States, but after completing several years of studies, his visa was running out, and not even his parents' money, which would be instantly cut off if they were to have any idea that his homosexual activities or even tendencies were ongoing, had the power to allay this process.

In Lauderdale, jealousy did rear its ugly head on one occasion, when I discovered an orgy in progress in our room with the same people who, fifteen minutes earlier on the beach, I'd presumed were so envious of our conjugal bliss, as evinced by the matching leather necklaces Stash and I paraded about in, arm-in-arm, as we cooed and nibbled at each other. Feeling that I should perhaps feel humiliated, I tossed my drink in Stash's face. His response was a giggle, at which point I abandoned my tragic posture and joined the orgy.

There were two trips to Key West, where I made the surprising discovery that Stash admired my being active in gay causes, even if that admiration never seemed to translate into any involvement of his own. Like so many of the post-Stonewall, pre-AIDS generation of gay men, Stash was not a gay libber or do gooder, just as he was not a screamer. He was one of the machos. The machos would admit they were gay to other gay machos and participate in the sexual – mostly leather – subculture, but that's as far as it went. The attitude was a lot like that of gay artists, most of whom still feel that the gay world is lucky enough to have them at all. Don't ask for anything else, like marching in demonstrations or being otherwise public. Like many of these cases, however, Stash did seem to respect what I was doing and even regarded me as a kind of role model. Conversely, Stash, who was the only younger gay man I'd ever fallen in love with, inspired my activism. Even though he represented a lot of what I was fighting to change, I felt deeply empathic for his being less experienced and less wise. Whether either of us liked it or not, he was my gay child. I was in love with him sexually, but I also loved him parentally. If I had been like the trying-to-be white daughter in *Imitation of Life* when I was growing up, I was now like her mother.

I remember the visceral sensation of that love as he lay in my arms. Sometimes I'd read to him from owl and puss poems I wrote about our romance or from a child's book I'd found called *Stanley, The Worldly Pig*. In those moments of real lover-with-lover, parent-with-child tenderness, he'd put his head on my chest and within minutes fall into a deep, untroubled sleep. One morning I watched him gulping down his cereal. He was 'all bright-eyed and bushy-tailed' (as Andy Bullen would say of me) and unaware that he had a thin line of milk on his mustache. My secret knowledge of his vulnerability made him seem so innocent and me so powerful. In a mediocre restaurant in Manhattan some months later, the same innocence and power repositioned themselves. Stash was devouring the driest, most depressing slab of veal parmiggiana I'd ever seen. I couldn't understand how he could like it so much, even if he were starving. Suddenly, I was suffused with that special tenderness as I reminded myself that Stash, whose family was blue-collar, hadn't yet seen or tasted very much of the world. Actually, I think he was the only gay man I'd ever met who'd never been to Europe and who knew nothing about cuisine.

Needless to say, Stash knew nothing about opera either. The doting parent in me was more charmed than offended by the Parsifal-like irreverence of his falling asleep when I played him the majestic Act I transformation scene of that opera. I was similarly charmed when he described the world premiere of Penderecki's *Paradise Lost*, which I forced him (and myself) to sit through all five hours of, as 'the worst experience of my entire life'. 'Talk about S & M!' he pleaded tearfully during an intermission.

Respecting the great sources of identity, pride and strength which Catholicism and being Polish were for Stash, I dutifully forced him to go to a few performances, such as the Penderecki and *Dialogues of the Carmelites*. What I couldn't see was that as a role model, I was giving him a confusing message. I was urging him to take pride in being Polish and Catholic. At the same time, he could see that although I took pride in being gay and although my respect for his ethnicity and religion could be interpreted as a way of encouraging the same respect for mine, I actually took little pride in being Jewish.

While Stash's ignorance of 'the finer things' may have seemed very butch to me, they failed to captivate D. J. Love. When we ran into D. J. on the first trip to Key West, he was initially friendly but even more volatile than usual, still deeply embittered about the gay community as he had satirized and stereotyped it in *The Sissy*. In a rare moment of calm, D. J. asked me, 'Do you love him?' 'Yes', I answered without hesitation. It was the only time I'd ever seen D. J. without a comeback. When D. J. asked Stash, who was seated next to him at a dinner at the original Claire's, how his blackened bluefish was, Stash jabbed him in the ribs and yahooed, his mouth full of food, that it was '*molto* tasty'. I don't think the otherwise very literary D. J. appreciated what a clever if unwitting put-down this was of a conversation, mostly about opera, theater, gourmet food and gay politics, that was liberally interlaced with European code words and that had otherwise completely excluded Stash. I beamed with pride. (But was it gay pride?)

On the exceedingly uncomfortable rocky flats gay Key Westers and visitors went to in the absence of a real beach, we played Othello, Stash's favorite game. When I reprimanded him for his coarseness at dinner and tried to explain how important a person D. J. was, he had the kind of puppylike comeback that was a lot more successful in disarming me, I was to learn too late, than the banks that were financing his real estate ventures: 'Remember, I'm like Charlie, the Starkist tuna. I may not have good taste, but I taste good.' Children in love.

Walking home from the rocks that afternoon, we were gay-baited by some of the local rednecks (our machismo notwithstanding), which has remained a common problem in Key West. We ducked into Shorty's, the popular diner, for a bite. On the menu was a special, 'Jewfish steak', which Stash thought was hilarious, even though it clearly made me uncomfortable. In fact, the more uncomfortable I became, the funnier Stash seemed to find it. The 'Jewfish', I later discovered, was so named in seventeenth century England because it was regarded as ideal for kosher diets. Meanwhile, however, it sounded like something anti-Semitic, and indeed, that's the way the word is mostly appreciated today – as a racial slur. When we ascertained that the fish in question was grouper, Stash began guffawing that I was in fact just like a grouper – serious and dour. 'You've both got the same face.'

This hurt more than I was able to admit to Stash, or even to myself at the time. But I got my revenge a few months later when we went to Cozumel. Stash was prematurely bald and wore a hairpiece. Recognizing this as an area of vulnerability, his friends would test and affirm their friendship, as friends are wont to do, by kidding him mercilessly. They'd say things like, 'Stash, you can't send away for hairpieces.' Or 'Is it true your hairpiece was made in Korea?' In Cozumel, we went diving off the spectacular Palencar reef. Though neither of us was a certified diver, they took us down to 110 feet. Now that I am certified, I realize how extremely dangerous this was. Stash was so nervous he forgot to wear his bathing cap. There were six or eight of us in about ten feet of water, waiting for Stash, who finally jumped in and began his descent to join us.

We all watched his descent which was slow and graceful and, as he reached our depth, perfectly mimicked by the balletic ascent of his hairpiece. It was so funny everyone had to resurface. Unfortunately for me, among the creatures we saw on the reef when the dive finally did get underway was every size and variety of grouper. Tat for tit, I thought, as I endured the next round of retaliatory barbs. It didn't occur to me until years later that a sensitivity about being bald wasn't really the equivalent of a vulnerability about being Jewish. And by the time I did realize it, I had already invested my life savings in a real estate syndication Stash had put together.

In San Francisco Stash and I 'checked out', as Stash liked to say, a private S/M club he'd heard about called the Catacombs. Mostly what went on there was fist-fucking, which Stash wasn't into at any level. More appealing to him were the hoists, harnesses, ties and paddles – accoutrements which, like such other traditional S & M paraphernalia as black leather boots, chaps and masks, likewise dominated the pornography one of Stash's older brothers kept hidden, we discovered, but which had never been part of my fantasy life and which had never aroused me in any formal role in practice. After an hour or so, overcome by the thick smog of marijuana, tobacco and nitrite vapors, we departed, never to return. Some dominance-and-submission fantasy play at home, occasional threesomes and orgies, visits to the leather bars and (most often) the baths: these were more our speed, at least together. In short, in matters of sexual taste and lifestyle, we were a fairly typical gay couple of our generation and place.

Back in Chicago, I tried to decide how I was going to make my life work, a challenge that was becoming more and more difficult to evade. The trip to the Catacombs inspired me to begin researching the medical literature on fist-fucking. As I continued my writing, mostly in the broad area of medical aspects of homosexuality and sexuality, I pondered the feasibility of doing a second residency in psychiatry, in which I had already done a lot of independent work and which I was a lot more interested in than anesthesia, even though it had the more serious disadvantage of being unlikely to be able to support me and my writing with part-time wages. The home in New York I'd always dreamed of having was now a reality, but I didn't want to be separated from Stash. That had become the first priority, at least for the short term, until Stash could relocate with me. So I proceeded to apply for a residency in psychiatry in the Chicago area, and I did so as an openly gay man.

The year was 1980. When I told the uniformly white, middle-class, mostly Jewish gentlemen who interviewed me at the Universities of Chicago, Illinois and Northwestern that the main reason I was looking at programs in Chicago, as opposed to other areas, was that I wanted to be with my lover whose business was there, they were flabbergasted and very angry. At Northwestern, the full professor who was head of resident training sneered, as if he were parodying how a kindergarten teacher might speak to a favorite pupil: 'Tell me, son, what does your mother think of you?' ('She thinks I'm too serious', I answered, taking him seriously.) As I was leaving a few minutes later, he brandished a letter of inquiry from my file in which I'd asked how many first year resident slots they had in their program. 'By the way', he snarled, 'we don't have SLOTS here!' Later that day, a lower-ranking interviewer threw his legs up on his desk so that the soles of his shoes were a few feet away from my face. In this position, he began chomping on some cashews from a bag, which he then offered to me: 'Do you see what I'm doing? I'm a man whose eating his own nuts right here in front of you, another man, and offering them to you to eat too, if you want. What do you think of that?' At the University of Chicago, the interviewers simply walked out. I wasn't even sent a rejection letter. At State, my *alma mater*, the interrogations were more indulgent in the hope that I might identify other faculty members there whom I knew to be gay. I fought back as best I could, as a writer – in essays, interviews and book reviews, and as newsletter editor of the caucus of gay and lesbian psychiatrists.

Meanwhile it was time for another trip, our last. In the early months of our affair, I eroticized everything that appeared to distinguish Stash from me: his blue-collar background, his hirsuteness, his being uncircumcised, his height, baldness and ignorance of *cuisine*, even the way he wiped his ass, from the scrotum toward the coccyx (literally ass-backwards). I likewise eroticized his being Polish, his Catholicism and his homophobic discomfort in the presence of 'screamers'. In the throes of this infatuation, which in my case was most definitely an irrational, physiologically altered state of consciousness (whatever the role of masochism in fanning it), I had promised to take him to Rome, to show him the churches and artworks he had dreamed of seeing as a seminarian. We had also planned to go to Naples and Sicily, but we arrived in Pompeii the very morning of the great *terremoto* and had to reroute ourselves north. As we sought to reconnect with our gay ancestors in the erotic tiles of the baths and catacombs, we were suddenly possessed by eerie resonances of ancient catastrophe. Even as the earth shook beneath our feet and officers hurried us away, however, the simplest insights into the impossibility of our predicament – as lovers with hopelessly divergent values and loyalties – remained elusive.

In Rome I accompanied Stash to three – three! – different mass audiences with Pope John Paul II, whose homophobia Stash simply ignored, especially during our evening jaunts to Roman baths, bars and orgies. He'd suggest that the gay issue was like contraception. Millions of Catholics ignored the Church's pronouncements on birth control and extramarital sex but were otherwise faithful. Whenever he saw how uncomfortable I was made by his surpassing affection for this pope who was, after all, a fellow Pole and the first Polish pope in history, Stash would delight in pointing out, especially if he were in a social situation, that I got even closer to the pontiff than he did 'just a few inches away', he would boast with the zeal of a fisherman describing the size of his catch. Lucky me.

I could accept and encourage Stash's pride in his ethnicity, which I unconsciously envied, but not at the cost of his inability to feel any pride in being gay. As I saw it in those days, my inability to feel proud about my ethnicity wasn't a problem of internalized anti-Semitism. Rather, it was a struggle to assert my more fundamental identity as a gay man. And that's the perspective I projected, or thought I was projecting, onto Stash.

I knew about Polish anti-Semitism, but Stash's deceased father had fought with the Allies in World War II and Stash's mother was very nice to me. Of course, I met her only once and she didn't know that I was Stash's lover, that Stash was gay or even what gay was. Stash said that she had always shown respect for Jews, but she probably didn't know that I was Jewish, an identity which, like my gayness, I'd been conditioned since earliest childhood to suppress. Hell, she didn't even speak English.

When we returned to Chicago something had changed. Stash seemed to be withdrawing from his stated commitment to try to relocate to New York with me within three years. At the same time, we were having less sex and arguing more. I was particularly upset by a Mr International Leather contest we attended, where one of the entertainers was sporting a swastika. As I did with almost everything in my life, as I'm still doing even now as I write, I tried to analyze and intellectualize what I was going through. Even as limerence continued to possess me, I conducted an interview with sexologist John Money on the subject of his book, *Love and Love Sickness*. But the resultant understanding of the so-called science of love was of little practical value. Like writing them, having insights is seldom empowering. Inexorably, our romance continued to deflate and when it finally became clear that Stash never had any intention of even trying to relocate to New York, I returned home. It all happened very suddenly, on New Year's Eve, 1980. The extent of his pain seemed surprising in view of his deceptiveness about our future plans – he must have imagined I would conform, like his brothers' dutiful wives, to whatever were his wishes and plans – but I was, on the other hand, his first lover. His parting words were, 'You can't commit murder and get away with it.'

Stash wouldn't speak to me for many months. We would never have spoken again, in fact, if it weren't for the small detail that my life-savings were tied up in his real-estate syndication. Back in New York, I took a job at a substance abuse clinic. During the six months I had to wait for my sublet apartment to become available to me again, I resided with a friend, a gay internist who, like me, had decided to do a second residency in psychiatry. But Harold Tartofsky and I held some very different points of view. Harold, whose hair transplants looked like an unplayed game of dots on pink paper, whose favorite store was Paul Stuart, who was still in the closet and whose taste for cocaine didn't seem so problematic at the time, remain convinced, until his death from AIDS five years later, that the psychoanalysts had been right after all, that homosexuality was indeed a mental disorder.

Harold's likewise closeted best friend, Egon, who lost his

entire family in the Holocaust, who was personally tortured by Dr Mengele, who survived to become a leading society photographer, who knew Mrs Onassis and who, like Harold, had once flirted and fallen out with D. J. Love, tended to agree with Harold that homosexuality was an illness. He was convinced, for example, that lesbians – and certainly his close friends, the sister heiresses of the leading publishing house that gave him one of the cushiest jobs in town – had even more contempt for gay men than straight men. 'They think we're weak and ineffectual', he asserted. 'Straight men they can at least respect.'

Like Egon, and for that matter our mutual friend D. J., Harold couldn't shake his contempt for the gay movement. He still wanted desperately to be straight and remained obsessed with the concept of homosexuality as always falling within a continuum of 'pathological narcissism', and with the pre-World-War-II theory that repressed homosexuality is, universally, the cause of paranoid schizophrenia. It was his acceptance of these viewpoints that gave him entrée into the notoriously homophobic New York City hospital departments in which he trained in the late 1970s. In the early 1980s, in an unwittingly successful attempt to prove the applicability of this theory, he made bizarre, distressing but fortunately unsuccessful efforts to undermine my recovery from depression. At the time, within months of his first hospitalization for KS, he was heavily addicted to cocaine.

Stash and I both went on to subsequent relationships. I saw Benjie, the Jewish astrologer who I'd met through Harold, for about a year before linking up with Arnie, my life-partner since 1982. The involvement with Benjie was my first with another Jew, albeit a self-negating one like me. My relationship with the man with whom I've shared my home for more than a decade, on the other hand, was and remains my first real love affair with a self-respecting Jew, a man who was and remains also, unlike the others, politically conscious, involved, and very openly and proudly gay. In between Benjie and Arnie there was another relationship. The subject of the next chapter, 'The Housemates Who Got Nailed', it would officially launch these memoirs, and my adulthood.

Stash's new lover was a poor white-trash type from rural

Mississippi named Hamilton Jackson. In the army, Ham had spent five years stationed in rural Germany where he had a protracted affair with a local whose father had been a high-ranking and unrepentant (as they all were) Nazi officer.

Because of the real estate partnership, I had to deal with Ham as well as Stash. When we first met, we talked about Germany and opera. In earlier times I'd been the stereotypic, unconsciously anti-Semitic Jewish Wagnerite. I now see how that worked. Worshiping at the shrine of your enemy, however objectively great or gifted that person may be, is otherwise known as masochism. It's a simple, common defense mechanism: if I, the Jew, am anti-Semitic, the real anti-Semite is less likely to feel the need to express his anti-Semitism toward me. My anti-Semitism defuses his. So if I, the Jewish Wagnerite, effusively proclaim my love for Wagner, notwithstanding or in spite of (excusing) the composer's anti-Semitism, the non-Jewish Wagnerite is less likely to feel the need to express any anti-Semitism toward me. Unfortunately, this tactic hasn't worked well, at least not in the cases of the two most famous Wagnerites in history: Richard Wagner and Adolf Hitler. Why am I the only one who sees this?

Both Ham and I had been to Bayreuth for the Wagner festival, our discussion of which concluded with Ham's detailed account of the day he and his lover visited Cosima Wagner's grave. Did Ham have any idea how anti-Semitic Cosima was? For that matter, did he know which side the United States fought on in World War II? Probably, I thought in answer to the first question, and not very clearly, I later concluded with regard to the second, when he said something about 'niggers' and then immediately apologized with tongue-in-cheek sincerity, acknowledging without my saying anything that I probably found that word offensive. In questions of anti-Semitism, I was undergoing a metamorphosis: from unconscious masochism to becoming easily suspicious and never confident of my impressions in a society that was consistently telling me I was either wrong or overreacting – i.e., paranoid. Like my affair with Benjie, Ham's romance with Stash lasted only about a year. Benjie and I soon lost contact. Ham, however, became even more strongly entangled with Stash, his new business partner.

By the spring of 1983 – two years into the AIDS epidemic,

an unprecedented catastrophe which demanded and appropriated everything I had as a physician, writer and activist – I was utterly burnt out and was hospitalized with a major depression. In the hospital, I received an unsolicited visit from my sister, with whom I'd shared an intense dislike of our patriarchal, corporally punitive father during our childhood and adolescence. The latest from medicine and science, incidentally, is that *all* physical punishment of children – like the spankings and slappings so many of us got (including, incidentally, D. J. Love) should be regarded as child abuse. With regard to my own experience I couldn't agree more. Although homophobia did not seem to be the core of my father's anger toward me, which seemed no different than that toward my sister (was misogyny its essence? internalized anti-Semitism?), the end result of what happened to me is not so unlike what happened to D. J. It taught me a hatred for my father I was eventually able to transcend intellectually, but never emotionally.

The other feeling I shared with Judith as well as my brother Howie was a profound childhood unhappiness and insecurity about being Jewish. I was never very close with either of my siblings. I suppose I resented them as heterosexuals, for all the years I had to pretend to them, as to everyone else, to be someone I wasn't. And, of course, I resented them for being older, stronger, smarter and having more privileges, and for teasing and otherwise taking advantage of me when we were children. What happened in early childhood was forgivable. But were childhood dynamics the reason I never got a phone call, to say nothing of a gift or even a card, when I graduated from college and medical school? Or was it something more complicated?

Actually, both dealt reasonably well with my coming out – certainly, neither has ever been overtly homophobic – but for a long time I had the sense that my being gay was OK not so much because they were progressive and accepting, but because it didn't really matter what I was or thought or did. Was such indifference the result of generic dysfunction in our relationships or did it have to do with much deeper issues of unhappiness and insecurity about acknowledging and accepting our family, with its ineradicably Jewish heritage (and fate)?

In the 1970s we began the (in our case glacially) slow, painful process of establishing adult relationships. Eventually my sister and I connected at the level of appreciating gay politics in the context of feminism and AIDS politics in the context of the need for socialized medicine. Howie, too, found a kind of detached appreciation of and compassion for gay people in his anarchic, dadaist and altogether childlike sense of the world as one huge joke – a place where power plays, authoritarianism and chaos were the rule, where outsiders always got screwed, where so-called nobility, heroism and other 'virtues' could always be deflated.

In the early 1980s, when my Jewish consciousness began to emerge from its long sleep, I had become newly uncomfortable with both of them, but especially with Judith, whom I was closer to and saw more of. Of course, she was having to deal with yet another of my identity transitions – this time from 'Judeo-Christian' to Jewish – and was raising a son who was not Jewish on his father's side. Even so, her inability to ever affirm her ethnicity seemed to mirror my own anti-Semitism, as I was finally beginning to see it, and to be the unconsciously determining factor in her anti-Israeli politics. An ostensible supporter of gay rights in this country and, simultaneously, an ardent or at least tacit defender, without qualification (that I ever heard), of communist dictatorships that brutally oppressed gay people (e.g. Cuba) and some of which were also manifestly anti-Semitic (e.g. Poland, Russia), she tended to bully people with her vision of socialism, in much the same way our fanatically religious grandmother (whom she resembled physically and who likewise bears some physical resemblance to Arnie) tended to dominate everyone with her Jewish fundamentalism.

How much of Judith's politics – from a socialism that de-emphasized the significance of ethnicity to the point of rewriting history, especially for Jews, to a multiculturalism that extolled every ethnicity and culture except the Jews – was the result of internalized anti-Semitism? I'd say a lot, but it's not as if Judith had been overtly victimized in childhood by her predominantly non-Jewish peers for her ethnicity. On the contrary, I vividly remember her girlhood successes in being elected a cheerleader and to an exclusive sorority. She was popular, respected and proud. It was not her failure but her success at assimilation that provides the window on her internalization of anti-Semitism, as on my own and that of so many (the majority?) of the Jews of our time and place. Not having ever really accepted our own roots, however, our ability to assimilate into other group(s) was compromised even more fundamentally. When the group you're trying to assimilate into can see that you've not been able to take an appropriate degree of pride in your ethnic birthright, that you can't look it in the face, it registers as something suspicious, neurotic, 'degenerate' (to racists) or at best 'pathetic' rather than sympathetic and deserving of respect, and it invites contempt and exploitation, even though such responses are evil. This is the way non-Jewish Wagnerites, I'm convinced, tend to regard their Jewish counterparts at varying levels of consciousness, if less often in public discourse since the Holocaust. Certainly, it's the way Wagner, who was both racist and evil, regarded Jews, in music as in society. It's likewise the way Hitler, the most famous and outspoken non-Jewish Wagnerite since Wagner, regarded us.

At a personal level, Judith's politics could be more flexible. As adults, why weren't we suddenly much closer now that she, as a struggling divorcée and single parent, really needed the nuclear family attachments her politics were otherwise so committed to obviating?

Among the gifts she brought to the hospital were fancy French candy, fruit (oranges), a copy of *Gay American History* and a March-For-Gay-Rights T-shirt. I was still so uncomfortable in my relations with Judith that, notwithstanding the book and T-shirt, the candy seemed a socialist comment on gay men as privileged white male capitalists and the oranges registered the old association with Anita Bryant. Even in my depressed, hypersensitive state, however, I could see through her tears and feel in her embrace that she genuinely cared. I was grateful and expressed my appreciation. But there was one other gift – the manuscript of a book her son (whom I likewise wasn't able to feel as close to as I might have liked because I never knew whether the feelings he was expressing were genuinely his or his mother's) had worked on about children's reactions to terminal illness called *The Child's Book of Death and Dying*. Even though his chapter was written under the auspices of his teacher, a prominent gay activist who is candid about his own Jewishness and about anti-Semitism, when I saw the title page of the manuscript, I entered into a tailspin of paranoia, wondering if the inclusion of this latter item were sadistic, however unconsciously so; or, worse, if it constituted an act, albeit likewise unconscious, of attempted murder. After all, if I were to die, that much more of my mother's estate and perhaps my own (in a legal contestation of my will during a time when gay domestic partnerships had no legal standing?) would go to Judith and my nephew ... For some years thence, our relations were very strained.

Howie, still mired in the demise of his night club, which had been a real force in the new waves of music and art in the 1970s, also came to visit me in the hospital, at my request. For whatever reason – perhaps because his nihilism, with its detachment from judgment, was so close to my own pessimism, as amplified by the depression – he was the only family member I could bear to have any direct contact with. For perhaps fifteen minutes he was more empathic than I'd ever seen him before or since. He even wrote a check to help me out. Otherwise he was typically out of touch, literally and figuratively. As in my own case, though I didn't know it yet, was chemical dependence the underlying reason Howie was so chronically depressed and disconnected, so zombieoid? Like his siblings' childhoods, Howie's was marked by considerable success at assimilation with peers, even with the German–American, confederate-descended buddy whose family estate, less than a mile from our home, had at one time welcomed visitors with a sign we'd seen in other parts of town: 'No Dogs Or Jews Allowed'. During the McCarthy era, Howie was an eagle scout and he made the state championship golf team, but at what cost? A boyhood in which pre-school mornings were divided between doing the phylacteries and polishing an M–1 rifle for 'Rot-C' (Reserved Officers Training Corps), while the news on the kitchen radio blared the alleged high treason and execution of the Rosenbergs, must have exacted a toll. Whatever the explanation for Howie's attitudes and habits and recurrent crises, he might continue to channel those drives into creative endeavors, the way artists are wont to do, but he wouldn't be able to perceive himself and resume the struggle for maturity he'd abandoned in his mid-teens until he could begin to feel the pain of that toll. Does maturity destroy creativity (the classic rationalization proferred by artists who can't face curtailing their addictions)? The evidence seems to be the contrary, but in any case, how many of the *many* artists who have been killed by their addictions ever made the effort to find out?

The other unsolicited visitor to the hospital was José Orlovsky. Stash, who sent me a puppy-dog-and-kitty-cat get-well card, had apparently called him. (Following my break-up with Stash and the simultaneous deterioration of my friendship with José, José invited Stash to visit him in New York and Fire Island. I have no idea what happened, but I'd be mightily surprised if Stash, who found José even more unattractive than I did, was able to respond to José's advances.) Instead of the fifty-dollar box of Belgian chocolates José would bring when he was trying to court me, I received a five-dollar box of Perugina hard candies. José, who was a psychiatrist, knew that the antidepressants I was on produced xerostomia (dryness of the mouth) as a principal side-effect, and the hard candies, he explained, would help to stimulate saliva. 'You just have to suck', he said with a sniggering edge my paranoia probably did not invent. 'You just have to suck.'

I was on antidepressants for about six months, during which time Stash persuaded me to take the life savings I already had invested with him and augment it with a mortgage on my home in an expanded syndication. Additional investors included Gene Thoreau and his lover, another Jewish doctor whose parents were Holocaust survivors and who kept changing his name, Arnie and Mick Johnson – a Vietnam war hero, Judy Tenuta groupie and analysand of one of the homophobic professors who had interviewed me for a residency in psychiatry. Mick thought it was very cute to refer to Chicago's Gold Coast as 'Judea', reassuring himself that he couldn't possibly be prejudiced because he'd once had an affair with a black man. On the other hand, Mick was the only member of this crowd who had ever purchased a gay book – *The Celluloid Closet* (which I don't think he ever got around to reading, though he did notice Vito's acknowledgement to Arnie). Actually, Mick's gay activism was regarded as genuinely path-breaking in Chicago, especially by Mick and even if the co-founding of the city's leading gay social club quickly degenerated into nothing but an occasional appearance in drag at a fundraiser. Two days after signing the partnership agreements, I admitted to myself that I was chemically dependent on alcohol, marijuana and cigarettes, and entered a twelve-step recovery program.

As his partnership with Stash prospered, Ham, who had had an affair with someone in Callas's inner circle and thus got to spend time with her on her farewell tour, became involved with a handsome closet case who eventually became an elected court judge. During the same time frame, Stash also became involved with a closeted, elected politician, but this one was much older, a lot less handsome and much higher ranking. In fact, hard-drinking, hard-playing Theodore Blarney was among the biggest wheels in the municipal machine and was becoming a force in national politics. Stash adored the limelight that came with being in Blarney's entourage, but like me with the Baron, had to squint his eyes shut the single, failed time Blarney was able to get Stash drunk enough to try to have sex. That was when they were traveling to Europe together, first class on the *QE II*, a trip I urged Stash to take with no questions about how it would be financed.

Everyone in town knew Blarney was gay except Blarney, and he dutifully showed up at every public event with a spinster escort whom everyone likewise knew to be lesbian. When Stash introduced me as a gay activist, Blarney wasn't the least bit fazed. 'I saw *La Cage Aux Folles* three times', he countered. Like Stash, Blarney was a devout Catholic. Was I paranoid to think that he was making a point of showing me the itinerary he had mapped out for their trip to Europe? It included a visit to Oberammergau, which had just been in the news amid renewed accusations of anti-Semitism. I said nothing and breathed a sigh of relief when Stash later explained that they had cancelled the trip to Oberammergau because of scheduling conflicts. The trip was to cost Stash approximately $10,000. (Notwithstanding that his personal finances had been the subject of public inquiry on more than one occasion, Blarney wouldn't have treated his own mother to a glass of beer.) But Stash needed the break. He had just moved into a fancy new office, which complemented the new condo he had just purchased and redesigned. The office was within walking distance of the condo, so there was no need to take the new Mercedes, a distinguished dark brown model that was in fine contrast to the red and white of Stash's old Buick, which actually had 'cherry and vanilla' written in script on both sides of the car. Things seemed to be going well for Stash, if less clearly so for our real estate partnership.

In fact, the real estate project wasn't going so well, thanks largely to the drastic new tax laws Reagan began implementing in 1985, which shook the entire real estate industry. Stash was a small fish who might be able to ride a few mild currents, but not these tidal waves. With each new piece of bad news about the syndication our communications deteriorated, hitting an all-time low when I made the foolish mistake of asking Stash, who had been reminiscing about his wonderful trip with Blarney to Austria, how he felt about Waldheim. Waldheim, whom Stash was so proud to have seen a number of times worshiping at St Patrick's in New York, was much in the news. 'Well', he answered, 'they elected him President, didn't they? The whole country can't be wrong.'

On their return from a subsequent trip to the Middle East, where Blarney was given some kind of award by Israel (in pathetic, desperate efforts at political good will?), Stash and Blarney made it a point of letting me know how much they loved Egypt and loathed Israel. As a Catholic archbishop who was a friend of Blarney's put it to me at a reception for Blarney in New York, 'Those Israelis sure learned their lessons. They're doing to the Palestinians exactly what the Nazis did to them.' Also at that reception were Ham, Ham's ex-lover (the unrepentant Nazi's son), the ex-lover's current lover (a very stoned black drag queen), and Dr Richard Littlehead, the brilliant physician to whom I'd been introduced by Gene Thoreau and who had introduced me to his (Littlehead's) good friend, the former lover of the closeted mayor of one of the world's biggest cities. (I met the lover just before he moved to the west coast, at the start of the mayoral campaign. Their break-up and the lover's relocation had been decreed – and financed? – by the candidate.) While still in the closet himself (I guess he still believed what he so often said with regard to the mayor – that a public figure's sexual orientation isn't appropriate for public discussion), Littlehead – also a closet Catholic whose mother made him dress in girls' clothes and once put him in a dryer as punishment, and who sadomasochistically abused the only lover any of us ever knew him to have had – took charge of one of the largest AIDS programs in the nation.

When I invited Littlehead, the only person I knew who was still regularly going to the baths, Stash, and Blarney to see D. J.'s AIDS play (Stash, whom Blarney was now growing tired of, suggested it), Blarney had a full-blown ulcer attack and couldn't drink for the next two days. I wondered if he would go into DT's. Three years later, Blarney, still in the closet, had his own float in Chicago's Gay Pride parade. Three months before his death some ten years later, Littlehead was brought out in the *New York Times* as a gay man and person with AIDS.

There was one aspect of my participation in the real estate project that complicated what might otherwise seem in my version of things to be the straightforward question of who might be trying to take advantage of whom. When Stash persuaded me to assume a mortgage on my co-op in order to invest in the new partnership, he offered to reimburse me for the monthly mortgage payments, which my income couldn't support. Stash promised to cover these payments, which were to be deducted from my profits, but only on condition that I not discuss our 'special agreement' with the other partners. Conversely, this feature of our alliance couldn't be written. It would have to be between gentlemen – a discomfiting proposition, to say the least. If he wasn't telling the others what he was doing with me, I wondered, then what's he doing with the others that he's not telling me about? Somehow blind, naive trust in Stash – masochism – won out again. There seemed to be no other choice.

Or was something else going on? As the partnership became increasingly indebted and precarious, Stash informed me that he could no longer cover the mortgage payments 'in fairness to the other partners'. By the time this long-dreaded catastrophe finally hit in 1988, it was almost anticlimactic. Much more surprising than it should have seemed (considering that I hadn't had a drink, joint, cigarette, or other drug in more than four years) was Stash's subtle and preposterous implication that it was *I* who had been trying to exploit him and the partnership, rather than the other way around.

But at some level was he right? Had I somehow provoked him into the clandestine arrangements which he had in fact proposed because the project needed my money and which I signed for within days of entering a program of recovery from chemical dependence? Confused and worried, I sought legal counsel. Whatever the answers, I needed to face them. Of course, I did want the answers to be the best ones. So I replaced my Bostonian attorney – a 'good friend' who was gay, misogynist, Catholic, a drunk and, like Stash, jocularly anti-Semitic – with a higher-powered New York lawyer – a stranger who was straight, misogynist, Jewish, sober, humorless and homophobic.

The questions persisted. While seeking legal counsel for clarification and self-protection, was I secretly hoping that there might be some way to be scrupulously honest and fair and at the same time still benefit from Stash's unwritten but (possibly) legal vulnerabilities in the matter of our 'special arrangement'? Even more disturbing was an underlying question. Was there a part of me that all along had been like Wagner's Mime, nurturing for my own purposes (and those of my communities and peoples) this oxymoronic Polish Siegfried, this alien child who claimed me as a role model and who, for better or worse, has remained subculturally gay and who always denied that he was anti-Semitic, but who in fact never gave a penny to a gay cause or ever participated in a gay demonstration during our time together and who did indeed turn out to be anti-Semitic?

As in some of the fantasies we shared the night we met, which weren't so unlike some of the Wagnerian and other operatic fantasies I used to be able to escape in and out of, these questions of exploitation and vulnerability, of who was the victim and who was the victimizer, of 'top' and 'bottom', didn't have immutable answers, not even when the real estate partnership finally went Chapter 11 (bankrupt) and I had to go into major debt to pay a staggering accumulation of back taxes that were consequently being 'recaptured'. There were, however, two big differences between the way we were in our fantasies that night at The Barracks and the way we were in reality ten years later. We were no longer in love and we were no longer children.

Chapter six

The Housemates
Who Got Nailed

IT happened in fragments. There was a message for me at the *New York Native*. I was to call a name I didn't recognize.

'Hi. The editor said I should talk to you. I was at my doctor's again yesterday for the amebas. I've had every treatment you can think of and then some. Now he's talking about putting me on some kind of anti-cancer drug! But that's not why I called. I'm not a gossip, and maybe I shouldn't be telling you this. Anyway, I overheard him say there are three – maybe it's five – gay men in New York City intensive care units. They've all got some weird pneumonia or something. I think he said two of them died.'

Later that afternoon there was a message on my machine to call David Rothenberg. David explained that he had spoken with a physician on the attending staff of St Vincent's hospital. 'You'd better call her and see if you can find out what's going on.'

I did. 'I'm sorry, but since you're asking me as a member of the press', said Dr Joyce Wallace, 'I can't talk about it now. Call me back next week.'

At a *Native* writers' conference (the only such conference I can recall ever having attended) some weeks later, each of us was asked to say something about our current projects. I explained that I was working on two pieces. One was entitled 'Chemical Castration'. Certain psychiatrists were broadly endorsing the use of a class of hormones called 'antiandrogen' to treat 'growing numbers' of 'sex offenders', most of whom were being even more grossly lumped together as 'male homosexual pedophiles'. Wallace Hamilton, whose positions on intergenerational relationships were a constant source of insecurity for him and his friends, shared my concern that proliferating medicolegal categories of 'sex offenses' would inevitably metastasize into the witchhunting of all adult men who have relationships with younger men.

The other project I was working on for the *Native* was about the mysterious new diseases in the gay community. For the same issue that would contain the piece on chemical castration, I was preparing what would become the first feature article on the epidemic to appear in any press (*Native*, July 27 1982). As Randy Shilts reminded me (I'd forgotten), in Arnie's presence, when he interviewed me for *And the Band Played On*, I'd also written the first news report on the epidemic (*Native*, May 18 1981, as documented in *Covering the Plague* by James Kinsella). 'You were the first', Shilts insisted. His tone was odd, as if he were trying to flatter me with something I would most want to hear. 'You were the first', he repeated. 'No one will ever be able to take that away from you.' When Randy (whom I regarded as a friend as well as a colleague) himself did precisely that in his book, obscuring the fact that he himself was not covering the epidemic during its first two years, I was shocked, and wrote him a letter expressing my indignation and hurt. He wrote me back that he was sorry, that my reaction 'bothered me because I honestly like you and respect your contribution and would never want to do anything to hurt you'. The problem, he explained, was that he simply couldn't include everyone and everything . . . He signed his letter 'with affection and respect'.

The weekend of the *Native* writers meeting, I marched with friends in the Christopher Street Gay Liberation Day Parade. The next day I read in the *New York Times* about how 'Homosexuals Parade in Celebration'. Then, on July 3, it hit the mainstream press. There, in the far left-hand column of a page in the 'A' section of the *New York Times* – coincidentally placed adjacent to a big department store ad for an Independence Day sale ('Sing Out for Independence!') – was that report by Dr Lawrence Altman. Entitled 'Rare Cancer Identified in Homosexuals', it was based on an article in the *Morbidity and Mortality Weekly Report* (MMWR) from the Centers for Disease Control in Atlanta that was published the same day: 'Kaposi's Sarcoma and *Pneumocystis Carinii* Pneumonia Among Homosexual Men – in New York City and California'. 'Skin or mucous membrane lesions', read the MMWR, 'often blue to violaceous plaques or nodules, were present in most of the patients on their initial physician visit. However, these lesions were not always present and often were considered benign by the patient and his physician.' This last sentence was one I remembered months later when I saw the movie, *Making Love*, the first American-made film to show two male lovers kissing on the mouth. In one scene, the gay writer is told by his physician (who later becomes his lover) not to worry about a pimple-like lesion on the back of his neck.

I heard about the *Times* article before I saw it, in Cherry Grove, where I was spending the holiday weekend. I was having my first 'adventure', as I got in the habit of referring to liaisons that were something between a one-night stand and an affair, since breaking up with Benjie. My host, Egbert Cissie, was a fast up-and-coming interior designer of English and German extraction who periodically decorated the display windows of the Axis Hotel in Tokyo as well as those of a chic, Jewish-owned, Manhattan department store. Every summer, Egbert shared a sprawling bayside gazebo with rotating housemates and what looked like moderately expensive department store *chinoiserie*. As I was to learn too late, one should never refer to an interior designer as an interior decorator, especially after one has already been redressed for this error.

The host, whom I'll also refer to as housemate Number One, liked to fancy himself dominant in business if not in bed, where, as he dictated, I served in the role of 'dominance'. Demonstrating just how tough a businessman he could be, he once bragged about the time he had all but physically assaulted an elderly Jewish woman who owed him $5,000. 'I *got* my money', he snarled, like Faye Dunaway in the television version of *Evita*.

Needless to say, Egbert and I weren't very well acquainted. In fact, we had first met just several weeks earlier at the Everard Baths. At the Soho 'power' restaurant he selected for our first date (my treat), where he spoke familiarly with the blowzy *maîtresse* who then seated us at the 'power' table, Egbert pretended to be unimpressed that the 'Home' section of the *Times* was planning to acknowledge his work. 'The worlds of taste and fashion are just like the rest of the world', Egbert explained. 'It's all money and connections. That's how it works. It's just that simple.'

For reasons known only to our collective unconscious, neither of us had yet admitted to ourselves, let alone to one another, that outside the arena of sexual fantasy, we had absolutely nothing to talk about. In addition to being struttingly unscrupulous, he was, with all due respect to the many self-affirming, politically conscious gay and lesbian people who also vacation there, the kind of self-hating Pines/Grove archetype who even in 1981 still disdained those of us who stayed in the city on sweltering summer weekends to demonstrate for gay rights. 'The *gays!*' Egbert sneered (not so unlike D. J.), implying that card-carrying movement people were nothing but a bunch of underachievers, malcontents and sissies.

Notwithstanding my denial of Egbert's homophobia (he *had* to be saying these things tongue-in-cheek), I said things I'd often written, about how inconsistent the *Times* could be in its treatment of minority concerns. I was speaking sincerely, unaware that in the jungle, sincerity is just another form of vulnerability, 'an exploitable weakness', as one of the reptile people put it in *V*, a television sci-fi soap about fascism.

'Issues of anti-Semitism', I proceeded, 'receive a degree and quality of attention in the *Times* that equivalent issues of racism, sexism and homophobia don't.' I don't remember his exact words, but as I was ordering our second or third Dubonnet aperitif (his preference), Egbert seemed to be in a little too much agreement about the *Times*' attention to anti-Semitism. For the first time in my adult life, in fact, I could actually feel, in a face-to-face confrontation, albeit through a grassy, alcoholic haze of paranoia, the wisps of anti-Semitism.

In the Grove that Independence Day weekend, those wisps became a cat-o'-nine tails. On Friday evening, after a dinner that might have been photographed for the Summer Gourmet pages of *New York*, I was effortfully small-talking with Egbert and the only other housemate present that weekend. Number Two, as I will call him, was wearing a studded black leather outfit that sadistically drew attention to rather than away from its master's sylphlike waist. Out of nowhere, Number Two began to bumble anxiously and incoherently about how what he called S and M had completely taken over his life. 'I haven't worked in three years,' he boasted.

Although it was instantly clear that Number Two – the owner of the multi-million dollar house? – was peculiar and hostile, I had no quarrel with what I imagined to be his sexual preferences. Whatever the details, they were presumably 'consensual', 'nonvictimizing', 'mutually responsible' and 'respectful of stated terms and limits' – all those vanilla words and phrases we so reflexively hurled at all those questions about the borderlines of what we called S and M. Those questions never did seem to get addressed clearly, no matter how much we continued to blabber about a subject that remains less understood than any other major phenomenon of human sexual behavior. I emphasize, however, that if there were bad vibes between myself and Number Two, I certainly wouldn't have presumed to blame them on the mere fact of his being 'into leather', as we so easily say. After all, so was I.

Not to be shrugged off, Number Two began to pontificate about politics and art. The misstatements were such that it quickly became impossible to remain passive. I tried not to sound condescending. 'Callas never sang Carmen on stage', I patiently explained.

'Yes, she did', he screeched.

'No', I repeated, firming my fist on the table, 'she did not.' In a sulk Number Two fled to the living room.

Alone for some minutes and very bored, I sat at the kitchen table playing with a Rubik's cube, unaware that it was the territorial possession of Number Two. Unable to align the colors, I twisted the object so determinedly that it broke. Number Two suddenly reappeared, inspected the damage with trembling, porcelain fingers, and then said to me with the unnatural whine of a frightened and enraged child to his sadistic father: 'Why did you break it? You're not supposed to be so rough. You sh- sh- should be ... gentle.'

Over fresh-squeezed Florida orange juice the next morning, Number Two proudly recounted his late-night adventures in the Meatrack, the sexual never-never land between Cherry Grove and the Pines that may be the only place left in the world where you can still see people having sex in trees. He had shared a sexual scene with someone that had climaxed in the driving of a spike through his penis. Since that was the only part of his body that wasn't on display that morning, and since I didn't ask to see it, I never found out which anatomical parts were involved. In those days, the only cockpiercing I'd seen was of foreskin. I had already begun working on a review of the medical literature on fist-fucking ('brachiopractic eroticism') injuries, which were being reported in alarming numbers in New York and San Francisco, in heterosexual men and women and lesbians as well as gay men. I wondered if infections and other problems were being encountered with piercing of the nipples and genitalia. It was an article I never got to, but I did complete the fist-fucking piece. Originally entitled 'Handballing: High Risk Sport' (*New York Native*, May 10 1982), it correctly dismissed as circumstantial popular associations between nitrites, used heavily by fisters, fisting itself, and the AIDS epidemic. Hence the *Native* headline – 'Handballing and KS: Is There a Link?' The piece concluded with an admonition the editors thought too salacious for such clinical reportage: 'If you're going to be forearmed, be forewarned.'

Dinner that evening was deceptively calm. After fresh fruit and coffee, Number Two asked us to join him in the living room to listen to one of his favorite tapes – 'a collector's item'. It sounded scratchy, suggesting that it dated from the 1940s or early 1950s. From what I could make out, the program consisted of military marches and fragments of some speeches with narrative and sound effects. As it played, I looked at the tape box I had been handed. It included brief summaries of the lives and exploits of 'History's Greatest Military Leaders: Attila the Hun, Genghis Khan, Alexander the Great, Napolean Bonaparte, Benito Mussolini, and Adolf Hitler'. (Mussolini?!)

As Hitler's voice began to rise and I began to sicken, the tape was removed. Number Two had already disappeared. I immediately confronted Number One, but with all the composure of a two-year old child in the presence of a giant, hissing crocodile. In these moments, I could feel the flickers of the most devastating truth about myself. This was how I, as a not atypically assimilationist Jew, had been reacting to a lifetime of more subtle expressions of anti-Semitism. The fear of being Jewish that I had learned during my upbringing in the rural South was so overwhelming that when I wasn't forced into direct physical combat, I instinctively dealt with it by regressing to the most primitive of childhood defense mechanisms: denial. Here I was twenty-five years later, the 'top' man', reacting like a frightened babe to the acid and stink of a couple of corroded queens.

'Don't be so sensitive', Number One protested with a reassuring tone; in fact, with the same words my mother so often used when admonishing me not to get so upset about things I disagreed with or disliked. His glistening eyes were at half-mast, like those of a pussycat that's been petted in just the right spot, in just the right way. They were eyes from a painting by Mel Odom. The expression on his face looked loving and trustworthy. For a moment, the child in me started to feel better.

'He just happens to be into military things', he continued politely and with a warm smile. 'It is, after all, a free country, and it doesn't necessarily mean any kind of prejudice.' The host, who was wearing a military crewcut and the most delicately embroidered white lace socks, seemed sympathetic with both of us. There was a long pause, and I began to regain my composure. 'But you do have to admit', he purred, 'that Hitler *was* one of history's most important military leaders. Whatever else might be said, you *do* have to admit', he began to hiss, 'that as a commanding officer, as a leader of his people, as a shaper of history, as a MAN, as a MASTER, ADOLF HITLER sho' did have his shit togethahhhh ...'

The host had prepared housemate Number Three for our final sexual encounter. In his bedroom, which he had decorated from top to bottom in his favorite color, white, he first insisted on photographing me with my arms horizontally outstretched. As the camera hammered away and Egbert sniggered, I felt the flames of another devastating truth: I, not Egbert, was at the bottom of this relationship. In the most Gordian entanglement of fantasy and reality I've ever experienced, I realized that I was deeply involved in a very ugly, 'consensual' against all reason and judgment, sadomasochistic relationship – not the theater-and-games-with-rules stuff that goes on in so much subcultural S/M, but the real thing. Unlike what we presume to be the majority of self-accepting and subculturally-identified sadomasochists, Egbert and I had never even attempted to discuss terms or define limits. Like most sadomasochistic relationships, however, ours was one that either of us was at any time technically free to unload.

The time had arrived for me to resume my role on top. 'So this is what you want, baby, a real MAN, a MASTER, to nail your ass to floor. You WASP SLIME! You STINKING KRAUT! You DISGUSTING TWAT! You PATHETIC, WORTHLESS, SNIVEL-ING, NAUSEATING, SHITEATING FAGGOT!!!' As I rammed my fist up an ass that was so greased and patulous it seemed to have no boundaries, the last embers of resistance disappeared from his gaze and I began to purr.

My psychotherapist during that time was a Jesuit priest who told me that one of his clients had been at the most notorious of Manhattan's after-hours club, where he witnessed the following ritual: the claws and teeth were wrenched from a gerbil, which was then smeared with Crisco and shoved up the ass of someone in a sling. The turn-on for 'the masochist' in the sling was supposed to be the death struggles of the suffocating creature inside his rectum. Now, I have no way of knowing if this story, which perpetuates one of the ugliest myths about gay people – a slander that got so out of hand it became the subject of an investigative feature in the *Advocate* – had *any* basis in truth, but even if it did, that wouldn't have meant that the club's management or the vast majority of its clientele, which had included me, wouldn't have been horrified by such criminal behavior. I certainly never saw or otherwise heard of any such thing at this or any other club, though I did see – and participate in – a number of sling scenes, fascinated, disturbed, and really turned on by the sometimes intense aggression that came out. In any event, the story reminded me of another club I'd attended that featured exhibitions of feeding live animals to piranha and reptiles, a memory that resonated when I saw a film by Rosa von Praunheim, the opening sequence of which features a mouse being devoured by a snake; and which in turn reverberated when I saw the Bertolucci film *1900*, the opening sequence of which shows a boy hunting frogs along a creek, wearing a belt of living captives, interconnected with a string through their legs, and wherein the protagonist warns: 'In Germany, they're crucifying kittens.' It was at one of these clubs, incidentally, that I first saw – or first noticed –

leatherfolk with Nazi regalia, trappings that made no more impression on me at the time than police insignia.

The priest had raised the question of evil, which, as I saw it then and continue to understand it, is primarily, mostly and simply the pursuit or experience of socially disapproved forms of aggression. The problem, of course, is that the forms of aggression which are approved or not approved vary from society to society if not from person to person. Atrocities such as what was alleged to have happened to the gerbil have been regularly committed against countless millions of human beings and other animals by all kinds of people and societies throughout history, and they continue today. Hasn't this history taught us *any* absolute definitions of evil? What about the torture and murder of children? That would certainly seem to qualify – unless you happened to be, among countless others, the Biblical God of the Hebrews in Pharaoh's Egypt, a Christian patriot during the Crusades, a Turkish patriot in 1915, a German patriot in the 1940s, a Palestinian patriot in the 1970s, a Serbian patriot in 1992. Dr Mengele would be regarded by the Nazis as a patriot rather than a psychopath and the same might now be said of Charles Manson since his forehead acquired a swastika. Likewise, John Wayne Gacy, the sexual sadist and serial killer of boys who regarded homosexuals as vermin to be exterminated, would be probably regarded by fascists as a hero. And to me, I must confess, harassers, murderers and even torturers of haters and fascists would likewise be heroes. No question about it. The saliva all but dribbles from my mouth at the fantasy of an aggressive force brutally murdering a core group of neo-Nazis (and their families?). Does this mean I'm the same as them? Does it also mean I fulfil the stereotype of the Jew (or the gay man) as eye-for-an-eye vindictive? Am I thus Shylock? Was Shakespeare anti-Semitic? In *The Merchant of Venice*, no question about it. Too bad (or is it good?) that I can no longer feel the kind of pain about fantasies of revenge that Vanessa Redgrave conveyed at the conclusion of *Playing for Time*, where she portrayed a concentration camp survivor who suddenly observes herself singing with the camp's liberators, '*Allons enfants de la patrie ...*' In an earlier, more naive time, such self-censure would have seemed the only appropriate response. Patriotism in any form – whether Confederate, Yankee, Nazi,

American, Israeli – is all the same stuff, I kept telling myself. 'The Nazis were human beings', I once upon a time told Arnie.

'Evil' tends to be correlated with dominance and sadism in much the same way that 'good', especially as defined by Judeo-Christianity, is so often linked with submission and masochism. What makes it so difficult to distinguish between good and evil is the fact that the seemingly opposed forces of dominance and submission are so inextricably entangled in their composite form, aggression, and that aggression is so inextricably entangled within the greater phenomenon of bonding.

'Fight or flight', is what adrenalin, the hormone that fuels the psychophysiological experience of aggression, is called; which is why these responses are so often observed together in the same persons (e.g., in priests, in the concept of 'passive-aggressive') and societies (ones that are simultaneously warlike and religiously submissive). In S/M sex play, as in other lovemaking and even social bonding, both roles stimulate release of the same hormones, the same excitement. In consensual circumstances, both sadist and masochist, like any other pair of lovers, are experiencing the excitement they crave and excitement, it's now clear, can be a pleasure-inducing, anxiety-relieving dependence. Some masochists and sadists are unquestionably reenacting exceedingly primitive, rigidly scripted, childhood traumas and fantasies that victimize themselves and/or others, and some may be matched lovers, but whatever else they are, many are, overridingly, excitement junkies. Extreme expressions of love and its constituent aggression, and the possibility of intoxication from and dependence on such expressions, are in all of us, but how and by whom released aggression is interpreted defines the difference between 'good' and 'evil'. It's just that simple.

Back in New York there was a message on my machine from D. J. Love, one of several gay Jewish writers who, I was later to discover, had had 'affairettes' (as D. J., who introduced me to that word, liked to call what I was calling 'adventures') with Egbert. If the repressed, denied or otherwise defended vulnerabilities that so often accompany being Jewish had been factors in these relationships, however, and certainly if there had been instances of overt anti-Semitism, neither D. J. nor Phil Lennon, the other gay Jewish ex-affairette writer I spoke with about Egbert, could recall them. 'The thing about Egbert', observed the ferociously ambitious Love, 'is ambition. He's extremely ambitious.'

Unlike Lennon, Love, who was a teenager during World War II, could not recall ever having personally experienced anti-Semitism. Certainly nothing with Egbert. Notwithstanding D. J.'s comparisons of the AIDS epidemic with the Holocaust, and his recounting of a family circumstance that involved anti-Semitism in *The Truth about Me* a decade later, D. J.'s writing confirmed that being Jewish was not regarded as a source of major pain, self-hatred or identity conflict, at least not consciously. The week of the premiere of *The Truth about Me*, D. J. did an interview with Gore Vidal for *NQ* (*New Queer*) that went further than any previous piece in confronting Vidal about his unwillingness to publicly identify himself as gay, but which didn't even mention the anti-Semitism controversies Vidal had unleashed several years earlier. In trying to nail the neo-cons (as we all referred to the dread neo-conservatives) with the same, eye-for-an-eye slander they had so often used against us – principally treason (e.g., extrapolating from Blunt, Burgess, etc. to 'homosexuals' in general) – Vidal had accused them ('the Pod people') of being less than American in having closeted, primary loyalties to Israel in an attack that was unequivocally anti-Semitic, no matter how otherwise sympathetic, no matter how often how many of us had had precisely the same thoughts in fantasies of revenge.

Far more ethnically conscious at that time (1981), Lennon was nevertheless also incapable of indicting any past experience with Egbert. 'He's got a gorgeous prick, don't you think? I know he has a thing for Jewish men', said the handsome, observant Lennon, 'but what you're attributing to him sounds like your own *mishe-gass*. Even if it's true, you can't blame him for something you were an equal partner in. If a crime was committed by Egbert, you weren't the victim. You were the accomplice.'

A collector and occasional merchant of antiques and *objets*, Lennon subsequently sold me an old World War II postcard I'd seen on the bathroom wall of his spare but interesting apartment, a home that achieves naturally what people pay decorators to imitate. The postcard, a reproduction of an oil painting of Hitler and a group of Nazis shaking their fists at a vision of Einstein, bears this inscription: 'Neither hatred nor persecution can stay the progress of science and civilization.'

At home I placed the card on a bookshelf, leaning against Richard Count de Moulin-Eckart's biography of Cosima Wagner. While that book remains on the shelf, together with her husband's rambling *Mein Leben*, Shaw's *The Perfect Wagnerite*, and too many other works about 'The Master' (as I myself, echoing Cosima, used to call him), of the books from those years, only Robert Gutman's study, *Richard Wagner: The Man, His Mind and His Music*, which perceives the centrality of the Wagners' anti-Semitism, is not gathering dust. When Arnie moved in some months after the 'affairette' with Egbert, some of these books went into the closet – they almost went into the trash compactor – as did all my most prominently displayed Wagneriana: a black and white postcard of his death mask, reproductions of a sketch of Wagner by Cosima and of a portrait by Renoir, and two magnificent porcelain friezes of scenes from *Lohengrin* – the most nationalistic, Gutman feels, of all Wagner's works.

In recent years, there have been some additions to the little library on Wagner. In *The Darker Side of Genius: Richard Wagner's Anti-Semitism*, Jakob Katz argues that there is little in Wagner's art that can be unequivocally related to his racist views, and states the inevitable reality that 'the time will no doubt come when the historical background of Wagner's art will have faded to such an extent that it will be possible to present his works detached from their moorings and solely on the basis of innate aesthetic value'. Meanwhile, however, he acknowledges that even if Wagner 'kept his distance from the [anti-Semitic] movement, it was obvious that his sentiments were in accord with it'. 'The historical condemnation of Wagner', Katz frankly concludes, 'by no means rests on the belated insight of the historian, but results from the correct understanding of [Wagner's] own statements and actions.'

Other additions are a collection of Wagner's essays that includes the proto-Nazi *Jews in Music*, and *Revolutionary Anti-Semitism in Germany: From Kant to Wagner* by Paul Lawrence Rose, a less equivocal assessment of Wagner's historical role than Katz's. 'Hitler', Rose reminds us, 'admitted only one real precursor

– Richard Wagner.' It is Rose's contention that Hitler's own estimation of the composer's importance in the evolution of anti-Semitism in Germany – in the greatest wave of racism in recorded history – was accurate. Surprisingly (in view of its hard line on the profundity and reach of Wagner's anti-Semitism), Rose's most recent book, *Wagner: Race and Revolution*, was reviewed in *Opera News*. Not surprisingly (in view of the depth and consistency of that magazine's conservatism), however, the review by Editor-in-Chief Patrick J. Smith was not favorable. In two short paragraphs the book is dismissed as a rant. 'I am surprised', Smith concludes, 'that a major academic publisher [Yale] would put its imprimatur on such tendentiousness.'

In a review I wrote of psychologist Dorothy Tennov's *Love and Limerence*, I criticized the author's 'flabbergasting' conclusion that Wagner may have been a lifelong nonlimerent – someone incapable of experiencing the primary event of pair-bonding in human primates (falling in love, limerence). As quoted by Tennov, 'Never in my life have I enjoyed the true felicity of love', Wagner wrote. 'What Tennov seems not to have appreciated here', I so unwittingly affirmed, 'is that for Wagner the true felicity of romantic love, that love to which he erected some of history's greatest artistic monuments, was a metaphysical experience. It was the ineffable experience of *Tristan und Isolde*. Tennov's clinical observation that "limerence at 100 percent may be ecstasy or it may be despair" at once simplifies and complicates the master's supreme vision of the two united.' In 1981 I was just beginning to consider what it meant to my people and therefore to me that this 'master' was – as Rose contends, as Hans-Jürgen Syberberg's documentary interview with Winifred Wagner affirms, as many other historical documents confirm, and as my conscience now reflexively reminds me every time I hear the music or even the name of the composer I, as a teenage, clinically anti-Semitic opera queen, had so fallen in love with – that this 'master' was nothing less than the acknowledged spiritual father of Adolf Hitler and the Nazis.

Months later I remembered something about Egbert, whom I saw only once again, at 'Showers', the first fund-raiser for Gay Men's Health Crisis. On returning from one of his quickie decorating trips to Tokyo about two weeks after our first encounter, Egbert had brought me three 'gifts'. The first was a small ceramic incense burner. Was it consciously or preconsciously intended to provoke racial discomfort? Was its airport-souvenir-stand cheapness likewise intended to comment on my ethnicity? Parenthetically, I had declined Egbert's offer to redecorate – oops, redesign – my apartment, which he had described with bullseye accuracy as looking as if it had been thrown together in about two weeks.

The second item was a book on the new-wave Japanese artist, Katsu (*Katsu-Sexus*), that featured a painting I'd seen as a poster on Egbert's wall which shows a pair of red high-heeled shoes being kicked off, crisscrossing each other in the air. Behind the shoes is a tensed, muscular male torso. What I saw in the painting was an effeminate gay *man*, casting off his drag, shedding his paradoxical camouflage in defiance and rage.

The third item was the most disturbing. It was a tube of toothpaste, brand-named 'Darkie', that displayed a cartoon minstrel figure in top hat and blackface. The subject of an exposé in *The Village Voice*, it was overtly racist.

In appreciation of these exquisitely subtle insults – that is, with the most primitive denial of my deepest fears – I gave the housemate who had been licking out my asshole with such dependable competence an exquisite and rather expensive bonsai tree.

Finally, or so it seemed, there was the lingering, overtly paranoid question of Egbert's friends. It was beginning to seem less paradoxical that one of the closest of them was not only a card-carrying gay man, but the officer of a gay organization, another member of which I remember more – or is it less? – for his affability and true grit than for his Aryan physicality and pierced nipples.

I suddenly recalled something else about my heavenly host. Shortly before we met, as he casually explained on our first date, he had been hospitalized with an unusual and very serious pneumonia. His recovery, he was told, had been complete.

In his book *Sexual Excitement*, Robert Stoller wrote that 'the desire to humiliate is the central feature of most people's sexual excitement all of the time, but not for all people's sexual excitement all of the time'. I thought back to that first encounter with Egbert at the baths. In what seemed at the time to be such unequivocally mutual sexual excitement I felt as if I'd never had a more responsive bottom. If Egbert were into worshiping my ass, I made sure, as I instructed him in tongue-in-cheek technique improvements, that he was always fully erect. Likewise, I always made sure that he got off. In fact, I can't recall a time when we didn't come together. In any case, I find a stiff, oozing dick a pretty dependable index of mutuality in a partner. The question that intrigues me is whether or not it is always and infallibly so. That is, can a person really resent what's happening if his dick is rock hard and dribbling with precum?

It was the intensity and mutual satisfaction of our initial encounter that set the stage for our subsequent meetings. After that first date at the Soho power restaurant, we retired to his place in Chelsea. The varyingly shaded gray walls, industrial wall-to-wall carpet, and few pieces of furniture in his austere yet comfortable medium-tech studio were dominated by a life-size statue of Buddha surrounded by lighted votive candles. At the time I thought nothing about this Buddha, at least not consciously.

Hypnotically, however, I was transported back to a time when I was intensely preoccupied with Japanese culture. It all had to do with Yukio Mishima's *Confessions of a Mask*, perhaps the most engaging and disturbing memoir in the history of gay literature. I believed Mishima's story was so revealing of a recurrent role played by *some* homosexuals in the history of patriotism (i.e., altruism or tribal, colony, herd, social, religious or moral aggression) that I wrote a kind of screenplay about Mishima based on *Confessions*, what I called 'a psychobiography after the story of Yukio Mishima'. In my interpretation, Mishima was what the American Psychiatric Association classified in the third edition of its Diagnostic and Statistical Manual of Mental Disorders as an 'ego-dystonic homosexual', a male whose acculturated aversion to his own androgyny and homoeroticism were at the heart of his machismo and bloody patriotism unto death by ritual *seppuku*, Samurai warrior suicide. I sent my version of *Confessions* to the only person who I believed – on the basis of his astounding film *In The Realm of The Senses* – could realize Mishima's life on screen: Nagisa Oshima.

But I was naive to think that Mr Oshima would share my view of Mishima as a clinical case whose sexuality determined his politics. When I saw Oshima's next film, *Merry Christmas, Mr Lawrence*, I began to understand what connected Mishima, Oshima, Egbert and myself. Here, relationships between the ability to endure pain and strength of character, between homoeroticism and gender identity, between homoeroticism and patriotism and, to a lesser extent, between pain and erotic pleasure, are seen to be complex and entangled. The film contains the observation that 'you don't know the Japanese until you've seen harakiri'. But once you've seen harakiri in *Merry Christmas, Mr Lawrence*, what exactly do you know?

In the film the two most androgynous characters are the most homoerotically involved with their fellow soldiers and each other. They are also the bravest and fiercest of warriors. David Bowie, playing the English Lieutenant Celliers, is described by his compatriot, Colonel Lawrence (played by Tom Conti), as a 'soldier's soldier'. It's tacitly clear that Celliers and the similarly androgynous Captain Yanoi (played by Bowie's artistic counterpart in Japan, Ryuichi Sakamoto), have been strengthened by gender-identity conflicts that may have been benchmark determinants of character in early childhood.

Early in the film a Korean guard is beaten for attempting to have sex with one of the prisoners, a Dutchman. Both guard and prisoner are denounced, humiliated and ordered to commit harakiri by the commanding Japanese Sergeant Hara − not because of the taboo on homosexuality but because of that against any kind of bonding between enemies. My thoughts flashed to *Romeo and Juliette* and *Aida*, two of the countless artworks that explore the subject of love across enemy lines. Although the cheerfully sadistic Sergeant Hara is clearly homophobic, he acknowledges the historical frequency of homosexuality among all classes of Japanese men, including, of course, the noblest Samurai warriors. It's *this* relationship, between homoeroticism and patriotism, that will probably be exhaustively explored if and when Mr Oshima ever does his own version of the Mishima story, an unlikely prospect in view of Oshima's conflicts with censors in Japan, the extreme volatility of the subject of Mishima there, and the ironclad grip on rights to Mishi-

ma's works by Madame Mishima, who wants to negate the importance of homosexuality in Mishima's life and works.

Although Oshima would seem to have explored every other
aspect of the relationship between pain and strength in *Merry
Christmas, Mr Lawrence*, he has virtually ignored that realm of the
senses that was a focus of his earlier masterpiece – that which exists
between pain and erotic pleasure. Anthropologists, psychiatrists,
sex researchers and other observers acknowledge the wide diversity
of this association throughout the animal kingdom and have postu-
lated that it may have multiple roots and is often a feature of
normal sex play. In other instances, however, this connection is
viewed as originating with sex-negative childrearing practices that
aversively condition behavior that becomes compulsive, progressive, self-destructive and/or injurious to others.

I don't know what, if anything, he ever wrote about the
origins of sadomasochism, but Magnus Hirschfeld, the gay Jewish
founding father of sexology, coined the term 'cisvestism', to denote,
according to anthropologist Edgar Gregerson in his book *Sexual
Practices*,

> a sexual interest in dressing in a style that would usually
> indicate an inappropriate age or social role ... Cisvestism
> seems to be restricted to highly advanced societies, particu-
> larly in the West. One variety of cisvestism is the wearing of
> diapers or other infantile clothes by adults in sexual scenes.
> Another, possibly more common, involves wearing
> uniforms. The accountant or business executive might, for
> example, choose to dress up as a construction worker,
> cowboy, policeman, sailor, marine or Nazi officer. The
> social inappropriateness of the styles is seen in the fact that
> many men who wear motorcycle garb – almost totally a
> homosexual, sadomasochistic style – do not own and cannot
> even ride a motorcycle.

Notwithstanding the need for updating of this primitive sexological
concept, a glance at the facts of his life, at the countless macho roles
he dressed up for but was otherwise uncomfortable and unsuccess-

ful inhabiting, reveals Mishima to have been a spectacular example of cisvestism.

In *Merry Christmas, Mr Lawrence*, it's the greater relationship between pain and strength of character that Oshima is most interested in displaying. It's his superior ability to endure pain and brave death that seems to set Celliers apart from his fellow men, both English and Japanese, in the film. Whether sexual or nonsexual, between warring armies or would-be lovers, it's his love-your-enemy masochism that divinizes Celliers', like Christ's, suffering and death, and that ultimately seems to defeat the spirit of his executioner, Captain Yanoi. Instead of crucifixion, Celliers is buried alive, up to his neck, and left to die of starvation and exposure. In the last moments of Celliers' life, Yanoi salutes him as he would a superior officer.

Would Mishima have attempted to eviscerate himself if his childhood homosexuality and androgyny hadn't been so aversively conditioned? Many Japanese, probably including Oshima, see World War II, Japan's humiliating defeat, and emperor worship (i.e., patriotism) as the overriding factors in Mishima's death. Others, myself included, suspect that the demise of Yukio Mishima had less to do with his political loyalties than with his sadomasochistic, cisvestic sexuality. He may have come to believe in the roles he was playing, and those roles may have seemed eminently worthy to many, but he was definitely playing roles, as in *Patriotism*, a short film he wrote, directed and starred in, based on his short story of that title, about a young lieutenant whose marriage prevents him from participating in an ultra-rightist military coup, in the name of the emperor, that was a signal event of World War II. To the strains of Wagner's *Liebestod*, the music Mishima selected to constitute the film's entire soundtrack, the lieutenant commits *seppuku*, foreshadowing the bungled public ritual in which Mishima's own life ended in Tokyo in 1970. On the other hand, there can be no question that what may have been personal for Mishima became political for Japan.

Though I never saw Egbert again, we continued our *danse macabre* surreptitiously. In mid-December, about the time Egbert returned to New York, I received a postcard from Tokyo on which he had written only 'Merry Christmas'. It was signed simply 'Egbert'. Suddenly I recalled an earlier card. It showed a thick-lipped princess kissing a frog and was accompanied by a legend: 'Princess with great hopes kisses the local frog.'

I called his office. 'I got your card, Egbert. Happy Hanuk-kah.' Silence. 'HAPPY HANUKKAH, EGBERT!'

'Okay', he muttered. 'Happy Hanukkah.'

'*Thaaaaaat's* right', I purred, then hung up.

A moment later he called back. 'Listen, if you have a problem . . .'

'We'll let the public decide what the problems are', I interrupted. 'Meanwhile, don't ever attempt to communicate with me again.' (He hasn't.) I delivered my warning in a tone of absolute calm, then slammed my (princess) phone down so hard that it literally burst its buttons.

About six months after receiving Egbert's Merry Christmas card, the film *Merry Christmas, Mr Lawrence* came to New York from Japan, where it had opened to acclaim. When Egbert sent me the card, was he making some kind of connection with this movie? Since Oshima had finally emerged as Japan's leading filmmaker, and since I had often told Egbert of my interest in both Mishima and Oshima, I began to suspect that something more than coincidence or paranoia was going on. I took another look at the card, which I found tucked away in a drawer. Sure enough, the first line of my address was no more than an inch to the right of Egbert's 'Merry Christmas' on the postcard. Despite his knowledge that I was a physician, it read 'Mr Lawrence . . .'

Enough fragments had now come together for me to perceive a realm of my existence I was heretofore only able to sense. As the film explores the inevitable problems of dominance and submission between peoples of differing race, class, and sexuality that had veered out of control in my own relationships with the world around me, I need to detail the forces which bring *Merry Christmas, Mr Lawrence* to a close. The quotations which follow are recreations of the actual dialogue.

The line 'Merry Christmas, Mr Lawrence' that closes Oshima's film recalls an earlier scene in which Sergeant Hara, ostensibly drunk, calls for his prisoners Celliers and Lawrence, to be brought from their cells. 'Today', Hara says with great good humor in heavily accented English, 'is Christmas and I am Father Christmas. Is that how you say?'

Lawrence smiles politely, then respectfully corrects him. 'You mean Santa Claus.'

'Yes', Hara giggles, amused at the thought of the naive occidental religion with its sentimental holidays and gods. 'So today', Hara continues, 'I am Father Christmas and I've decided to give you your freedom.' For the moment Hara has become the occidental god. Santa Claus is Japanese.

As the prisoners leave, ostensibly free, everyone is laughing. Moments later Celliers and Lawrence are brusquely rearrested by Yanoi. For having participated in such a gross breach of military conduct, however, Hara is only mildly censured by the otherwise ferocious Yanoi. This is because Hara, who claimed earlier to believe that only harakiri can expiate the sin of an officer who has failed in the line of duty, pleaded with Yanoi that since he, Hara, was a high-ranking officer, his censure should be minimal or eliminated altogether.

In the movie's final sequence the war is over, and Hara is awaiting execution. A less than ebulliently victorious but subtly sadistic Colonel Lawrence visits Hara in his prison cell. They discuss Yanoi and Celliers. Yanoi has already been executed, shot by a military tribunal. 'Too bad for that', Lawrence muses. 'Celliers planted a seed that would have been sown had Yanoi been allowed to live.' But Lawrence's conjecture is undermined by Hara, who recounts the postwar religious ceremony in which Yanoi burned incense and a lock of Celliers' hair. The lock had been snipped by Yanoi as Celliers watched, moments before Yanoi saluted him in the final moments of Celliers' life.

'I'm sorry I couldn't save you', Lawrence smiles with English courtesy.

With Japanese humility, Hara thanks him for trying. They rather stiffly bid farewell. Then, as Lawrence is walking out the cell door, he is startled to hear the voice of his captor Sergeant Hara, as stern, confident and godlike as it had sounded on that Christmas day in Java during war: 'MR LAWRENCE!' In response, Lawrence reflexively turns around, as if to attention, and is wearing the same slumped shoulders, partially bowed head and fearful, submissive look on his face that he wore when he was Hara's prisoner. When Hara sees this demeanor, his authoritarian posture and tone are mitigated by a crooked smile. The movie's final still is a blowup to godlike proportions of Hara's face and the equivocal expression on it after he speaks the drama's final sentence: 'MERRY CHRIST-MAS, MR LAWRENCE.'

There are no longer any questions about why Oshima's film is called *Merry Christmas, Mr Lawrence* rather than *The Seed and The Sower*. Likewise, the double meaning of Egbert's message to me could now be divined without reservations. MERRY CHRIST-MAS, MR JEW.

In the crowd as Arnie and I left the movie theater were Ron Reagan, Jr and his wife, who was carrying a copy of the Radosh book about the Rosenbergs, the premise of which is that Julius was guilty. The simultaneity of coincidence and paranoia, I've too often found in my own experience, is what Jung called synchronicity – a meaningful coincidence of two or more events where something other than the probability of chance is involved.

What Egbert had discovered was that just as I was able to dominate him, however 'consensually', because of his largely un-conscious sensitivity about being androgynous, he could likewise dominate me, however 'consensually', because of my largely uncon-scious sensitivity about being Jewish. When Egbert was a child, he was ridiculed and humiliated for being a sissy. When I was a boy, I was never attacked for being a sissy, not even in the rural South where I cross-dressed during childhood and was homosexual from my earliest memories. But I did get into fights for being Jewish. For Egbert the most fearful nightmare from childhood is that God will turn out to be the Biblical Patriarch who hates homosexuals. For me the equivalent dread is that He will turn out to be the Nazi Antichrist.

After seeing *Merry Christmas, Mr Lawrence* I mailed Egbert – who continued to show up in the glossies and gossip columns, usually in association with prominent Jewish clients – a copy of an article that appeared in the August 22 1983 issue of *Newsweek*.

The Aryan avenger of Cleveland, Ohio was two very different people. As Frankie Ann Spisak, Jr., he was a one man war against blacks and Jews, a fervent disciple of Adolf Hitler (right down to the toothbrush mustache) who killed three innocent people in utterly cold blood and last week was sentenced to death in the electric chair. 'Even though this court may pronounce me guilty a thousand times, the higher court of our great Aryan warrior god pronounces me innocent,' shouted Spisak, 32, snapping a Nazi salute. 'Heil Hitler!'

The article was headlined 'Nazi Killer is Sentenced to Death'. I circled the word 'Death' and dropped the envelope containing the article and affixed with a Scott Joplin commemorative stamp in the mail.

Some months later Arnie and I saw the Israeli film *Drifting* at the New York Gay Film Festival. Its antihero is drifting into extreme social alienation. As a homosexual he is rejected by his own tribe. When two Arab commandoes, one wounded, seek refuge, he lets them in. They are sexually attractive, and he is masochistic.

With sadistic sympathy, the more available Arab, having already succumbed to the Israeli's crotch-groping, purrs that in his village they traditionally slice off the heads of captured enemies. Shortly thereafter the Israeli presents his ass to the Arab for fucking. As he does so, the Arab, confident that his sexual captive won't betray him, lovingly pecks the vulnerable nape of his Jewish enemy's neck.

By the standards of the Japanese, according to Sargeant Hara, homosexuality is taboo only across enemy lines because that is treason. One of the intended messages of *Drifting*, I think, is that treasonous liaisons are forced on the Israeli because homosexuality is so taboo in Israeli society.

But that's not all that's going on in *Drifting*. You can see the pleasure on the Arab's face as he fucks the Israeli from behind. The Israeli, by contrast, maintains a stern, guarded expression, a face the Arab cannot see. Love across enemy lines may complicate what racists, tribalists and other patriots will always define, without reservation, as treason. But the treason that may lurk within that love can abruptly uncomplicate it. This is not *Romeo and Juliet*, *Aida*, or *The Seed and the Sower*, after all. It's more like *Judith and Holofernes*, *Samson and Delilah*, *Merry Christmas, Mr Lawrence*, or *The Housemates Who Got Nailed*.

Chapter seven

Chocolate Operas of the Coral Reefs

IN an offbeat, low-budget and little-known film called *Carnival of Souls*, the main character is a woman who gradually discovers and learns to accept that she is dead. Like so many perceptions, her awareness happens gradually rather than as a revelation. At first she's frightened by sights and feelings she can't understand. In dreamlike moments following a car accident, she sees what seems to be a phantom, a man with chalky skin and dark eye sockets who appears out of and disappears into thin air, but she's even more disturbed by the way he looks at her, tacitly beckoning as if in some kind of recognition. Eventually, she gets used to his increasing presence and even tries to return a smile and join him in a dance with other phantoms. By this time, though she probably hasn't noticed it yet, her skin has begun to turn chalky and her eye sockets have darkened.

I've been a member of the McBurney YMCA since 1979, when I moved to New York from Boston. Seven years later, unable to endure the boredom of regular workouts, I began playing paddle-ball (the New York version of racquet ball), often, though I didn't notice it at first, with people in their fifties and sixties, and even some in their seventies. When I did notice it, I was initially resentful of having to expend so much social and competitive energy with contemporaries of my father. Most of the elder players belong to the Men's Health and Fitness Club, a fancier membership within the Y that has one large disadvantage the older, often Jewish, heterosexual gentlemen who keep urging me to join can't see: most of its members are like them – older and heterosexual. Now the comforts of that membership – better facilities, more room, larger lockers, the provision of towels and gym clothes, less rudeness and noise – have started to seem as attractive as the greater presence of younger men and gay men in the regular membership. Over time, as I've grown more aware of the prejudice of ageism from the direct experience of my own accumulating years, less angry about my childhood, homophobia, anti-Semitism and the world in general, and as my game has improved, I've become more comfortable with the older players. Gradually, as I settle into my mid-forties, the distinctions between their generations and mine have begun to blur. Is my body starting to look like theirs?

Something parallel is discernible in my sexuality. It still tyrannizes me and remains mostly frustrated and compulsive, but for the first time in my life there has begun a subtly appreciable, decreasingly intermittent, diminution of intensity of sexual desire as well as experience, even as I expend more time and energy in pursuit of satisfaction. Once, when I mentioned this to Arnie, my senior by six years, and became wistful about the deliquescence of sexual intimacy between us, he comforted me with his loving, teacherly wisdom. He invoked Edna St Vincent Millay's poem 'What Lips My Lips Have Kissed, and Where, and Why', in which the passage of the heyday of one's sexual life is compared to the passage of summer. I asked him to find the poem and he read it me: ' . . . I cannot say what loves have come and gone, / I only know that summer sang in me / A little while, that in me sings no more.' That special moment was two years ago, in late autumn. Now, it's July 1990. The summer is back, possessing me with its hotness and unquenchable thirsts, beckoning to me in mirages of satisfaction.

Reverend Bullen, my senior by twenty years, was very critical of the social structures of gay life, especially the baths. Xenophobically a 'one-on-one man', he deplored the leather scene and promiscuity (a word I always used to place in quotes) – three-ways, orgies, anonymous encounters – but with the exception, at least for himself, that there might be several one-on-one relationships going on simultaneously. He avoided the baths – I was about to say like the plague, which eventually provided such perfect validation of his sexual conservatism, older generation closetedness and staunch, right-wing Republicanism. As Andy saw it, at least in those days before anyone, including Andy, had a sense of the real dangers of sexually transmitted diseases, the debate about promiscuity all boiled down to this simple aphorism: 'You'll never meet a lover in the baths.' In my case, though Andy was my first lover and we did not meet in the baths, he was wrong.

Arnie and I met in a dark cubicle at the Everard. The connection was strong and memorable, so much so that when we recognized each other again while pretending not to in the identical circumstances a year later, we decided to get acquainted after sex. In the gritty little coffee shop across from the check-in window, we were the only pair. But like us, everyone else there was a regular. Among the most regular of the regulars were the properly-married-with-kids manager of one of the world's most famous opera singers, a writer who would later throw together a junk-food biography of that singer, and an executive producer of high-culture television programs, all of whom had something else in common besides their regularity at the baths: they were all closet cases. The manager would later have an affair with one of our community's most viciously *roman-à-clef* short story writers – *roman-à-clef*, that is, about everyone in his life except his closet-case lover and, ultimately, himself. The producer was invisible and silent in the numerous debates that took place, throughout the 1980s and into the 1990s, over public television's failure to affirm gay life. Of course, those debates were mostly in the gay press, for which the producer had such contempt. And the hack, still in the closet like the others, continues to earn a living writing junk-food bios that get $50,000 advances and allow him to keep a vacation house.

Arnie Kantrowitz. In an S/M scene at the Everard, Arnie, who was blindfolded and among whose favorite songs are 'It Might As Well Be Spring' and 'Embraceable You', was asked, 'What's the worst thing you've ever done?' 'I gave away my cat', he confessed. He may have been telling the truth.

I remember the moment my fate with Arnie was sealed, the

moment I knew I was very deeply in love. It was the summer of 1982. We were walking along 72nd Street near the apartment Arnie would soon give up so we could live happily forevermore together, and so he could better care for me through the burnout and life-threatening depression I was already sinking into. Unquestionably, it was Arnie's love, with no small help from his wonderful cat, Sid, that pulled me through. Could I ever have made it without them? Passing by the Famous Dairy Restaurant, now famous for having been the hangout of Isaac Bashevis Singer, Arnie suggested we stop for tea and ruggelach. 'What's that?' I asked, revealing to Arnie if not yet to myself the extent of my disconnectedness from my ethnicity. In the eyes of the *mensch* I'd connected with at the baths, I saw a twinkle that deepened my love a hundredfold, as he shyly explained, looking alternately at me and at the ground, that a ruggelach is 'a little Jewish pastry'. His tone was almost apologetic, as if he already understood that proclaiming something as Jewish might be a problem for me; as if he were being challenged to affirmatively explain something about Jewishness to a gentile. Or anti-Semite. I put my hand under his chin and lifted up. What did I see in those eyes at that moment? Was it myself? 'That's what *you* are', I said, 'my little Jewish pastry.' Nine years later, Ruggy (pronounced Roogy) remains my principal term of endearment for Arnie.

Every year, Arnie comes out to his classes at the College of Staten Island where he is an associate professor of English. One year he discovered that he fared much better on the teacher evaluations if he came out after the evaluations were completed. With his priestly (rabbinical?) gift for disarmament, he sometimes begins by saying 'Not all gay men wear dresses. Besides, I look terrible in a black cocktail dress.' Even funnier is the thought of Arnie as a little boy, dressed as Aunt Jemimah, replete with spatula – his immigrant mother's unconsciously and simultaneously assimilationist and racist choice for a Halloween costume. It was the only time he ever cross-dressed, something he never had any desire to do, though he did drawings, as I did, of women and fashion.

This year one student wrote, 'I don't know what I'd do if my son turned out to be gay', to which Arnie responded: 'Well, I'm glad you're not my father.' Another student reasoned that she didn't have to know if her teacher was a woman or black. 'But you *do* know', Arnie pointed out. 'One of the main reasons for prejudice is invisibility. A lot of bigots are proud of the fact that they don't associate with gays, but they do.' 'That's why it's so important for gays to be out', I added, attempting to steal the last word in our outing dialectic, in which Arnie is more defensive than I of a public person's right to remain in the closet.

When another student reiterated the cliché that 'God created Adam and Eve, not Adam and Steve', Arnie responded without missing a beat: 'So who created Steve?'

Unfortunately, ignorance and bigotry at CSI are by no means limited to the students. Well aware of Arnie's sensitivities about anti-Semitism, one of his colleagues, who prides herself on being a WASP, delighted in telling Arnie the joke she'd just heard: 'Why did God make *goyim?*' Answer: 'So somebody would buy retail.' When Arnie expressed his concern that this was anti-Semitic, she demurred that she was told the joke by a Jewish friend (some of my best friends ...). When Arnie then apologized, masochistically acknowledging that perhaps he had overreacted, she immediately proceeded to tell another joke from the friend: 'What did one mink say to the other?' Answer: 'I'm gonna get myself a full-length Jew.' Arnie told her that the second joke was definitely anti-Semitic and not funny in a world where Jewish skins were actually made into lampshades.

In the fall of 1989, Arnie, Vito Russo, Jim Owles and I drove upstate to see the leaves, between brunch at the Hudson Inn and dinner at the Bird and Bottle Inn. Vito, who had AIDS, and Jim had been, with Arnie, leading figures of the early post-Stonewall gay liberation movement, and they were Arnie's two closest friends. When Arnie became my life partner, Vito and Jim became family. Approaching Cold Spring, we stopped to take pictures. At one point the three of them were standing against a forest ablaze with color. With their gold, crimson and orange shirts, they became the autumn leaves our camera would preserve. The autumn leaves of the gay liberation movement as we knew it.

Two years later, almost marking the anniversary of Vito's death, Arnie, Jim, who now has AIDS, and I visited the same area. The leaves were fewer, and because it was cloudy, their colors were muted. Again we took pictures and I thought of the autumn leaves analogy. Was I one of them?

Arnie has recurrent dreams about Vito and Jim. 'They're visiting you', says Annie, Vito's mother. Pondering his future – without Vito and Jim – Arnie likened himself to Dorothy being without the Scarecrow and the Tin Man. The analogy brought tears to my eyes. In the early gay liberation period when Arnie wrote *Under the Rainbow*, gay people were wandering children who sought their identities and homes – denied everywhere else – in the realms of Judy Garland and *The Wizard of Oz*. But when I realized that Arnie's analogy made no mention of me, the child I become in our love talk expressed his insecurity. 'What about *me*?' I pleaded. Kissing me gently on the lips, his rejoinder was a characteristically reassuring, loving, incisive, put-down: 'You can be the cowardly lion.'

In July 1989 Arnie and I took a little trip through upstate New York to Niagara Falls. The day we left I awakened to Arnie's chirpings: 'Good morning to you. You still are a Jew.' Our first stopover was the postcard-pretty town of Skaneateles, where we dined at the Krebs Inn, a landmark that has been visited by many dignitaries and aristocrats, including several presidents. On a shelf next to our table was a German beer stein which was inscribed as follows: '*Dem sei dies Seidl bier gebracht / Der über seine Pflichten wacht.*' Framing the inscription were painted scenes that prominently featured Stars of David. Did the hostess seat us next to the beer stein because she assumed we were Jewish? And if so, was this good or bad?

Returning from the Falls, we stayed at the lovely Corning Hilton. During dinner at the hotel, I noticed that the carpet had what I call a swastikaoid pattern, which I would define as any pattern that bears similarity to a swastika, and which similarity would be denied by its designers, who would claim, sometimes truthfully, never to have thought of or even noticed such a connection. Several months later, I learned that the lover of a gay Jewish doctor, both of them friends of Vito's with whom we developed some closeness during Vito's illness, is half-German, half-Polish and from Corning. The lover candidly acknowledged that his father is anti-Semitic. A year later, the lover and the doctor had separated. I ran into the lover who, sweet and friendly as ever, was wearing a Jesus T-shirt. At the Rainbow Mountain Lodge, a large gay resort just outside Stroudsberg and our last stopover on the Falls trek, a fellow we assumed was lonely struck up a conversation with us. He was wearing a cross with a Star of David superimposed on it. I asked him about the symbol, which I'd never seen before. He was from New Jersey and a member of the Christ The Liberator branch of the Metropolitan Community Church. 'The star of David', he explained, 'is to emphasize that Jesus was a Jew. I'm not one of those Christians who want to . . . exclude Jews or deny that Jesus was a Jew.'

Back in New York, Arnie and I attended a screening of a Hollywood movie about the Manhattan Project called *Fat Man and Little Boy*. On the way to the screening Arnie wanted to stop in a nearby record store to see if they had a cassette he'd recently become obsessed with obtaining: variations for guitar on the Haydn theme that is popularly known as 'Deutschland über Alles'. The young, hip, black attendant of the store, which specialized in hard rock, didn't know what Arnie was talking about. When I asked Arnie why he wanted to keep subjecting himself to this music, with its terrible associations, he said, 'Because it's so beautiful.' Masochism in action, I thought. You learn to love that which oppresses you. Ironically, it was Arnie who made me aware of the masochism in my Wagnerism. Meanwhile, in *New York* magazine that same week, there was an item called 'Nazi Notes Ring from West Side Church' about how Rutgers Presbyterian Church at Broadway and 73rd Street had been chiming the Haydn theme, which is also the melody of a Christian hymn called 'Glorious Things of Thee Are Spoken', for weeks, offending some neighborhood residents. Two weeks later, in an op-ed piece in the *New York Times* expressing his fears about the reunification of Germany, Elie Wiesel concluded: 'What should one feel when hearing old-new Germany's anthem . . .?' Is this true? Is it really still the same anthem?

At the campus where Arnie teaches, someone painted a hate message on a men's room stall: a Star of David and a swastika with an equals sign between them. It's an equation I've seen many places, including the elevator at the McBurney YMCA, where it's so deeply etched I haven't found a way to obscure it (no one else seems to have tried). Like most of the YMCAs in New York, the McBurney has a large Jewish clientele. Another graffito at the school said: 'Hitler had the right idea.' It's been a long time since I've seen the hate word 'nigger' in graffiti. By contrast, swastikas are commonplace and becoming more so. One of the scariest of the anti-Semitic graffiti I've seen recently was on the back of a trash compactor. On four horizontal panels were the following: yes / [cross] / [Star of David] / no. What was especially frightening was that it was all in the same bright yellow paint the Nazis used to deface Jewish homes and businesses.

My dictionary defines paranoia as 'delusions of persecution', but also as 'oversuspiciousness', implying that some of the suspiciousness within oversuspiciousness may be reality-based. As Arnie was hardly the first to point out, even paranoids have actual enemies. On a long drive south from Miami, entering Key Largo, I passed the largest shell store I'd ever seen. In the parking area of the store there was a truck the size of a moving van, the side of which read, in gigantic letters: 'SHELLS, CORAL, JEWELRY'. The rear door of the truck was open all the way around to the side, obscuring the letters 'ELRY'. My heart pounded when I saw the word 'JEW' in such boldly public script. Inside the warehouse the inventory included numerous lacquered tortoise shells among the calcereous exteriors and prepared skins of at least a half-dozen other endangered species. As I saw myself reflected in the high gloss of the lacquered tortoise carapace, as lampshades made of Jewish skins flashed on in my unconscious, I wondered if Jews, like the American Indians whose swastika symbols leather people and wealthy Santa Feans ostensibly expect everyone to be unreservedly comfortable with, are also an endangered species.

A conditioned response, the fear of being publicly identified as Jewish, was such that during our childhood in Macon, Georgia, my brother, who otherwise appears to have so little awareness of his own or anyone else's anti-Semitism and who probably thinks that his girlfriend's status as the child of a Holocaust survivor has nothing to do with their relationship, clinically recalls that he always walked on the other side of the street our temple was on, lest anyone see him there. Lest he get 'caught', the way he did one day when he attended a Catholic church with a friend. When confronted with the wafer dish, he didn't realize what it was and dropped in a quarter, which landed on the pewter with a loud clank. Everyone turned and glowered. Everyone knew.

As for the swastika and the aristocratic gay life that flourishes around the Santa Fe Opera ... At a reception for Kenneth Lewes at the home of Dr Herb Cohen, I noticed a beautiful American Indian ceramic, the design of which was dominated by swastikas. I wrote Herb a thank you note for the invitation, adding that I was curious to know more about the vase. At a subsequent gathering, he explained that he had purchased it at a GMHC auction. I remembered Herb's vase when I saw the Woody Allen film, *Crimes and Misdemeanors*, in which there's a framed patch of Indian fabric with a swastika pattern in the apartment of the mistress (Anjelica Huston) who's blackmailing the ophthalmologist (Martin Landau). It's just there on her wall. Though the camera makes sure you see it for long stretches, nobody ever says anything about it, which is almost certainly the way she dealt with it; that is, by telling herself and anyone else who might ask that she liked the pattern, thought it was pretty, and that it's an ancient Indian symbol for good things. At Dr Cohen's reception, incidentally, I asked Lewes if he thought there was any validity to my own supposition that the virulence of psychiatric homophobia that peaked in the 1950s and 1960s could be partly explained by the mythology among psychoanalysts, so many of whom were Jewish, that the Nazi leadership was riddled with homosexuals, that homosexuality was a principal cause of Nazism. 'Yes', he said.

This situation in *Crimes and Misdemeanors* reminded me of Arnie's close friend, Marshal, a Jewish playwright from Brooklyn whose mother was Jewish—English and who is married to Millicent, a non-Jewish Scotswoman. Millicent completed a quilt which now decorates their living room wall. Its traditional windmill pattern appeared swastikaoid to me. Paranoid, perhaps, but in this case both Marshal and Arnie, who's usually pretty aggressive about diagnosing my paranoia, had independently made the same observation.

I know I'm not the only one who's hypersensitive to the public appearance of the symbol. In Hull, Massachusetts, which is home to a small Jewish community, the city council voted to carpet over the town hall's inlaid mosaic tile floor, which prominently featured swastikas, presumably exclusively American Indian in association, though the floor was constructed in 1924. The action was taken in response to protests from the Jewish Defense League. But no such action has ever been proposed, to my knowledge, to cover the swastika designs that adorn the proscenium of the Newark Opera House, which was constructed in the late 1920s, those which adorn several buildings on Fifth and Park Avenues, or those which permeate the lobby of the recently restored Brooklyn academy of Music. During the restoration, did the swastika designs ever become an issue? Did the people who paid for the project know of their existence? Are swastikaoid designs appearing in today's fashions in much the same way that swastikas themselves were in vogue in the architectural designs of the 1920s?

The trip to Miami was part of a trend. In my twenties, I spent most of my vacations in Europe. Culture – and the epitome of culture, opera – was my highest priority. Anti-Semitism was of little concern. Over time the priorities have changed. Comfort and adventure, sun and sea, have become more important. I no longer care so much about Europe or its culture, during the height and in the cradle of which the worst atrocities ever committed by human beings took place. And I no longer care as much about its opera, so bitterly poisoned for me by my adult knowledge of Wagner and Strauss.

Everywhere you turn for escape in the arts as in society at large, there's old or resurgent anti-Semitism and concomitant homophobia.

Even in sleep, I have a lot of dreams that are unpleasant if not true nightmares. Sometimes they're funny when I think about them later, like the one where my mother took the stage at a concert to tell the audience how disappointing and ungrateful her son is. Sometimes you can have a sense of humor about an event during a dream, but not this time. Recently, I dreamt I was with a hustler type who had a swastika tattoo. I fled, then tried to find him again. I wanted to explain why the tattoo was distressing to me, meanwhile anticipating his defense of the swastika as fashion. At the substance abuse clinics where I work there are several ex-prisoners and bikers with swastika tattoos. One of them is Jewish. My first reaction was one of complete rejection. Then I realized that they are within their rights to have whatever tattoos they please and that I'm not within mine to refuse to treat them.

In most of my dreams I am riding – on a bus, train, boat, plane or in a car, trying (and often failing) to get somewhere (often to another form of transportation) on time. Arnie says my unconscious has sketched 'riding' as a homonym of, and metaphor for, my writing. Sometimes nightmares are living and walking up 7th Avenue near 17th Street, across the street from Barney's, and wearing neo-Nazi T-shirts. This one was the double lightning-bolt symbol of the SS. I was so upset that I confronted the man, a truck driver type twice my size and half my age: 'DO YOU KNOW WHAT THAT STANDS FOR!?' I demanded. 'YEA', he said, 'IT STANDS FOR WHAT I STAND FOR!' I told him to go fuck himself, then had the good sense to keep trotting. Meanwhile, I could have been killed in a confrontation that achieved nothing except empowerment of the enemy.

At the substance abuse recovery meeting I was on my way to, I shared the experience with the mostly black members and friends who were there: 'It's a little like how a black person must feel when he or she sees a white person wearing a confederate-flag hat or shirt', though I've encountered no such anger from the black men I've met at the Dugout, the gay bar on Christopher Street that prominently displays a large confederate flag with a biker at its center. Is this decor in response to the increasing predominance of black people on lower Christopher and West Streets? Does the fact that the doorman there is black prove that racism isn't an issue? At home later, I told Arnie about the incident with the neo-Nazi and we shared our anger. 'Why can't we execute these people?' I asked with complete sincerity. 'It would make an interesting trial', Arnie suggested. Then, like one of the Jews fleeing the Nazis in the Holocaust films Arnie watches and collects so obsessively (by now, his must be one of the largest private collections around), he turns to me and says: 'They're after us. This isn't leather people doing theater with these symbols. It's the real thing and I'm afraid.' Tacitly, we both realize that we can't just exterminate neo-Nazis on the streets. As long as they aren't caught breaking specific laws, we will have to tolerate their presence.

The 'extermination' of six million Jews. It's mind-boggling to me that the William Safire types have never looked at this phraseology. I can understand the use of the word *extermination* for an appropriate subject, like Nazis or neo-Nazis, but when applied to their victims, without being placed in quotes, it endorses the Nazi concept of Jews, gypsies, gays, etc. as vermin to be exterminated. The Nazi atrocities should be referred to as genocide or mass-murder or slaughter or annihilation, but never 'extermination', unless that word or its derivatives is placed in quotes. I've written to the *New York Times* to protest their perpetuation of this usage, but none of my letters were ever printed or answered.

At that twelve-step program meeting, the qualifier (the speaker who tells the story of her or his 'experience, strength and hope', which is called the qualification) was an attractive young woman who was wearing crucifix earrings and who spoke candidly of her difficulties as the daughter of Holocaust survivors. After the meeting, I asked her about the significance of her earrings. Had she converted to Christianity? 'No', she explained. 'It's just fashion. I wouldn't wear a cross around my neck. *That* would mean I was Christian.' Even Arnie's cousin Cathy Kent (Arnie's uncle Albert changed his surname from Kantrowitz), who is so extrovertedly Jewish (her brother says she has a voice like a dentist's drill), wears cruciform earrings. At least, she was wearing them the last time I saw her – at the annual family gathering to break the Yom Kippur fast so few of us actually observe. It must be extremely painful for Jewish young people, I've often thought, to be so incessantly bombarded with crucifix imagery. On the surface, a lot of the current imagery is parody, fashion and criticism – e.g., Madonna. Overriding all that, however, is the power of the crucifix as an expression of bonding that, notwithstanding Sandra Bernhardt, Liz Rosenberg, Steven Meisel, Woody Allen and all the other Jews who have been in Madonna's entourage, must inevitably exclude Jews at subtle and not-so-subtle levels. After ten years of Madonna, the number of people wearing crucifixes, the vast majority of them now middle class, must have increased by many millions. I think *Bundeswehr* tank tops and *keffiyehs* all tap into this exclusionary sensibility.

Tacitly, often pre-consciously and in the name of fashion, they toy with anti-Semitism.

Robert Chambers, the defendant in the so-called preppie murder case of Jennifer Levin, wore a *keffiyeh*, as a scarf, to his trial, and photos of him wearing it appeared in all the papers. Was this simply a matter of political conviction – deep sympathy for the disenfranchised (ve von't say nozzing about anti-Semitism), or of the other principal explanation of those who wear them: just fashion? Two weeks before the war in the Persian Gulf, a secretary at one of the clinics wore a *keffiyeh*, draped broadly over her shoulders, to our staff meeting. Several weeks later she had replaced the *keffiyeh* with a yellow ribbon. Was it my imagination or did the wearing of *keffiyehs* diminish by approximately sixty percent during and immediately following the war with Iraq?

Unquestionably, there are people, including Jews, who wear the *keffiyeh* with consciousness of its political symbolism but who would deny any connectedness to anti-Semitism, just as there are people who really do believe that the wearing of *keffiyehs* has only to do with fashion. With regard to the latter, consider the case of a patient at one of my clinics – a very overweight, unattractive young Jewish woman with a mouthful of rotten teeth. A diabetic and addict recently diagnosed with AIDS, she was wearing a *keffiyeh*. When I asked her about it, she was surprised. She'd never thought about it having any meaning other than fashion. Extremely gentle and sweet, she considered the issue and concluded that if there were a political issue involved in the wearing of *keffiyehs*, then her wearing one should help defuse any negative associations. Notwithstanding that there are many Jews, including myself, who are varyingly pro-Palestinian, and although the swastika and the *keffiyeh* are *not* comparable in numerous important aspects, I must confess that I've wondered if there were Jews in the early years of Nazi Germany who wanted to wear swastikas with the same rationale – i.e., as a symbol of and for the poor and dispossessed, and/or as fashion.

Synchronicities. Arnie and I went to see the film of the opera, *The Man Who Mistook His Wife for a Hat*. It's about a singer who loses his ability to recognize certain objects. His musical perceptions remain unimpaired as other mental capacities deteriorate. He has Alzheimer's. In one scene, he has trouble recognizing his coffee, but he does identify it, finally, by virtue of its smell. Earlier that day, Arnie had concluded a disagreement we were having by admonishing me to 'wake up and smell the coffee'. The next day, I attended Rosh Hashanah services with my mother for the first time in many years. Not surprisingly, the rabbi's sermon emphasized that the Jewish New Year holiday is a time of awakening, of waking up to the reality of one's circumstances and one's responsibilities. Meanwhile, the refrain in skinhead rock lyrics as in neo-Nazi rallies, echoes the calls of the past: 'Germany Awake!'

In my commentary for *Opera Monthly* on the opera *Frederick Douglass*, which had its world premiere in Newark in the spring of 1991, I said that being gay and Jewish made me more interested in the subject of minority experience in music and opera. But in postulating contemporary American minority heroes as subjects for new operas, I was stymied when it came to thinking of a great Jewish hero/martyr, an American whose stature is equivalent to that of Dr Martin Luther King, Jr, or Harvey Milk (who was Jewish, but whose martyrdom had primarily to do with his being gay). When I asked my brother, he suggested that the Lubavitcher rebbes of Brooklyn would certainly have candidates from among their own. Meanwhile, neither Howie nor Arnie was able to come up with an example. My internalized anti-Semitic self was thrilled with this major proof of the badness and inferiority of Jews. Two years later, when I crossed this by my friend, the philosopher Paul Asman, he observed that Mickey Schwerner and Andrew Goodman, the two Jewish martyrs of the civil rights movement, would be more widely recognized than Harvey Milk, and would qualify as suitable subjects for opera. But in my absolute assurance that their stature isn't worthy of comparison with Dr King's, am I still being anti-Semitic? (Golda Meir?)

Rearranging a pile of papers on my desk, I stashed a copy of *Jewish Currents* underneath the medical journals. I did this unconsciously, and the reason I did it was not because it was low on the priority list of things to be read (which it was), but because it was a reflexive response of childhood to hide any prominent displays of

Jewishness, just as it became reflexive to hide any prominent displays of queerness.

Jews have repeatedly been set up and then scapegoated throughout history (e.g., the Nazi burning of the Reichstag). We're not very far from the times when Jews were widely believed to eat Christian babies in rituals, the so-called 'blood libel' that continues to resurface, most recently among black Muslims in America, and which was the subtext of the media feeding frenzy in the Joel Steinberg/Hedda Nussbaum child abuse and murder case. Even though horrific child abuse is common in other minority populations, here it was proof, albeit tacit in the media which are otherwise always being accused of being Jewish-dominated, of the old medieval myths. This tacitness about the Jewishness of Jewish criminals and their crimes was likewise the subtext of the Leona Helmsley story, and of the motor vehicle accident that resulted in the killing of a black child in Crown Heights, the spark that ignited one of the worst outbreaks of anti-Semitism – and as close as we've come to a full-scale pogrom against Jews – in American history.

On the subway, a poster for the Job Corps read: 'Come Join The Program'. The display showed silhouettes of workers walking toward the viewer. Some were wearing hard hats, some carried shovels, and others had pitchforks. When I first saw it, my heart began to pound. I thought it read: 'Come Join The Pogrom'.

On the flight from New York to Miami ('God's Waiting Room'), the plane was packed, mostly with elderly New York Jews. Some were indeed loud and demanding. I thought to myself about how the stereotypes of 'Jewish vulgarity' are based in truth; then I caught myself. My burgeoning Jewish consciousness reminded me that I've been on many flights with sports groups and business groups, with screaming, brawling, drunken yahoos who make these people seem like model passengers.

At the Club Baths in Miami that week, I sat in the hot tub with an airline steward from Texas who had been cruising me. The attraction wasn't mutual and would have been destroyed in any case by a staggering case of halitosis, which wafted its way around me as we spoke and for which he apologized in advance, explaining that he was in the midst of having major dental work. I wasn't attracted to him at all, but he kept pursuing me and we left the premises together for dinner, with me silently congratulating myself for my goodness. After ascertaining that I was a physician, he talked about his job, how broke he was, how expensive the dental work was, and, after ascertaining that I was from New York, how difficult and exhausting it is to deal with groups of kosher Jews on flights in and out of New York. His comments about their rudeness seemed pointed and extended. I then asserted that I was Jewish and proposed that centuries of prejudice may have conditioned these people to be the way they are – nervously, insecurely loud and aggressive. 'Like the screaming queen, you mean', he said with what appeared to be genuine perspicacity. 'Yes', I said, 'precisely.' When confronted, he backed off, but I couldn't help wondering about our encounter. Had he decided I was Jewish before I told him? Was he pursuing me anti-Semitically? To punish me for sexually rejecting him?

Just before leaving New York on the Miami trip, my first vacation in the new decade, there was a phone call from Ned Rorem, whom I had confronted in my interview with him (the full text is in Volume II of *Dialogues of the Sexual Revolution* and in *Queering the Pitch*) about passages in the *Nantucket Diary* I thought were anti-Semitic (e.g., the old neo-Nazi canard that the diary of Anne Frank is a fake that was created by her relatives to make money). He wanted to know where he could get a copy of our interview, an abridged version of which was just being published in *Opera Monthly*, and to invite me, with Quentin Crisp and Tom Steele, to tea. I told him I was on my way to Miami. 'So you're going on a Jewish vacation', he quipped affectionately. My dialectic with Ned, conscious and unconscious, at once playful and serious, rich and challenging, is ineluctably about the uses and excesses, the legitimacy and illegitimacy, of group identities (aka identity politics). The phraseology of going on a Mediterranean or European vacation wouldn't arouse comment or thought, but to speak of going on a French, German or Jewish vacation sounds funny. 'No', I reassured him and my internalized, anti-Semitic self. 'This vacation is going to be more gay than Jewish.' As it turns out, we were both right.

196: *Confessions of a Jewish Wagnerite*

Sitting in the Holiday Inn restaurant by the gay beach on Collins Avenue and 21st Street, kitty-corner from Wolfson's deli (where I stopped having breakfast because the coffee was so terrible), I noticed a hunky, Teutonic-looking man at a nearby table. I cruised him. Not only didn't he return the cruise, he looked displeased. I thought to myself: he's straight, homophobic, knows I'm a faggot and doesn't like it. Better stop. Just at that moment I happened to notice that I had been reading an article in the *New York Times* about resurgent anti-Semitism in Russia. The thought flashed through my mind that maybe his distaste for me was anti-Semitic rather than, or in addition to being, homophobic. For most of my life, it never occurred to me that people might type me as Jewish and that I might experience their displeasure, often subtle, as a result. For one thing, I always prided myself on how often I was told I looked Italian or Mediterranean or Spanish. No one except Arnie had ever said, 'You look Jewish.'

The cries of the seagulls on what used to be the only gay beach in Miami (at 21st Street) sounded like those of children. As I ate my hot dog, they hovered around me, begging for scraps. Suddenly, they became children at Auschwitz, pleading for food, and I was a kapo. For a moment, I felt intense pain and profound compassion, but it wasn't enough to get me to part with any of my food. Later that day, when I related this episode to Arnie, he pointed out that there may have been another, unconscious factor at work: my mother's 'maiden name' (is that phrase still legal terminology?) is Segal. The next day I ate more junk food, this time at a junk movie called *Hard to Kill*, a cops-and-robbers action film starring someone named Steven Seagal (pronounced SeaGAL, with the accent opposite to where most Jews place it, analogous to such eccentric pronunciations as ShaPIEro, LeVYNE and BernSTYNE) Is he a relative? We have East German cousins who survived the Holocaust. One was in the *Kindertransport* of children who were raised in London. Otherwise I don't know of any relatives who were pursued or killed by the Nazis. But my inquiries haven't been very aggressive. In fact, I never asked my mother or father the simple question: Did we have any relatives who died in the Holocaust? In fact, we never discussed the Holocaust.

In the television dramatization of *The Winds of War*, one of the Jewish deportees reminded me of my Aunt Jenny Segal. In the drama, the character is the familiar type of smart, strong, noble Jewish woman who is always outspoken, respected and in a position of leadership – of her family, business and/or community. Here, she became the leader of her freight car to Auschwitz. I will never forget the look of pain on her face as she finally began to accept that there was nothing she could do to help her brood. I began to weep as I imagined my confused, frightened mother among those in her flock. The next morning, these images of my poor little old Jewish mother as a victim of the Nazis with Aunt Jenny trying to protect her still fresh in my head, my mother called and our typically dysfunctional communication managed to upset me so badly that I found myself consciously wishing she were dead. Likewise in reality, Aunt Jenny, a mathematics wiz who graduated first in her class from a leading university, has had a hard time accepting her closest relatives, especially her in-laws and (deceased) parents, whom she continues to resent for their parochialism despite her years in therapy – as a client and, more recently as a therapist (she has a Master's degree in social work). But perhaps my heart perceives the greater truth about the nobility and bondedness of these people beneath all the dysfunction, put to the test in circumstances of extremity. That's what De Sica showed in his film about the Finzi-Contini family.

Meanwhile, my relations with Jenny are strained, at some level over my unwillingness to reject my mother to the extent that she (Jenny) rejected hers, and our communications became even more strained when her daughter, Helen, confided to her what I had confided to Helen: I've always wondered whether Jenny and Lester (Jenny's husband) might have had their own issues of sexual orientation conflict during the years of extensive psychoanalysis they underwent in the late 1950s and early 1960s, when psychiatry was so profoundly homophobic. (They are the only relatives about whom I've ever asked myself: Could he have been gay? was she lesbian?) The proverbial straw for Jenny came when I asserted that while she, Jenny, was free to maintain her surprisingly ignorant and simplistic belief in the bad-mother origins of homosexuality (she never read my collections on homosexuality and sexuality, which my mother had sent her – I didn't bother – just as she never read any other contemporary works on homosexuality, so far as I've been able to glean), I was not yet ready to alter my own perspective about her and Lester, notwithstanding her denial that sexual orientation conflicts were ever any kind of issue for either of them, or that she could possibly be homophobic.

Our confrontation occurred on the occasion of Jenny's most recent visit to New York from Chicago, to be with her daughter. Over lunch earlier that day, Jenny talked about how heartbreaking it is to try to counsel a mother who recently lost both sons to AIDS. Heartbreaking indeed, but Jenny's perspective reminded me of the circumstance of Beverly Sills. On a talk show, the legendary diva was asked how she dealt with her daughter's deafness and her other child's retardation. For so many years, she explained, she was unhappy. 'Why me?' she kept asking herself. Her outlook was completely transformed, she felt, when her question changed to 'Why them?' Meanwhile, the otherwise brilliant and inquisitive Jenny, who is completing doctoral work on the mothers of children with learning disabilities, was concerned about Helen, whose closest friend is a gay man, and who was doing volunteer work for POWARS, an organization that provides pet care services for persons with AIDS. It was 1991 and Jenny, whose husband is a physician, wanted to know if pets could be a vector for AIDS.

During my teens and early years in college, Jenny was someone with whom I could confide, especially about my unhappy relations with my mother, from whom I was in a long-term and not atypical process of detachment. Jenny was a confidante and friend – more so than any other relative – who helped me to see the importance of this transition, but my detachment was less empathic than it needed to be, a development Jenny's own inability to accept the limitations of her parents tacitly encouraged.

I remember Mignon's delight at being called 'Mizz Mays' by a black gas station attendant in Macon, Georgia, where I grew up and where she and my stepfather still live for part of the year. Mignon is the name my mother used up to the time of her first trip to Russia with my sister, several years before *perestroika*. Prior to this time, I never knew that Masha was her given name. As she finally explained to me only recently and after much prodding, she chose the name herself. Raised in poverty – her father was a shoemaker and may have been alcoholic – in a fiercely anti-Semitic Polish neighborhood in Chicago, she didn't want to be who and what she was. Her given name, Masha, seemed to be a source of contempt, and her nickname, Minnie, didn't feel right. So she adopted Mignon, after the name of a glamorous Jewish girl she knew of, just as Arnie's mother changed her first name from Jenke to Jean.

The gas station attendant thought of Mignon Mass (a derivation of Mazurosky, my father's Russian name) not the way most whites saw her, as Jewish, but simply as white, which is what her internalized self wanted almost as much as I did. Not that my mother had no Jewish consciousness. Even now, though she and her WASP husband are sometime Unitarians, and her politics, like those of Mother Kusters (of the Fassbinder film), are the socialist politics of my sister, Masha/Mignon Segal Thorpe can still be articulate about anti-Semitism in a way that my sister cannot. The tenant who was going to be staying at the house in Macon when Mom and Bill returned to their home in Upper Montclair, New Jersey, told my mother not to be so 'pushy' with questions and demands. Although Mom's insecurity may have caused her to be inappropriately aggressive with the tenant, she correctly sensed anti-Semitism in that word. In the same conversation in which she told me about the tenant in Georgia, however, she could observe of her relatives, the Mandels: 'I think they're sentimental about Israel.' Meanwhile, when I complained to Arnie that the Israeli Film Festival attendant was 'pushy', Arnie pointed out that 'Israelis aren't about being polite.' I guess for people who are so immersed in the question of their very survival, the subtleties of etiquette and *politesse* aren't the number one priority, especially considering where etiquette and *politesse* have gotten them in the past.

Like Miss Daisy, Mom was quite assertive about being Jewish when we lived in the South, even though we were members of a small minority in a sometimes fiercely hostile environment. To me, who wanted more than anything else not to have to be Jewish, she seemed to flaunt it, often to my great embarrassment and shame. Why can't she be more 'discreet' about it, I always wished. Ironically, when we moved up north to Chicago, where we lived and socialized in communities that were predominantly Jewish, my mother's assimilationist leanings became stronger and have continued, especially under the influence of my sister, while I've moved in the opposite direction of wanting to better understand and reclaim my ethnicity.

Arnie showed me some old grainy photo proofs from his bar mitzvah. They were never developed because the family didn't have the money or just didn't bother. He remembers being afraid to try to have the film developed himself because he was terrified of going outside his house, lest the bullies in his Newark, New Jersey neighborhood beat him up again. As we looked over the photos, he told me a joke from his childhood in the early 1940s: 'Question. What did Hitler say when his son was born?' 'Answer. Hotsy Totsy, A brand new Nazi.' These are the people the Germans tortured and murdered in the millions.

When Arnie recalls those days, he's quick to point out that the worst of these neighborhood bullies were Jewish, albeit German–Jewish – 'two brothers from a family named Kampf, as in *Mein Kampf*'. Of course, neither Arnie nor the bullies had any awareness of Jewishness as an issue in their dynamic. Which brought me back to seventh grade in the predominantly Jewish Budlong Woods area of Chicago's north side, where I delighted in tormenting David Littleman, the weakest, nerdiest, lispiest and sickliest Ashkenazic Jew in our class. And to my first year in college at the University of Wisconsin in Madison, when I wholeheartedly joined my dormitory mates, virtually all of them, like the majority of Wisconsinites, German–Americans, in the persecutions of our homely, gentle, Jewish floor master, Melvin, often in the presence of his similarly homely, gentle Jewish girlfriend, Rebecca. PFM, we called him: 'Poor Fat Melvin'. A deep pain lacerated my heart as my conscience sadistically flirted with the notion that I was one of Arnie's bully neighbors.

Mein Kampf. The Jews in the camps may not have had much humor about their circumstances, but that's one of the ways I dealt with my earliest knowledge of Hitler and the camps when I was an adolescent. During one episode of my favorite TV show, *Rocky and His Friends*, Boris and Natasha, the Russian spy caricatures, wrote out their plans for conquering the good guys, in this case a community of mice, in a book they called *Mice Kampf*. So hysterically funny did this seem that I remember it as if it were a peak experience. I wonder if Art Spiegelman, author of *Maus*, who is approximately my age, saw that episode.

Just before the Miami trip, I helped Craig Rowland move to Boston. We rented a diesel van that was so outsized (it was the only vehicle they had left) we had to take an alternative route. On the Trump Shuttle back to New York, I thought to myself that this wouldn't be such a bad circumstance to die in – returning from helping a friend with AIDS. Several days later, on the flight to Miami, I thought to myself that this would be a lousy situation to die in – a co-founder of GMHC on his way to an escape vacation, much of it to be spent at the Club Baths in Miami and Fort Lauderdale.

Revisiting Miami for the first time since my parents took me there in 1955, in the town's art deco heyday, I drove the entire length of Miami Beach along Collins Avenue, amazed at how many of the motels I remembered were still there. What magical, glittering citadels of fantasy and adventure these Kewpie palaces – with names like Thunderbird, Suez, Sahara, Saxony, *Sans Souci*, Eden Roc, Marco Polo, Casablanca and *Fontainebleau* – were to a nine-year-old. However glitzy and tacky, the *faux* totempoles, sphinxes, mermaids and sheiks which adorned their façades have acquired a patina of glamour, like the props in the Ridiculous Theater's *Salambo*. All the excitement of the Miami trip from childhood returned several years later when we bought a new car – a lavender Thunderbird. Unwittingly, I had pushed for the color as well as for the car, which in the 1950s and in a place like Macon, was a major symbol of prestige. But we weren't staying at the Thunderbird or at any of the other places mentioned on that family trip. Like our houses in Macon and Chicago and my mother's house in Upper Montclair now, the motel we were at was the least glamorous among its neighbors. Like me even now, I always wanted to be staying or living in one of these other places. I never wanted to be who or what or where I was – a middle-class Jewish queer in Macon, Chicago, San Francisco, Boston and New York.

At the baths in Fort Lauderdale, an attendant was wearing a T-Shirt advertising Bolt poppers, the symbol of which is an S-shaped lightning bolt. In the hot tub, an Hispanic man and I exchanged pleasantries. It was raining, and he said – or I thought he said – 'I feel sorry for all those "Jews" who came down from New York for the sun.' 'You feel sorry for *what*!?' I demanded. 'For the tourists', he said, not noticing or ignoring my consternation. In the hot tub later I was joined by a German from Mainz whose nipples were pierced and who was very self-assured. I volunteered that I was from New York. Unlike so many others one meets, he didn't ask about ethnicity. Was that because he could care less or because he was being diplomatic? On the beach in Fort Lauderdale someone had drawn flags in the sand. There were American and British flags, a skull-and-crossbones flag and one that had been treaded on so that only a few random lines remained. Was it a swastika?

Edmund White once wrote that humor is out of place in dealing with AIDS. Edmund and Rosa von Praunheim have also observed that humor helped Jews survive in the camps. Arnie disagreed with both opinions, despite our having recently exploded in laughter together, the peculiar face of nearly a decade of pain, at Arnie's suggestion that in our vigilance about avoiding the word victim, we should henceforth refer to those who were murdered by the Nazis, like AIDS casualties, as 'persons with death'. A similar outburst occurred when I told Arnie that an opera friend with whom I'd had the inevitable disagreements about Wagner had died of AIDS. 'So when's the next death?' he asked. In the gay and AIDS communities we know how important and helpful humor has been. With the Jews in the camps, Arnie believed, it was a different story. He knew of no examples of Jewish humor from the Holocaust – stories, letters, cartoons – at least not from the camps. In our generation, of course, there has been Jewish humor about the Holocaust – for example, in the works of Isaac Bashevis Singer and in the films of Mel Brooks, Woody Allen and Paul Mazursky – if not specifically from or about the camps. One of the best films about the Holocaust, Lina Wertmuller's *Seven Beauties*, is filled with humor. But as it turns out, Edmund and Rosa were right. The most recent addition to Arnie's Holocaust library is a book called *Laughter in Hell: The Use of Humor During the Holocaust* (Lipman, Jason Aronson, 1991).

In Miami, I passed a Jewish wedding party emerging from one of the hotels. The bride was aglow with happiness. My preconscious selected 'Matchmaker, matchmaker, make me a match ...' to accompany the scene. Then, suddenly, it put me inside the mind of a virulent anti-Semite/Nazi, who sneered: 'I'll make you more than a match, ya fuckin' kike bitch! How about an oven!' When I returned to Miami the following year for the premiere of Floyd's *The Passion of Jonathan Wade*, I visited the Holocaust Memorial, a profoundly upsetting experience. In the photo of a skeletally emaciated inmate whose limbs had been severed in some kind of medical experiment, I suddenly saw the bride's face.

Periodically, with an exaggeratedly shrill and very endearing Yiddish accent that always makes people laugh, Arnie sings a little song his childhood friend, whose parents were socialist, made up. Sung to the theme of the Israeli national anthem, it goes like this:

> *Had a little candy store*
> *Business very bad*
> *Asked mein froo*
> *What to do*
> *This is what she said*
> *Grab a little gasoline*
> *Pour it on the floor*
> *Take a match*
> *Give a scratch*
> *Candy store no more.*

Actually, though I spent most of my free time at the saunas, as I now euphemistically refer to the baths, the Miami trip was centered upon a conference on substance abuse medicine. In one of the talks, a review of recent animal experiments, the speaker described protocols in which hamsters, rabbits, mice and monkeys had their appetite, thirst, pleasure and satiety centers variously 'obliterated', resulting in their starving or dying of thirst or overeating or drinking themselves to death. The findings were described with ice-cold detachment. Not one word of ethical concern for the creatures was expressed, not by the speaker nor any of the discussants. I found this silence so upsetting I became nauseous.

A year later, my cousin Helen Segal, who is working on her Ph.D. at NYU in psychology and education and who has made the monumental discovery that a learning disability and associated attention deficit disorder runs in the Segal family, confided that she thinks animal rights activists go too far. Because she believes animal research cannot be abandoned, she's been labeled a 'speciesist' by colleagues. In 1946, the year I was born, Nazi physicians and medical personnel were tried by a US military tribunal for their role in experiments that maimed or killed thousands. Now there's controversy about the ethical utilization (citation/application) of the results of these experiments in no less august a forum than the *New England Journal of Medicine*. And how do I respond when one of my dearest friends, a person with AIDS and no less humanitarian a figure than Vito Russo, is angry at antivivisectionists protesting the use of chimpanzees in AIDS experiments? As we both see it, these experiments can mean life or death for him and our people. As a physician and certainly as a gay man, I understand that animal research is important and cannot be abandoned. As a Jew (and also as a gay man), as someone whose people have been the subjects of such experiments, however, I simultaneously believe the ethics of animal experimentation should be similar, if not identical, to those applying to human beings who are, after all, absolutely nothing other or more than animals.

That's what my father, the distinguished physician, the mammography pioneer and scholar believed: that human beings are nothing other or more than animals. An ardent devotee of H. L. Mencken, whose rationalism, cynicism, and dryness of humor he reflected, what would he have thought, had he lived, about the revelations of anti-Semitism in the Mencken diaries? I really don't know. Dad never discussed anti-Semitism, not even in regard to my infatuation with Wagner – another anti-Semite whose virulent prejudices are universally rationalized and excused, often cynically, in the names of that's-what-everybody-thought-in-those-days ignorance and/or art; as in an op-ed piece in the *New York Times*

(December 13 1989) by Mencken scholar and apologist Gwinn Owens, which concluded by proposing that we henceforth think of Mencken the way we do of Wagner: 'One can still listen to Wagner's operas and appreciate their beauty. The work is separated from the man.' Undermining everything Owens has said up to that point, the piece then suddenly concludes by asking, 'Or is it?'

Unlike my mother, who refused to enter Germany on a tour of Europe, my father never expressed any anti-German feelings, not even in the diary he kept on that trip. Rather, his cynicism was global. Instead of inveighing against Germans and Nazis, he perceived:

> Robber barons and their captive villages ... The history of these vassal states is entirely that of murder, rape and subjection, and from this arose people devoid of frivolity, with the keen instincts of hunted animals. Here is the distillate of genius, of tireless application: here is the substrate of the renaissance ... And what comes after the ages of materialism? ... Can a domestic animal live in a wilderness? ... I know of no power or system except one of destruction and renaissance.

'Little Max', they used to call me. But that's not who I wanted to be when I was growing up. For one thing, I wanted to be Christian. Like a Jewish *converso* during the Inquisition, I secretly celebrated Christmas with my own little box of decorations. One year I insisted on putting up a stocking, which my mother half-filled during the night with a few dimestore toys and candies. It was the most depressing stocking I'd ever seen. There was no way I could match my friends – be really together with them – when they bragged about all the bicycles, Lionel trains, coats, sweaters and other spectacular things with which they were rewarded for being Christian. Unless I lied.

Another year my sister and I, like the Patty Lupone and Dan Ackroyd couple in *Driving Miss Daisy*, were so determined to celebrate Christmas like everybody else that we persuaded my mother to buy a tree, which we decorated and which lasted one day before my father insisted on throwing it out. 'But, Dad', we pleaded, 'why can't you think of it as a "Hanukkah bush"?' Dad was not very religious, but he was respectful of his Jewish heritage and offended, like Miss Daisy, by the spectacle of people desperately trying to be more or other than what they were.

When I was growing up I knew that I didn't want to be who I was underneath – a Jew boy who wanted to dress up in girls' clothes – and I also knew I didn't want to be like my father, who was so much more critical and punitive than my mother. From my late teens through my years in college (Dad died of cancer of the pancreas during my senior year at Berkeley), my sense of closeness and identification shifted from my mother to my father, to the extent that it was my father to whom I first confided my homosexuality. Though my adolescent resentment of him remained such that I wasn't able to mourn properly when he died some six months later, my feelings had come a long way from the terror I had experienced as an adolescent when he caught me playing with my sister's falsies. 'What are you doing?' he had demanded. Placing one of them on my head, I explained that I was ... uh ... 'just trying them on'.

Even in my pre-teen years, the idea of Dad catching me being bad was one of the worst weapons my mother could wield. In our new home in Chicago, where we had moved in 1958 – I was twelve – I was jerking off in my bedroom in front of the closet door mirror, observing myself as I inserted a discarded lipstick case in and out of my anus, not realizing that my mother could see directly in from the garden. Suddenly there was that piercing scream: 'MAX, DO YOU KNOW WHAT YOUR SON IS DOING!?' In most things Mom was on my side against Dad, who seemed to be as much her enemy as mine, but not this time. As in so many of these confrontations, though, I came out OK. When my mother tacitly ascertained that my attitude was sufficiently suppliant and my primary allegiance to her reconfirmed, she backed off, telling my father the alarm was false. Sometimes, when my father sensed this partnership with my mother, he would become even more angry and punitive. Like my sister, whose sense of independence and stubbornness were awesome and an endless source of friction with my father, I endured a lot of corporal punishment. The slapping of faces and 'strappings' (we never got spanked like normal children on TV, which seemed another manifestation of our alienness) came to an end during those pre-teen years in Chicago, when my sister told my father how much she hated him after he'd slapped her again for being willful, and when I threw a paperweight at him, missing his head by about an inch, after being slapped for spying, for telling Mom that Dad was sneaking cigarettes again in the basement (if he hadn't died of cancer of the pancreas he probably would have died within years from emphysema). The latest from science and medicine, incidentally, is that *all* physical punishment of children should be regarded as child abuse. With regard to my own experience, I couldn't agree more. It taught me a hatred of my father I was eventually able to transcend intellectually, but never emotionally.

Like virtually everyone else in America, my parents were sexually ignorant, inhibited, intolerant and fearful. My cross-dressing, the last vestiges of which finally died (either naturally or from suffocation, I'm still not sure) around the time of our move to Chicago, was, like my homosexuality, profoundly taboo and carefully hidden. There was enough negativity about what little in the area of sexuality was speakable; for example, the subject of pre-marital sex, as it pertained to my sister and me. In the years of the film *Blue Denim*, teenage pregnancy was regarded as the penultimate nightmare for a daughter in white America, the worst being teenage pregnancy with a 'colored' person. There was similar concern about my girlfriends, especially Shelley, a nice Jewish girl no less, but one with whom they correctly sensed I was becoming sexual.

During my junior year at Berkeley, in 1968, things had changed in society and in my relations with my father so radically that I felt able to speak frankly to him about my homosexuality and the love affair I was in the midst of – my first (with Andy Bullen). Dad's response was compassionate but very concerned: 'You'll be found out', he warned. Had he never felt any attraction for his own sex, I asked. Unlike brother Howie, who has acknowledged some homosexual responsiveness and play into high school, Dad could not recall any such feelings. It's a measure of just how stigmatized homosexuality was in 1969 – five years before the APA declassification – that Andy's being a Christian priest elicited no comment from my father, who used to read the New Testament, and who must have seen the fact of Andy's being a priest, alongside the overwhelming fact of our being homosexual, as relatively insignificant.

Dad had a second warning about my homosexuality: 'Don't tell your mother.' He didn't want to see her hurt and with his alternating passivity and paternalism toward women, especially toward her, he didn't think she could ever understand or handle it. He was wrong. In 1974, five years following his death, as the post-Stonewall gay liberation movement began to take shape, as I grew more distant from the family, my mother began to probe. Within weeks, it seemed, her questions became so bold and direct that it was clear she knew and could deal with it. So I took advantage of the next occasion, her birthday, to formally confide the facts of my life. I took her to dinner at the Russian Tea Room and at precisely the right moment, with precisely the right words and tone, I looked in her eyes and said, 'Mother, I'm gay.' But as so often happens with my mother when important feelings are being expressed by others, she got distracted. 'Look,' she said, 'Isn't that Lena Horne?'

Over time, my mother, like my brother and sister, has been very decent about my homosexuality, as she has about anything I might feel identified with, so long as we don't take too long to get back to what's really important – 'the family' (her issues, needs and priorities). At least on the surface, everyone in our family is fairly tolerant of one another's social identities or lack thereof. But the problems that pursue our family – my relationship with my mother, sister, brother an their relationships with each other – *are* about identity politics, the alternating absence and unrecognized presence of which in all our childhoods set the stage for more fundamental levels of dysfunction.

Now, I realize that what I always regarded as my mother's narcissism was really something more complex: an attention deficit disorder that may have a genetic component, as well as an adaptation to the profound insecurity of her early childhood. Hence her easily-triggered distractedness and reflexive distrust of people, especially strangers. The latter was primarily a conditioned response, the acting out of society's distrust of and contempt for her ethnicity, femininity and poverty. When Arnie and I talked to her about our discomfort with holidays, especially Christmas, Mom confessed that throughout her life, she never felt like she really belonged anywhere. She had to agree that this probably had mostly to do with our being Jewish. Now, try to imagine the courage of this woman from a pogrom-fleeing, extremely poor, orthodox Jewish background, intelligent and gifted but who never completed college (a 'proof' of inferiority that would haunt her for the rest of her life), who made the effort, however imperfect or distracted, to understand and who was willing to accept, in 1975, her son's homosexual identity, even as she secretly continued to battle the suspicion that she was somehow to blame, a notion that was subtly and not so subtly encouraged by Jenny, among other relatives and friends from the psychoanalytic 1950s and 1960s, and my sister, whose old-leftie socialism tacitly embraced the same neo-Freudian concepts of the bad-mother origins of homosexuality.

It's mid evening. The clunking noises from the upstairs neighbors have subsided. The phone calls have been returned, the other chores taken care of. We've eaten and have that post-prandial contentment. It's our quiet time together. Some of it we spend together, doing separate things we've been doing since childhood, when we learned they gave us solace. Arnie likes to cut out pictures from magazines. My habit with magazines (after looking over the pages with the beautiful houses, antiques and *chotchkas* with which my childhood fantasies still wish I could somehow be bestowed, like the prizes that were just given away on 'Queen for a Day') is to crinkle them. Arnie's pictures go into files he rarely if ever consults. The crinkling feels good to my fingers and puts me in a semi-hypnotic state. Arnie is the only person I've ever allowed to see my magazine crinkling. It must look – and in fact be – pretty bizarre, I've always figured. Confessions of a (closet) magazine crinkler.

In the early years of our love, before Arnie developed diabetes, before my hypertension, our quiet time would begin with chocolate, sometimes homemade brownies, and proceed with our ongoing ritual of lying together in front of the TV. The old couch was easy to unfold and cradled our cradling of each other. When I hastily bought the new L-shaped couch (without Arnie's input), which doesn't unfold (my mistake and one that never occurred to either of us until now – a simple demonstration of how writing helps the writer to see things), we had to invent new ways of snuggling while lying end-to-end, a challenge that would have been facilitated by an intermediate course in acrobatics. What we watch has never mattered so much, as long as it's not the heavy Holocaust films Arnie has collected so assiduously, or opera, which Arnie simply can't abide. Arnie says that soprano high notes hurt his ears, though there's no wincing when he's listening to Judy Garland. My theory is that opera was aversively conditioned for Arnie by his closest boyhood friend, a German–American, anti-Semitic opera queen who converted from Presbyterian to Episcopalian because he was in love with an Episcopal boy, who had contempt for Arnie's activism, and who literally and repeatedly told Arnie that Wagner was a lot more important than six million Jews.

Like my mother, whom I used to deride for wanting to avoid films with serious content, I want to spend our quiet time being soothed, pleasantly entertained, rather than challenged, enlightened or even edified. With rare exceptions, the Holocaust documentaries are, like my opera tapes, off-limits, although in the course of watching one of the growing number of those exceptions, *The Shop on Main Street*, in which the innocence and defenselessness of the civilian victims of fascist atrocities are captured with such indelible realism, I've come to see that the secret mainstay of our relationship is Arnie's slowly helping me to come to grips with Jewish history and reality.

How can he keep watching films about war and pain generally and the Holocaust specifically, I keep asking myself and him. Can his answer – that looking at the much worse trials and tribulations of others helps you appreciate your own survival, especially as it grows ever more precarious – really be the whole story? Or is something else going on, some process of expiation, of survivor's guilt?

Among the shows we can mutually enjoy are musicals from the 1940s (with their simple, healing, often subtextual politics) and 1950s, and the Japanese science fiction movies that seemed so consistently fake and disappointing to me even in my adolescence, when I learned to anticipate them with such fervor. There must have been an initial thrill (one of the Godzilla films, *Rodan*?!), long since forgotten, that I keep trying to recapture, like the addict I already was. But even more than the tacky sci-fi and musicals or operas, I prefer nature shows, especially those dealing with sea life, which has beckoned to me since my earliest childhood.

'What do you want to watch?' Arnie, keeper of the VCR and videotapes, asked ritually, as I sprinkled a second packet of Equal on my fruit salad. Unlike Arnie, who has seen *Gone with the Wind* more than fifty times, I don't have a single favorite film. But I do have an equivalent, at least in fantasy, which I likewise ritually proffer: 'How about *Chocolate Operas of the Coral Reefs*?'

It was our fifth anniversary, and we were bickering during the intermission of Harvey Fierstein's play, *Safe Sex*, when I suddenly realized what I would call the story about him and us and me.

On the way to break the Yom Kippur fast with Arnie's relatives, the Kents, in Connecticut, my 'hypercriticality', as it has been called, joined my masochism for a look at this holiday. Why is the Day of Atonement the holiest day for Jews? To encourage Jewish guilt and masochism? Atonement is an important aspect of most religions, but in what other is it given such preeminence? My hypercriticality has the answer. In Catholicism, confession and penance are far more pronounced, and Easter, the holiest day of the year, reminds Christians that Christ died for their sins. And the hypercriticality that Jews so characteristically apply to themselves as well as others – the always asking why, the psychology of which Wagner and his Nazi minions believed he had 'exposed' in his portrait of Mime – what does it signify? As Wagner recognized, it does have to do with survival, and it may utilize what thousands of years of the struggle to survive have rendered genetic gifts of intellect and reasoning. What Wagner didn't see at all, however, was the overwhelming extent to which Jewish inquisitiveness and analyticalness reflects society's 'hypercriticality' of Jews.

As we drove past the West Side Highway sewage facility, Roger, Arnie's cousin, said, 'Watch out for the smell. Hold your nose.' To which Arnie replied, 'Breathe deep, my lambs.' I caught the reference. It's from Andre Schwarz-Bart's novel, *The Last of the Just*, about the persecution, courage and survival of the Jews in Europe from the Middle Ages through the Holocaust. According to

Jewish legend, there will always be thirty-six just men, the *Lamed Vov*, often unknown to themselves, who 'are the hearts of the world multiplied, and into them, as into one receptacle, pour all our griefs'. If one of them were lacking, 'the sufferings of mankind would poison even the souls of the newborn, and humanity would suffocate with a single cry'. In the novel, a rabbi prophesies that there would be one of the Just in each generation of the (fictional) Levy family. (Arnie believes Elie Wiesel is one of these men. Is Arnie? Could they also be women?) The book chronicles the story of the *Lamed Vov* in each of the many tidal waves of European anti-Semitism and persecution, culminating in the Holocaust. The quote about the lambs is from the final chapter. Ernie Levy, a French Jew, hides out in the French countryside until he sees a busload of French Jewish children on their way to a camp. Overwhelmed with compassion, he presents himself to the authorities so he can accompany the children to their death. Inside the gas chambers, he shepherds his flock: 'Breathe deep, my lambs.'

During Arnie's first stint as a teacher in Cortland, New York, he taught this novel, which is so painful I couldn't finish half of it, in a literature course. In their final session on the book, one of the students asked, 'He seems to be mad at the Christians. Why?'

In the film and novel, *The Silence of the Lambs*, the title refers to the Jodie Foster/investigator character's childhood trauma of discovering that the lambs on her farm were all eventually to be slaughtered. Their sweetness and innocence seemed compounded by their silence. Intensely identified with both minorities, gays and Jews, I'm conflicted about whom I metaphorize the lambs to be. They are all the innocent creatures, great and small, past, present and future, who are victimized, persecuted, exploited, slaughtered, yes, but they're also specifically gays and Jews. My conflict is not about whether or not the two are analogously suffering minorities – clearly they are in many ways – but about the conflict my paranoia perceives *between* them. That is, my paranoia fears, on the one hand, that a monolithic Hollywood run by Jews (I sound like Spike Lee and Leonard Jeffries) is intentionally fostering the scapegoating of gays (does Spike Lee give a shit about gays and lesbians? Is Spike Lee gay?) by continuously perpetuating the myth of gender identity confusion as the cause of murderous psychosis, to say nothing of the gross fag-baiting that still goes on in so many Hollywood films. Although there have been a few homosexual, lesbian and bisexual serial killers in history, I know of none who were what we would call a transvestite or transsexual. So much for *Psycho*, *Dressed to Kill*, *Silence of the Lambs* and countless other such films (and novels) suggesting the contrary. Why would Jewish Hollywood moguls want to scapegoat gays? Well, for two reasons, my paranoia tells me. First, so that queers will be preferentially scapegoated in the next big economic/political crisis. In this scenario, Hollywood clearly doesn't know what historian John Boswell documented so impressively in *Christianity, Social Tolerance and Homosexuality*: that ever since the fourteenth century, at least in Western Europe, gay people have been scapegoated in tandem with Jews, gypsies and other minorities; who went first (usually Jews) was irrelevant.

The second reason in the paranoid scenario for Hollywood to want to scapegoat gay people would be for revenge, based on the myth, perpetuated by the World War II historians (e.g., Shirer) who, like the psychoanalysts, have had such an impact on the previous generation of thinkers about Jewish experience, that many high-ranking Nazis were homosexual; that Nazism was, in some very fundamental regard, a phenomenon of homosexuality. Richard Plant, a leading historian of the Nazi persecutions of homosexuals, calls this common, widespread phenomenon of making the villain homosexual or feminine 'the faggification of the enemy'. Of course, my better judgment understands what Vito Russo and Arnie have always pointed out, that more than anything else, Hollywood, which is not monolithic, is simply responding, like the rest of the culture, to the cash register. For example, in the rock music biz you have gay, Jewish David Geffen representing homophobic, anti-Semitic Guns 'N Roses (not unlike the way Angelo Neumann, who was Jewish, represented Richard Wagner). Bigotry sells. Plant and other historians have now documented a much bigger, more complex picture than Visconti portrayed in *The Damned*. In the infamous Night of the Long Knives in 1934, the Nazis murdered Roehm and his Brown Shirts, thus purging their ranks of all known homosexuals. The Nazis then specifically legislated the anti-homosexual persecutions that continued through the end of the war. So the principle perspective to have is that homosexuals were *victims* of the Nazis.

On the other hand, I can't help thinking about the role homosexuals did play in the early metastasization of Nazi ideology and power. Boldly homosexual Ernst Roehm (who did not identify with the gay minority or its emancipation movement in Germany) was, after all, Hitler's closest confidant and the architect of his early career, and there was plenty of homosexuality among the Brown Shirts. As a gay man, I identify with the lambs, victims of the anti-gay violence I sincerely believe Hollywood's *The Silence of The Lambs*, among a flotilla of other homophobic films, will contribute to. As a Jew, I also identify with the lambs as victims of xenophobia and fascism, the priests of which have often enough been homosexual. In both identities, my paranoia can't stop wondering to what extent reactionary, non-Jewish gays, like reactionary, non-gay Jews, are my real or potential enemies. Of course, even when they are gay and Jewish they can still be reactionary and very real enemies. Like Roy Cohn and who knows how many Hollywood moguls.

A new production of *Parsifal* at the Met (March 14 1991). The program notes by David Hamilton have this single reference to anti-Semitism: 'The anti-Semitism evident in some of Wagner's late essays has been detected in *Parsifal* by both his opponents and his more obnoxious disciples.' Does this imply that anyone in between these two extremes could not detect anti-Semitism in the opera, that it's not possible to be an objective admirer of the composer and simultaneously decry the anti-Semitism?

There's a second essay in the *Parsifal* program by Barry Millington, who has elsewhere written in depth about the anti-Semitism *within* as well as surrounding *Die Meistersinger*. The *Parsifal* essay, called 'Zen and the Art of Wagner', proposes that *Parsifal* is as much Buddhist as Christian. On this occasion, there's little discussion in the program, or even in the more critical analyses that did appear in *Opera News* and the *New York Times*, of the obvious, heavy interconnections of the Buddhism, Aryan Christianity, sexism and anti-Semitism which waft in and around *Parsifal* (notwithstanding the opera's explicit expression of compassion 'for all creatures') with what developed in Germany during the fifty years that followed Wagner's death. Not so unlike the way the blood libel myth hovered in the background of the Joel Steinberg case, the relationships to Nazism of the themes, messages and context of *Parsifal* are tacit, in the press and audience as in the opera itself, ready to explode forth again under the right constellation of circumstances, as they did in the ravings of Adolf Hitler.

Reviewing the new Met production, Bruce-Michael Gelbert acknowledged that some of the messages of *Parsifal* have grown 'increasingly abhorrent'. He then concludes: 'Heretic that I am, I go to *Parsifal* for the sublime music.' This review followed by some months a serious falling-out between Bruce-Michael and me. At some point in what had been a more or less mutually supportive and enriching if never truly comfortable friendship, Bruce-Michael (as he told me he preferred to be called, though other close friends called him Bruce), decided he'd had enough of my obsessing about Wagner, anti-Semitism and political unconsciousness among opera queens, which must have seemed at some level personally accusatory. On top of which were my concerns about political consciousness in the leather world, specifically about the public display of Nazi or Nazi-associated paraphernalia (which Arnie wrote a chapter about for Mark Thompson's collection, *Leatherfolk*, and which is also the subject of my interview with Arnie – 'Nazis and Gay Men II' – in *Homosexuality and Sexuality: Dialogues of the Sexual Revolution*, Volume I). For example, I pointed out that the eagle medal (different from American bald eagle insignia) Bruce-Michael wears on his cap when he appears in public in full leather, as he so often does (at work, at the opera) looks just like the eagle that identified the Nazi deportation trains. Likewise, the Eagle's Nest, the name of a number of gay leather bars in various cities, some of which (like New York City's Eagle Bar) have shortened their name (like Jews trying to pass), was the name of Hitler's lair in Berchtesgaden. I don't think Bruce-Michael, like many (most?) leather people, had ever given much thought to the possibility of such associations. And when he did, I believe, the pain that resulted became anger that was turned against me. That said, let me point out that Bruce-Michael, boldly up front about being gay in the gay press, has more political consciousness than most of the gay men who have written about opera in the gay press (e.g., 'Ivan Martinson') and a lot more than most of the *many* gay persons writing about music and opera in the mainstream press, *not one* of whom (not even K. Robert Schwarz?) has ever therein explicitly identified her or himself as lesbian or gay. (Correction: In addition to Ned Rorem, there is Alex Ross, who came out in an uninhibited discussion of Koestenbaum, Mohr, opera queenery, homosexuality, Jewishness, Wagner and *Parsifal* – the whole *megillah* – in the *New Yorker*.) On the other hand, I don't recall Bruce-Michael ever identifying himself as Jewish in any of his pieces, neither for the gay press nor for Axios – a gay Greek Orthodox Christian group his lover Joe (who liked to be called Joachim) belonged to – for whose newsletter he wrote opera reviews in the years before I helped get him his first assignments with the *Native*.

At the very touching memorial service for Joe, who died of AIDS, at the Lesbian and Gay Community Services Center, Bruce, casually dressed in the leathers and political jewelry in which he is most comfortable, most at home, warmly recalled that Joe's encouragement and Axios had given him an outlet for his writing when all other doors seemed closed. He then sang his own renditions of 'Somewhere', 'Where or When' and 'I am what I am'. The program included two other songs, 'Close Every Door' from *Joseph and the Amazing Technicolor Dreamcoat* and 'A Simple Song' from Bernstein's *Mass*, sung by the afternoon's other stellar baritone soloist, their friend Richard Holmes. With its allusions to chosen people, if not for more conscious reasons, the former was a favorite of Joe's and the song he most wanted Bruce to sing in his memory. But it lay too high.

It's springtime (Mel Brooks cuts me off: 'It's springtime for Hitler' ...), the season of the paschal lamb, time to start fretting about whether or not we'll be invited to Seder at Arnie's Aunt June's. Alternatively, will we attend a Seder with our gay Jewish friends? ('Queer Seder' chez Gregg Bordowitz is the most recent option.) On holidays we're so often left jostling. Where do we belong? Definitely not at the Met's new *Parsifal*. Like a gay person trying to fit into straight life, a Jew trying to be a Wagnerite is an awkward fit at best: imagine a Jew leading the orchestra for the passion play at Oberammergau. At worst – watching politically unconscious James Levine (like Hermann Levi, the first conductor of *Parsifal*) leading the soulless Met production nowhere, it's a spectacle of masochism. What seems so obvious to me, if not to anyone else, is that for Nazis, seeing a Jew conduct Wagner can have a certain thrill, like that of having Jewish instrumentalists play Wagner as their people were marched past them to the gas chambers and ovens.

In the Mel Brooks film, *History of the World – Part 1*, there's a musical comedy sequence in which manacled orthodox Jews are being tortured by the Spanish Inquisition. This blackest of black humor was in the same vein as 'Springtime for Hitler' (from Brooks's *The Producers*), but I was able to laugh at the latter. When confronted with the former, with actual images of the sufferings of these poor old Jewish peasants, who looked like my grandparents, images with a vividness my unconscious censors had never come close to permitting, any humor was superseded by an epiphanic moment of personal identification and deep, visceral pain. Clearly, comedy can be deadly serious business.

Chitchatting with opera people about the new *Parsifal*, I eschew what really concerns me – my pain about the composer's, and his last opera's, role in the development of Nazism. Since Hitler and the Nazis acknowledged it, why don't we? Within our prattle about the singers, the sets, the opera's interminable length, etc., my pain, like Wagner's intentions within the murk of *Parsifal*, is tacit. The music world simply does not attempt to deal with the extremely difficult subject of how much pain Wagner causes self-aware Jews who are genuinely knowledgeable about music, opera and German history. And with the rarest of exceptions, Jewish musicians and operaphiles only deal with it by denial and or masochistically.

Richard Mohr's book, *Gay Ideas: Outing and Other Controversies*, is dominated by an essay that focuses on *Parsifal* called 'Knights, Young Men, Boys: Masculine Worlds and Democratic Values'. While Mohr is principally interested in the work's implicit or projected (it seems to me) homoeroticism and theoretical links between homoeroticism and democratic values (à la Whitman), I want to know more about the gay men who find homoeroticism in

Wagner. How has this sensibility played into the cultism that has always surrounded Wagner and that became so intrinsically linked with the metastasization of Nazism? On the other hand, does the fact that Mohr has such a cultish vision of *Parsifal* merely reinforce the work's value and status as great art? (That is, like most art, the greater and more enduring it is, the more diversely it can be interpreted.)

'If you blame Wagner for the Nazis, must you blame Einstein for the bomb?' asks Paul Asman. No, I can answer with absolute certainty. As *I* see it, it's dangerously evasive not to blame Wagner for the evil he inflamed and that was carried out in his name. Einstein, by contrast, is exculpated by his contribution to the struggle against that evil. Could anything be more clear? Of course, if you're a German or Japanese partisan, *your* view may be precisely the opposite. Does this mean that I'm a kind of partisan, much too involved in blame and accountability to hold more complex, less temporal perspectives? On the other hand, are those who hold less partisan perspectives in times and locations that are or that remain politically volatile – e.g., so many artists, most mainstream music critics – evading moral accountability?

Has *Opera News* ever published a balanced piece on Israeli feelings about Wagner? Morris Springer, who covers opera in Israel for *Opera News*, wrote one, but it never made it into that publication. It's called 'Why Israel Bans Wagner'. It was published in *Midstream*, an Anglo-Jewish magazine, in 1988, and we reprinted it in *Opera Monthly* in early 1992. Here's what Springer concludes about Wagner, Jews, paranoia and the irrational:

> Given the thousands like my wife who live in a Jewish state the size of New Jersey, the concentrated antipathy to Wagner acquires formidable proportions far outweighing any question of art for art's sake or the opinion of any individually prominent musicians or groups of musicians. If this is a species of paranoia, so be it: but it should at least be an understandable one. For the survivors, the Wagner issue is, right or wrong, simply one of association. Most Jews associate Wagner with Nazism, much as they do Eichmann; in their own country they prefer not to have his music arouse

atrocious memories ... Since Wagner worship, like the worship of anyone or anything, has its irrational aspect, why is it regarded as astonishing and reprehensible that there exists a group representing the other side of the Wagner coin?

I tried to explain my feelings about Wagner and my disenchantment with the opera world to Manfred (Manny), an opera queen friend from twelve-step meetings. When I first met him, not having any clear sense of his ethnicity but curious about his name – I'd heard someone else call him Manny – I asked if he were Jewish. 'No', he proclaimed. 'I hate that name. Please call me Manfred from now on.'

'Knowing what I now know about Wagner and Strauss', I told Manfred in a moment of letting my guard down, 'I feel like the entire opera world has been poisoned for me.' A churchgoing Southern Baptist with little minority consciousness, he didn't seem to connect. In any case, he never said anything empathic. On the contrary, he seemed to actively ignore – that is, to subtly manipulate – my vulnerabilities in this area in communications that became more competitive than mutually comforting (a relationship, Arnie points, out I've had with more than few people in my life). Within weeks of my pouring my heart out to him about Wagner and Strauss and notwithstanding a more recent discussion of Vanessa Redgrave's politics, he couldn't wait to tell me his impression of the new *Walküre* production at the Met: 'Behrens was just wonderful. She sang beautifully and was a totally convincing warrioress. She reminded me of the young Vanessa Redgrave.'

When Norman Laurila agreed with me that the best comeuppance to Wagner was the irrelevance of his politics to the (still slowly growing) multiculturalism of contemporary casting, I thought immediately of that Met *Walküre*, the première of which we attended together. The casting of Jessye Norman as Sieglinde does make a mishmash of the racial theories that are at this work's heart, in the same way that the casting of Martina Arroyo as Elsa tacitly undid the nationalism of *Lohengrin*. On the other hand, racial casting can, however inadvertently or coincidentally, enhance the kind of prejudice that so deeply motivated Wagner. When Grace Bumbry became the first black singer to appear at Bayreuth, that was a milestone for the integration of opera, but Venus, the role in which she was cast, is a seductress whose attractions the hero must resist. I can't be the only one to have pondered the racial implications of that casting and staging by Wieland Wagner: the hero, an analogue for Germans as well as for Wagner himself, resists the temptation to miscegenate. Comparable implications can be drawn from some of the stagings of *Der Fliegende Holländer* that have featured Simon Estes. Ultimately, there will be more and more stagings of Wagner's operas, like the Met's *Walküre* (in which Estes was also to be cast as Wotan), that will make the case for the triumph of Wagner's art over his politics. At the same time, will there be more and more productions, like the Chéreau, that will make clear and render potent the inextricability of Wagner's politics from his art?

On another occasion Manfred was waxing ecstatic and without qualification about a recording of soprano Germaine Lubin, the Nazi collaborationist and sympathizer better known in our time as Régine Crespin's mentor. (What did Crespin have to say about Lubin's politics? I hope it was less superficial than her public dismissal of homosexuals as backstage pests, a remark her biggest fan, Peter G. Davis, declined to criticize.) Ten years ago, I would have enthusiastically joined in this conversation, completely and comfortably separating Lubin the artist from her shadowy past. Following a performance of Strauss's *Elektra* by the Vienna Philharmonic at Carnegie Hall, Manfred and I had coffee. He had been diagnosed with AIDS and was having ongoing substance abuse problems, neither of which he'd been able to face. Instead of talking about what was dominating him, he completely dominated our conversation with a manic recital of opera gossip (Barbara Bonney's Sophie, Josephine Barstow's new recital, etc., etc.), which wove itself into a full-blown made scene of tacit pain and escapism.

Shadowy. Shadow is a Jungian concept that refers to one's dark side. In Jungian psychology, one is urged not to negate or eliminate the shadow in one's life, but to acknowledge, accept and even rejoice in it. At least, that's what I understood from the few programs I attended at the Jung Foundation here in New York. The first of these featured two films about Jung: 'The Story of Carl Jung', which was narrated by Laurens van der Post, and 'Times

Remembered', a BBC interview with Ruth Lee Bailey, Jung's house-keeper and mistress in his later years. 'Jung would never say always about anything', Miss Bailey observed, 'because he was always open-minded.' It's Miss Bailey who made the point about the Jungian concept of accepting and integrating the shadow in one's life. When asked, 'Do you believe in God?', Jung, whose father was a minister, told van der Post, 'I don't *believe*. I *know*!' The film opened with a symbol: a red cross surrounded by yellow and red flames. In the background throughout the film was the Grail theme from *Parsifal*.

In his writing, Jung feels little or no pain about anti-Semitism. It's simply not there. Like Richard Strauss, he may have helped a few Jews and may not have been the most ardent collaborationist, but neither, clearly, was he passionately anti-Nazi. I mean, it's Jung's shadow that still lingers around the awarding of the Bollingen Prize for Poetry to Ezra Pound in 1949, an event that – OK – did not *directly* involve Jung or the Jung Foundation. On the other hand, it's Jung who wrote a letter that was one of the foundational events in the evolution of the spiritual program of substance abuse recovery that saved and has continuously renewed my own life.

In my twelve-step recovery program, however, my conviction and faith are continuously bombarded by my suspicion that I'm involved with a phenomenon, of not a discrete sect, of Christianity, that I'm still trying to fulfill my childhood fantasy of being Christian, that I don't and never really can, belong. The program's preamble states that it 'is not allied with any sect, denomination, politics, organization or institution, does not wish to engage in any controversy, neither endorses or opposes any causes', but not that it is not allied with any religion. And what is *de facto* the official prayer of the program, the Serenity Prayer, is taken from a longer, specifically Christian poem by Reinhold Niehbur. Something like seventy-five per cent of our meetings take place in churches. Many members are not practicing Christians, but many are and some of those are zealots. And as a newly recovering Irish-Catholic member who probably read earlier published chapters of these memoirs seemed to take delight in pointing out to me recently, there are fewer gay and lesbian Jews in these programs, proportionately, than you'd expect to find in view of their numbers in the greater Greenwich Village and Chelsea populations, a phenomenon that may or may not reflect a lower incidence of alcoholism and drug addiction among Jews. I doubt that his observation is accurate – certainly not for Overeaters Anonymous. (Is *this* observation anti-Semitic?)

And my former sponsee, Percy, the son of a small-town Southern Baptist minister, from a family he (Percy) characterized as 'poor white trash', even though his parents were both educated, was he not anti-Semitic? If he was, and to whatever extent he was, it was largely from ignorance. There was so much he simply didn't know. How painful it is to realize you have to keep trying to teach the lessons of history to each new generation. Percy has to work to see things from a Jewish perspective, but he can be very good at it because of his exceptional intelligence and profound sensitivity to homophobia. Once I tried to explain the kind of pain I experience when I hear unqualified adoration of Wagner. In a perfect analogy. Percy suggested it was similar to the kind of pain he and I experience, as gay people, when there's unqualified praise for Cardinal O'Connor or Pope John Paul II. Having said that, however, Percy, probably unconsciously, was provocative in subsequent discussions of Jung and Wagner, going so far as to joke that James Levine looked like Alberich after I had educated him about Wagner's caricaturing of the Jews as Nibelungs. This upset me, all the more so because the same observation, dripping with self-loathing, had more than once occurred to me.

A temporary split developed between Percy and me, and was specifically over the question of whether or not Jung was anti-Semitic. When I confessed my concerns to Percy after attending a series on Jungians, Freudians and anti-Semitism at the Jung Foundation in 1989, he was defensive. For Percy, a New Age vegetarian who attends Radical Fairy retreats and flirts with astrology, Jung is a cultural hero. The question of anti-Semitism in Jung and Jung's defensiveness was likewise at the heart of Freud's split from Jung, which was marked with the publication of Jung's book, *The Psychology of the Unconscious*. Recapitulating this conflict that has pursued Jews throughout their history, Percy and I began to recognize the presence of some as yet inarticulatable level of irreconcilable differences between us. Soon, we decided to stop calling each other sponsor and sponsee. We disengaged, but have remained connected, often very lovingly so, through the program that saved and continues to save both our lives. For us to resent each other, not to love each other, is, at a very fundamental level, a life and death issue for both of us. Percy is his own person now and has gone his own way. He may even find himself allied with some forces, ideologies or politics that are inimical to me, as Jung found himself at least passively allied with some forces, ideologies or politics that were inimical to Freud. So be it. But for better or worse, Percy is still my family, just as psychiatry, psychoanalysis and psychotherapy remain the greater family that keeps Jung connected with Freud, just as music is the greater family that keeps Wagner connected with Mahler and von Karajan with Klemperer.

Meanwhile, another sponsee, who is Irish-Lithuanian and whose scars as the child of homophobic alcoholics are as bad as I've seen, wears yellow shoes that remind me of the San Francisco Opera production, directed by Francis Ford Coppola, of Gottfried von Einem's opera, *The Visit of the Old Woman* (based on the Dürrenmatt play), in which the townsfolk signal their acquiescence to fascism by wearing the yellow shoes the protagonist has distributed as gifts. After more than a year, he had another slip, and by mutual agreement, he got a new sponsor. Michael G., my newest sponsee – actually we're 'co-sponsoring' each other (is this something we invented?) – is the son of a Lithuanian-Jewish father who survived the Holocaust and a German Catholic mother who converted to Judaism and was a PFLAG (Parents and Friends of Lesbians and Gays) activist in a small town where being in any way supportive of gays took life-and-death courage. Her death this summer hit Michael hard. In his grief, Michael, who told me there's now a twelve-step program for children of Holocaust survivors, is battling a clinical depression, which is not helped by his uninterrupted quest to come to grips with what the Lithuanians did to his father, his father's people, and, after the war, to his father's property and memory. Michael's story, which he is slowly putting together as a film documentary, as well as in poems and other writings, is not for the faint-hearted.

The latest commentary on twelve-step recovery programs is

to be found in Philip Roth's *Operation Shylock*, in which the protagonist has an affair with a 'recovering anti-Semite'. At first, the
notion of 'Anti-Semites Anonymous' seems hilarious. Vintage
Philip Roth. Bill Hoffman laughed when I told him about it, and
later thought up an even better one – 'Jews Anonymous' (for people
who were addicted to Jews) – for his play *Riga*. Arnie also laughed,
but not Paul Asman. 'It's too real', he said, and he's right. The
concept of prejudice as compulsion/addiction may be witty (notwithstanding that there are now over two hundred different twelve-
step recovery programs – you name it, there's a twelve-step program for it), but it's also brilliantly incisive. Prejudice *is* a spiritual
ailment and it *does* have the cardinal features of a compulsive
disorder.

Germany was reunited on November 9, which is also *Kris-
tallnacht*. Henceforth, on the same day the world commemorates
the official beginning of the Nazi persecutions of the Jews, the
Germans will be also celebrating the reunification of their country.
So much for German contrition, although neither Arnie nor Bill
Hoffman thinks this coincidence necessarily represents an inten-
tional slight.

In his review of *The Ghosts of Versailles* for *Opera
Monthly*, Erick Neher wrote, 'And anyone who still believes the
French Revolution was simply a righteous uprising of oppressed
peasants against evil aristocrats probably still longs for the good
old days before the Berlin Wall fell.' Erick had read my 1985 essay,
'Confessions of a Jewish Wagnerite', and I had read excerpts of his
Master's thesis on Wieland Wagner. While we both had critical
observations, there was mutual respect and we seemed to have
developed a friendship, albeit a more vocational than entirely
natural one, like that between Bruce-Michael and me. As in the
latter relationship, there seemed to be some level of strain over
political perspectives which peaked with the publication of my
interview with Gottfried Wagner in *Opera Monthly*. Why? Was it
because Dr Wagner denounced the Wagner societies – where Erick
had been invited to repeat his lecture on Wieland Wagner's Bayreuth – as bastions of political conservatism if not overt anti-Semitism? During this period, our communications ground to a halt, but

resumed when *Twilight of the Golds* came to New York. The play, by Erick's close friend, Jonathan Tolins, engages some of the same subjects with which these memoirs are preoccupied – homosexuality, Judaism, genetics and Wagner – with situations, comedy and metaphors that are as theatrically compelling as they are incisive. I know of no other work that so successfully exposes liberal 'tolerance' of homosexuality. But what most intrigued me was the ease with which *Twilight* acknowledges but then moves beyond the ethical and moral questions that flicker around Wagner in our time. Whatever one's answers, the play does suggest one perspective I've never doubted: that Wagner is here to stay. Can the same be said for the Jews?

One thing you won't find in Wagner's epochally anti-Semitic essay *Jewry in Music*: subtextual analysis of Meyerbeer's opera, *Les Huguenots*. It all came together for me when I saw a documentary called *Weapons of the Spirit* about a French town that protected Jews during the war. The entire town was united in this endeavor to an extraordinary degree. Why? Well, as it turns out, they were all descended from Huguenots, who had themselves experienced extreme religious persecution. So Meyerbeer's *Les Huguenots* wasn't just a mindless spectacle after all. It was subtextually concerned with serious, pressing realities – in the composer's life and society. (I guess this makes me a deconstructionist.) The film was introduced by Bill Moyers who had been the target of Jewish criticism a year or so earlier for his association with Joseph Campbell, alleged to have been an anti-Semite by Brenda Gill in the *New York Review of Books*.

Several years ago, on a visit to New York from God's country, where he now lives and teaches, Howard called and we got together. He was taking advantage of a frequent-flier discount, he said, to see Vanessa Redgrave in *Orpheus Descending* and *The Dybbuk* in a film version from pre-World War II Poland. I had already seen the former and joined him for the latter. Deconstructing the film later (à la Eve Sedgwick) as really being about the repressed homosexuality of the two friends, Howard observed, 'It's amazing how the Jewish mind works'. He was referring to the inability of the characters to express their affection for each other.

Was this as grossly anti-Semitic as it sounds, I asked myself (so I esked meinself ..., as Arnie might quip). Let's see. We talk about the British mind, the American mind, the Christian mind, I guess, but we often get into trouble when we start talking about female or black or gay mentality. Howard, a classic post-modernist whose years in the English Department at Yale coincided with those of Paul De Man, and who was in analysis for many years, had a Freudian slip, I think. But what did the slip mean?

The blur in my relations with Howard began to thicken when I met Daniel Zvi Margalioth, an English professor doing postdoctoral work on what was more or less Howard's subject: ethics and moral character in the literature of the late nineteenth century. Daniel's Ph.D. thesis for Columbia was entitled 'Taste and Morality: A Study of the Works of Henry James'. In genuine if inconclusive contrast to Howard, Daniel was deeply concerned with the casual-to-virulent anti-Semitism in European literature and sensibility that so preoccupied George Eliot and motivated her great novel, *Daniel Deronda*. I never heard Howard express a single word of concern about anti-Semitism in his beloved Dickens, our beloved Wagner, or elsewhere. On the other hand, during the years when we were closest, I never expressed any such concerns either. Quite the contrary, for my own anti-Semitism was deeply internalized – not so unlike that of Proust, to whom Howard introduced me.

Daniel was born and reared in Israel. The only son of Holocaust survivors, he was excommunicated from the family when he told them he was gay. Like the proverbial dog returning to the master who mistreats him, however, Daniel remained steadfastly loyal to his family and to being Jewish, an identity and awareness that motivated his life's work in comparative literature. Having read 'Confessions of a Jewish Wagnerite' when it was published in *Christopher Street*, he sounded deliriously enthusiastic when he sought me out. Literally delirious, for as it turns out, Daniel had a serious speech disorder, the consequence of his having been fag-bashed with a brick several months earlier. Alternatively, the impediment was due to HIV encephalopathy. It would take several more months before the latter would be clearly diagnosed as progressive. Communication with Daniel, nearly impossible to start with, rapidly deteriorated to nothing. His writing was as impaired as his speech, but we kept making the effort because he had such important things to impart: mainly, to confirm my feelings about the deadly seriousness and ongoing danger of Wagner's anti-Semitism. I became a care partner during the little time that remained. Daniel's body was shipped back to Israel. On our trip there that summer, Arnie and I visited his sister, with whom he'd remained in contact, and his grave, on which we placed stones from the closest members of his extended family. The memorabilia that were given to me by Terry Sandholzer, his life partner who also recently died of AIDS, were a copy of the Ph.D. thesis on Henry James, volume XX of a twenty-five-volume collection of the writings of George Eliot, Eliot's *Romola* and Thomas Carlyle's three-volume study, *The French Revolution*, which I subsequently gave to Bill Hoffman, a co-believer in coincidences, in tribute to his magnificent opera.

The trip to Israel was Arnie's first and my second. Arnie, who isn't religiously observant, was so moved by the experience of setting foot in Israel that he wept during the disembarkation in Tel Aviv, a stopover on the way to our first destination, Cairo. I, too, was on the verge of tears, but over less spiritual matters. Our luggage was lost. It was Ramadan, the Moslem high holiday, and all stores were closed, but Arnie made do with a T-shirt and I managed to find a *djellaba*, which I wore with considerable aplomb until our luggage was returned to us toward the end of our stay in Egypt, on our return from Luxor. As with the satisfaction I had derived from 'passing' for being straight, Christian, Italian, etc., my internalized anti-Semitism was very pleased with the notion of appearing to be Arabic. My ethnic sensibility was awakened, however, when we visited the old Ben Ezra synagogue, the oldest (and only?) Jewish temple in Cairo. Our guide, who gave endless lectures about every other site on this tour of the older parts of the city, had nothing to say about the temple, which we discovered in the midst of the old quarter and which was either being restored or torn down (we couldn't tell which), or about whatever Jewish community may be left in Cairo. Not a word. At the Islamic Art Museum, I inquired about the 'swastikaoid' (I didn't use that word) patterns in some of the rugs. With the graciousness we encountered everywhere in Egypt, he explained that it was an ancient symbol

228: *Confessions of a Jewish Wagnerite*

that had no more to do with modern usages than parallel images of crosses in Islamic art had to do with Christianity. At Karnak and Luxor, I asked our guide if he knew anything about ancient attitudes toward homosexuality. Clearly uncomfortable, he said he knew only that Akhnaten, the pharaoh of monotheism, was said to have been homosexual. Back at our hotel, Arnie was having a crisis with an ointment that had leaked, turning the contents of his toilet kit into a gooey mess. 'A romantic comment on our domesticity,' I proposed. As always, there was the instant comeback: 'So look what the other half of this romantic marriage is doing – lying in a dress, like a mummy, staring into space.' Bitch.

In Luxor we visited the ruins of the great temples, the monumentality of which nothing can prepare you for. In one of the walls of Karnak, a sculpted pharaoh kept watch over his various slave populations, each represented in small tiles facing him from the opposite wall. Among these, of course, were the Hebrews. I felt a stab of identification when this was pointed out by the guide and Arnie. Even when you already know something, some unanticipated way of encountering it may make it real, felt, in a way or to a degree that is new. Do African–Americans feel this way when they visit the old slave quarters in Charleston? What makes the pain so acute in both situations, even more than the fact of the slavery, is that it facilitated the creation of splendid edifices (the Egyptian temples and southern plantations) that are widely regarded as pinnacles of civilization and culture. Yet again – as always? Yes (alas) – the triumph of art over politics. Even the Nazi and Stalinist propaganda art that is currently denigrated as such will eventually be revered, like Greek and Roman art (both societies were military and imperialist states and both were slaveowners), for its quality, with less and less in the way of qualification. No one will care. But then I have to ask: do I care about whatever slave labor may have been involved when I look at the Parthenon? Do I reject the Coliseum because of the Roman persecutions of the early Christians? Do Christians?

On the way to the Valley of the Queens, our guide told us about Queen Hatshepsut – 'Queen Hotchickensoup', he said. Very charming, but does he say that for all the tourists, I wondered, or only the ones he perceives to be Jewish, with the ultimate aim of

augmenting his tips. That's racist and paranoid, I decided. It's also
the stuff of Jewish humor. That is, someone will say something
innocuous, friendly or complimentary and you immediately, reflexively question it. For example, what did the Jewish mother say
when she saw her son wearing one of the two shirts she gave him
for his birthday? Answer: 'So you didn't like the other one?' (from
Dan Greenburg's *How to Be a Jewish Mother*).

Jewish humor can be very dark. Like Arnie, Morris, his
father, had diabetes. Eventually, over many years and many procedures, Morris lost both his legs, a dread Arnie must continuously
experience with regard to his own future. When he and his brother
went to purchase the coffin, Arnie recalled, he wondered if they
would realize that his father would only occupy half its length, and
if not, would he then slide back and forth inside as the casket was
moved about, possibly causing it to disgorge its contents in a gro-
tesque accident in the middle of the funeral? The image of his own
father in this ridiculous situation is as black as Arnie's humor gets.
Apart from the one reference to 'persons with death', I don't
remember Arnie ever cracking a joke about Holocaust victims.

Arnie told me this story when we were on the most recent of
our trips to Washington to see the AIDS quilt. We were both
convulsed with laughter when I suggested how funny Vito would
have found it. Vito, whose spirit is still so with us. At the quilt, with
its eight or nine panels memorializing him, and his name remembered by more speakers than any other, our laughter seemed a
distant memory, as did our bitterness at the time of the funeral over
Arnie's brother's refusal to allow Vito, whom he knew to have
AIDS (which he believed might be contagious, notwithstanding my
physicianly reassurances), to attend, and the rabbi's refusal, likewise at Arnie's brother's insistence, to acknowledge Arnie's life-
partnership with me. (If everyone else were going to be identified as
husband and wife, Arnie wanted us at least to be designated as
partners.)

Rather naively driving around the Arab quarter of Jerusalem, which was virtually deserted at night, Arnie and I looked for a
restaurant for dinner. The one we found was decent, but we were
the only patrons there. On the wall above our table there was a
painting of an old Arab, bent over by the weight of the bundle on

his back. On closer inspection the bundle turned out to be a fish-eye view of Jerusalem. Then we discovered that the restaurant wasn't as empty as we'd thought. The loud laughter we kept hearing turned out to be a large party of German tourists dining in another room. When Arnie asked the waiter for a soft drink and was offered Sprite, he got momentarily nervous, thinking that perhaps the waiter had said 'spite'. Back in our room that night, we felt warm and secure and happy as we lit a little sabbath candle (something we've never done before or since) and watched Diana Ross falling in love with Billy Dee Williams in *Lady Sings The Blues* on Israeli television.

Though we don't light sabbath candles, we do light Yahrzeit candles – for deceased parents and for Vito – and Hanukkah candles. Last season, I bought a 'Happy Hanukkah' display to add to the Christmas decorations at one of my clinics. It was the first time in my adult life I'd ever shopped for such a thing, and it turned out to be an adventure. Considering how many Jews there are in New York, you'd think the selection would be great, but that wasn't the case. On the contrary, the paucity of items and their drabness were truly eye-opening. The other interesting aspect of this little adventure is that I did not seek to be reimbursed by the clinic, as if I'd done something to be ashamed of.

On our trek north, just outside of Jerusalem a rock the size of an orange smashed against our rent-a-car window. Because we weren't immediately able to exchange the car, something like a third of our views of Israel were through a spiderweb of cracked glass. Although this trip predated the Intifada, we were told the media hadn't reported that several tourists had been killed when their rented cars were firebombed. On the news, there were reports of the Klaus Barbie trial, which had just opened in Lyons, and the wholesale torture and executions of sex deviates in Iran.

Throughout Israel we dined on St Peter's fish, from the Sea of Galilee. Each time, my unconscious would compare this nomenclature with the term Jewfish, which had caused me such anxiety when I first encountered it – 'Jewfish steak'– on the menu at Shorty's, the Key West eatery. (Today, Shorty's is a T-shirt emporium owned and operated by Israelis.) Eight years later, the year after the trip to Israel, the Jewfish loomed much larger in my consciousness when I traveled to the Cayman Islands for a scuba certification course. The group I was with was made up mostly of Texans. The references to 'Jewfish' were ubiquitous, from the postcards in the shops to the smirking asides of the dive instructors. Even the popular guide to reef fishes by Idaz Greenberg used the term. When I saw that, I began to wonder if I were being paranoid again. Is 'Jewfish' any different from 'St Peter's fish' or 'monkfish'? Both make fun of appearances, but 'Jewfish' would seem to be referring to physical characteristics (large lips, demeanor, girth, etc.). Certainly, that was the case on the Caymans trip when the dive instructor told us about 'Sweetlips', the lone and very tame giant grouper among the denizens of an old marijuana wreck called the *Oro Verde*. Everyone laughed at the cuteness of the name, except me. After the dive, a Texas minister in our group gave the fish a new name: Judas. So contemptuous did this seem that I confronted him. Later, at dinner, his wife made a point of loudly talking about the JEWFISH everyone had seen as she and her table partners walked past me. Was this the same woman who sang 'That's a moray (*amore*)' when her husband told everyone about Gumby, the spotted moray eel that lives in the wreck and is so tame you can pet him (her?)?

The next day I calmly asked the senior instructor, who had advanced degrees in marine biology, about the term. He pointed out that in Australia they call this fish 'potato cod'. He couldn't see that 'Jewfish' was an ethnic slur. But this was the same instructor who said nothing when I complained to him several days later about our boatswain who, in a radiophone altercation with a nearby vessel, had suddenly slammed down his receiver and screamed, in a thick Texas accent, '*Fuckin'* NIGGERS!'

On another dive, the minister's wife asked me, with that utterly false Southern sweetness from my worst nightmare memories of growing up in Georgia, if I were single. 'Yes', I told her. I didn't say I was gay or that I lived with my lover, Arnie Kantrowitz. Where was my minority identity, courage and conviction? In the presence of these reptiles, I regressed to being that terrified child in Macon in the early 1950s, afraid of people and afraid to tell the truth. Meanwhile, the Texas yahoos weren't the only homophobes in the Caymans. When the gay RSVP cruise stopped over in Grand Cayman – the drug-money capital of the world – the following year, the headlines screamed: POUFTERS INVADE! And in case the poufters didn't get the message, RSVP was officially asked not to come back.

'Of course "Jewfish" is a racial slur', Rudi reassured me, 'but I wouldn't let a few creeps bother me.' I hadn't seen German–American Rudi Weiblisch, my closest friend in medical school, in years. Among the earliest gay punks, he'd show up for classes – often late, making an entrance – blowing large pink bubbles of gum and usually wearing the notorious Levi jacket he'd lined with thrift-shop mink and studded with a hundred patches from leather bars. It was the early 1970s and we were sisters. But Rudi never became very interested in or even sympathetic to the whole business of gay liberation and we drifted apart. Now he had AIDS and we arranged to rendezvous for the scuba course.

The last time I had seen him was in New York, when he was shopping for a second residency in psychiatry. Following medical school, he'd trained in pathology with the navy in California. Despite the new interest in psychiatry, which he would eventually practice in California prisons, he remained politically conservative and disconnected from civil rights and AIDS struggles. In psychiatry, he was less interested in the debates about homosexuality than in new age spiritualism and the teachings of its founding father, Carl Jung, who had become a guru. In New York we don't take Shirley Maclaine too seriously. In Southern California, things are very different.

Of course, my growing awareness of Rudi's interest in Jung and new age philosophy, his Southern California materialism, political conservatism and solid German ethnicity, made me uncomfortable, but Rudi had twelve-stepped me (as we say when a member tries to bring another addict into recovery) when I was bottoming-out. In addition to his having been my closest friend in medical school, he had helped save my life.

On Grand Cayman, I hardly recognized Rudi when we met at the hotel. In Chicago, he was this little slip of a thing with, as I always teased him, tiger-skin hair (proto-Madonna bleached blond with sloppy black roots). Now, he still had the blond hair, without the black roots and cut very short, skinheadoid, and he was twice his former size. Steroids. I didn't have to ask, but I was curious as to how this fit in with his recovery from substance abuse. He was still abstinent, he claimed, but no longer attended meetings.

Like Mishima, Rudi was one of these feminine gay men who wanted to be the opposite of who they *really* wanted to be when they were children. As little boys, both were cross-dressers. In adulthood, both wanted to be the kind of man they desired sexually and that society always told them they themselves should and could be. That's who I was seeing. Despite several serious accidents requiring hospitalizations and surgery, Rudi drove one of the largest Harley-Davidsons made. His shoes were for trench warfare. It must have taken a half hour to get them on or off. And his T-shirts were usually these super-macho things with bulldogs and bears. Otherwise he was the same person with the same sense of humor: 'It's nice to be in a place where a sign that says "Free Margarita" has nothing to do with politics', he quipped. For a moment we were giggly sisters again, until I thought about just what it was we were laughing about.

We talked a lot. He asked about my writing, which I tried to explain. We talked about Jung and Germany and Hitler. Like AIDS, Rudi said, he accepts what happened in Germany. That's the only way he can deal with it. 'But that's *not* the way to deal with it!' I shrieked. 'Resistance and protest, politics and involvement, *that's* the way to deal with a crisis, with AIDS, with the Nazis, with any kind of injustice or disaster!' But the truth is that we were both right. Every day I pray for acceptance of 'the things I cannot change' (a line from the Serenity Prayer), 'courage to change the things I can, and wisdom to know the difference'. Among the things I cannot change are World War II and what's already happened to Rudi.

Anxious to learn more about the derivation of 'Jewfish' – as it is so designated in Fort Lauderdale's new Science Museum – I did some research. Upon discovering that the term was first used in Elizabethan England to describe fish favored by Jews for dietary reasons, I wrote to the *New Yorker* to propose a paper on the odyssey of the term in the English-speaking world. The proposal became the quickest rejection I've ever received. So there's no paper about the Jewfish, only memories, the strongest of which is my final encounter with Sweetlips, the lonely custodian of the *Oro Verde*, who was so close to me I could reach out and pet him.

The encounter was transcendant, and I all but forgot about the graffiti on the hulk of the wreck beneath us, which included a Star of David and, nearby, a square with a cross inside (like a window with four panes), a symbol I've often created myself in efforts to transform a swastika that can't be erased (like the one in the McBurney elevator), painted over, or otherwise obscured. Like Jacques Cousteau, the Fort Lauderdale museum also characterizes these fish as 'gentle giants' that have been hunted to the brink of extinction.

Sometime in the late 1980s I ran into the gay, Jewish psychiatry resident who was assigned to me during my hospitalization for depression in 1983. Allen had just returned from rural Minnesota and Wisconsin, where he had spent two years practicing in fulfillment of a government-sponsored scholarship agreement. Knowing the extent to which coming to grips with being Jewish and anti-Semitism was a catalyst for my depression, he confided how isolated and uncomfortable he had been there. 'The anti-Semitism is so thick', he said, 'you can cut it with a knife.' My thoughts flashed scenes from *God's Country*, Louis Malle's documentary about the roots of anti-Semitism in the northern American states where Allen worked – where my father lived much of his early life (in St Paul, Minnesota) and where I did my first two years of college (University of Wisconsin at Madison). Then I remembered that I had relatives in this region – farmers on my mother's side, my father's sister's family, people I met once but never knew. What became of them? Cousin Donnie, I heard, changed his name from Zwigoff to Carter, just as some of Arnie's relatives changed their names. Do we still have our 'Cousins Club'? How much of my estrangement from my biological family stems from my being gay? How much from being Jewish? How much is just me?

At dinner the following week, Allen had more to confide. Since finding out he was antibody positive, he'd been unable to curtail his baths attendance and masochistic sexual preferences. His self-esteem couldn't have been lower. We talked about pornography among safer sex options. Like Arnie and me, Allen had begun to notice how much of American gay porn is ethnocentric and how little of that ethnocentricity is ever Jewish. But perhaps this just reflects subpopulation size – a good explanation that left none of us convinced.

Ethnicity as hotness is a similarly prominent feature of casual and trade sex. Often, it's one of the first things asked. In my own case, I've consistently been mistaken for Italian or Spanish. In all the encounters over the years, no one ever asked me if I were Jewish, just as no one, except Arnie, ever told me I looked Jewish. In these kinds of encounters, of course, you want to satisfy your partner's fantasy. But as time has passed and I've become more self-aware, it's increasingly difficult for me to lie about who and what I am, even for and in fantasy. Saying I'm Italian is a little like saying I'm married and have kids. It may be what turns the other person on, but acting out the latter fantasy enlists homophobia, just as acting out the former involves anti-Semitism. So one day I made it with a hot Latin-appearing man who identified himself proudly as Cuban–American. When I similarly asserted myself as Jewish–American, his face stiffened slightly. We made arrangements to see each other again, but he never showed. That slight change of facial expression or tone of voice when the word Jew or Jewish comes out is something I'm getting used to, but there are plenty of occasions when the other person turns on to my self-assertiveness and honesty about who and what I am. Or what I've become – proudly ethnocentric?

New Year's Eve at Victor Bumbalo's. On his bathroom wall, there's a poster of an Italian soccer team. Would Arnie and I ever think of displaying a poster of an Israeli team? Perhaps the one that was massacred at the Munich Olympics? Revising *Medical Answers about AIDS* for GMHC, I worked with a medical editor from McGraw-Hill. By coincidence, I'd recently met one of her supervisors whose name I couldn't remember. 'Ellen something', I fumbled. 'She has very black hair and ...' 'Oh, yes', she said, 'and she's very Jewish looking.' One says so and so looks very German or Italian, so there's no issue with saying someone looks very Jewish, is there?

No, except that a principal manifestation of anti-Semitism is the preconception of Jews as physically unattractive (the stereotype of the 'dirty Jew' – e.g., Fagin). At some level, of course, I always had my own sense of physical repulsion as a central feature of anti-Semitism, but I remember when it first knocked at my unconscious. I was visiting Kostas, a wealthy gay Greek/Turkish–American friend in Boston who was waxing ecstatic about how beautiful Greek men are. 'I'd say Greeks, Turks and Italians are the most beautiful men in the world', he proposed. 'What do you think?' 'Well', I hesitated, for my three, 'I guess I'd choose ... uh ... the Oriental Jews of Israel, Italians and Greeks or Hispanics.' Kostas was nonplussed by the reference to Oriental (Sephardic) Jews (he didn't know enough about Jews to be conversant with words like 'Sephardic', 'Ashkenazic', or 'Hassidic', even though his sister was about to marry a Jew). To him, Jewish meant an Eastern European stereotype, and he seemed amazed that anybody's reality, even Jewish reality, could be so far off as to rank Jews among the world's most beautiful people. (Actually, my anti-Semitic self was almost as surprised as Kostas at my response.) It was as if I'd said that marigolds are as beautiful as orchids.

Nothwithstanding this incident, I didn't really perceive that Kostas, like Nicky, our mutual friend and lawyer, was anti-Semitic until much later. After all, Kostas seemed to like his brother-in-law to be, who was Jewish, as was Heshy, one of his closest friends from childhood. And I'd had good, mutual sex with both Kostas and Nicky. But Heshy once warned me that Kostas, whose fortune was inherited under dubious circumstances and who liked to sneer about people who believe fortunes are made by savings, was anti-Semitic. That finally became indisputable when, over dinner at Maison Robert, as he and Nicky shared a toast *à deux*, Kostas casually observed that a loud Jewish clientele was invading some of the finer New York restaurants. Stunned by the remark, I was overcome with reflexive pain and fear and said nothing.

That was when it became conscious. On that trip – I was living in New York and visiting Boston for a medical conference – I stayed with Nicky. One night we got very drunk and he told me hair-raising stories of the anti-Semitism of his Catholic upbringing. What was especially chilling is that they were neutrally described, sometimes even with relish. There was no condemnation or judgment. And there was another confession. The lawyer he'd arranged years earlier, at my request, to consult with my sister regarding her divorce and child-custody battle was grossly misogynist. And then I realized the connection. Beyond the anti-Semitism, Nicky, who was Albanian, was resentful of my sister's strongly socialist politics, as I had characterized them. What I finally came to realize after I'd moved to New York is that there was this huge subtext to my relationships with these people, a subtext I was only just beginning to read.

On a recent getaway to Montreal, I met an Episcopalian Irish-American gay man who told me about his best friend, a Jew who gets upset when someone says so and so is a Jew instead of saying that person is Jewish. On television, there was an entertainment show spot about the reunion of Dean Martin and Jerry Lewis. When asked why they split up, Martin said: 'Well, I was the dago and he was the Jew, or was it the other way around?' What struck me most here was how the word Jew had the same ability to stigmatize as the epithet 'dago'. Of course, I'm curious to know more about how ethnicity influenced their friendship, artistic partnership and estrangement.

'Jew be swell ...' sings Googie Gomez in Terrence McNally's bathscapade, *The Ritz*. Arnie and I sing her refrain and make up others: 'Eat hahd to be Jew ...' 'But I only have eyes for JEW ...' In New York, ethnic cabbies are always listening to ethnic radio stations. This includes Israelis, but what about second or more generation Americans? What do we listen to? People of various ethnic backgrounds, including Jews, take palpable pride in their musical heritage, but not in all areas. This came to light at the recent Metropolitan Opera premiere of Janacek's *Káťa Kabanová*. As proclaimed in a banner callout, the Met's program notes by Yveta Synek Graff were mostly about how 'the glorious but difficult Czech language is gaining its rightful place on opera stages around the world'. Aside from the subject of supertitles and of opera in the original language versus that of the audience, could such a statement ever be made about opera in Hebrew or Yiddish? *Is* there an opera in Hebrew or Yiddish? For the anti-Semite (e.g., Wagner), this divorce of Jewish music from language is just one more proof of the innate falseness, the derivativeness of Jewish art.

On seeing Bernard Holland's impassioned and morally conscious *New York Times* review of Zimmerman's opera, *The White Rose*, about a tiny, very uncharacteristic youth movement of German resistance to the Nazis ('The [protagonists] were in fact an aberration', states Holland, 'in a Germany that overwhelmingly embraced Nazism'), Arnie asked 'Why aren't there any operas about the Nazis or World War II? It would seem to follow logically from *Die Götterdämmerung.*' Why indeed.

Rosa von Praunheim confided to me that his father died an unrepentant Nazi, as his mother, who lives with him, remains, but he couldn't understand why Arnie and I don't want to visit Germany. Likewise Vito Russo, who was otherwise so incredibly sensitive to anti-Semitism, couldn't comprehend Arnie's unwillingness, like my mother's, to ever set foot on German soil, where (as everywhere), Vito had so many friends and fans. Now, of course, no one would expect any Jew, or for that matter any non-German, to feel unreservedly comfortable about visiting Germany. After endeavoring to explain to Rosa the passage of my infatuation with so much of German culture (e.g., Wagner), I suddenly found myself saying something a lot less differentiated, from the gut: 'Do you have any idea how much we hate your father?' (As I'm writing this, my masochism selects 'Nibelungs' hate', Wagner's *leitmotif*, from the preconscious jukebox.) Almost immediately, we both agreed that while it was important to express that kind of anger, it was a lot more important to direct it affirmatively for change. Overall, I think I'd feel a lot more comfortable about Rosa – whose politics would seem to be in just the right place but who simultaneously acknowledges that while Germans may not deal enough with their past, they are nonetheless saturated with the Holocaust – if he'd direct a film about his parents. My suggestion was realized, at least in concept, in Rosa's next film, *Affengeil*, one short scene of which deals with his mother's reactions to the Jewish actress and Holocaust survivor, Lotte Huber, who lived with Rosa and his mother during the period of the filming. Perhaps Rosa's best film, *Affengeil* is a loving and moving tribute to Lotte, the star of so many of Rosa's films, and a documentary of her life in contemporary Germany. Despite a political subtext of enormous artistic power, however, there is virtually no direct confrontation of his mother with political questions or accusations.

Meanwhile, as I actually told Rosa, it's difficult for me, as the stereotypically (in German eyes) 'hypersensitive' Jew, not to worry that as counter-cultural German artists become more successful, more establishment, as seems to be happening, and as they age, they could go the way of all flesh and become more conservative. German nationalism and Catholic prejudices, inculcated in childhood, are not the easiest things to purge. Rosa countered by acknowledging that many of his Jewish friends were self-effacing to the point of masochism regarding their Jewishness and that a lot of Americans, non-Jewish as well as Jewish, project Nazi fantasies onto most Germans, including him. A related phenomenon we both agreed was especially sad is the spectacle of Jewish people participating in the kinds of prejudice that have historically been inflicted on them – e.g., against gay people by Hassidic Jews in Brooklyn; against the Turkish *gastarbeiter* in Germany by some conservative German Jews (according to Rosa, and I don't doubt it); against Palestinians and other Arabs by Jewish Israelis (nothing was said by either of us about the pervasiveness of virulent anti-Semitism and the demonizing of Israel in the Arab world). And Israel, he noted, is strongly supported by German conservatives. In addition to its truth, what I heard in this remonstrance was the standard German response to criticism by non-Germans – that the nations of the critics have been involved in atrocities too (e.g., was what America did in Viet Nam really any different, in essence, from what the Nazis did? Or as a prominent German actress recently told a friend, 'Are the neo-Nazi reactions to the asylum-seekers really any worse than the way New York treats its homeless?'). Rosa and I have had little contact since before the dismantling of the Berlin wall and the reunification of Germany, events Arnie and I were not able to celebrate. But having had this discussion with Rosa, and here, I feel I'm in that process of directing my anger for affirmative change we both agreed was so important.

My next trip to Florida was to Orlando, where I go once or twice a year for medical conferences and/or to pig out at Parliament

House, which may be the largest gay resort in the world. This time I met a local redneck alcoholic of mostly German extraction – very butchly handsome, alas – who couldn't have dropped his asides about 'sissies' and 'the coming new order' with more sweetness or courtesy. 'So what do you think of Germans?' he asked after he'd downed several beers at the local leather bar, which is decorated with an old red, white and black German flag with an iron cross. 'Well, what do you think of Jews?' I answered. The conversation had reached an impasse. I then tried to tell him a little bit about what the Nazis did to homosexuals, something I correctly surmised he knew nothing about. When we met again a few days later, I asked him if he knew what the pink triangle was. He said he recognized it as a gay symbol, but didn't know what it meant. My explanation completely disarmed him, and left me with a new appreciation of the depth of meaning and power of this symbol of our oppression.

On that recent sojourn to Montreal, my evolving Jewish sensibility likewise asserted itself, in dialogue with an Italian–American philosophy intellectual who knows a lot about Wagner and opera as well as with the Episcopalian gay Irish–American. The former, like Marcel, seemed Semitophilic. The latter, who was socially and professionally closeted but had just begun, in late middle age, to explore his homosexuality, and who casually mentioned that he worked on Middle East affairs for the United Nations as he reminisced about the wonderful years of his upbringing in pre-World War II Vienna (we were coincidentally seated next to one another at a performance of *The Merry Widow*, which he knew every word and note of), was possibly more like Egbert, a gentleman anti-Semite on the surface, a Nazi reptile underneath. 'And how do *you* feel about Vienna?' he asked after the performance over drinks. When I said that Vienna can't be a comfortable place for a Jew with any degree of consciousness, he was soothing: 'But so much of the best of what Vienna became was from the contributions of Jewish intellectuals and artists.' Albeit like water and rest between torture sessions, this seemed a lot more reassuring than his earlier, similarly cheerful observation, after I stated my ethnicity and retraced the various places I've lived, that I was the proverbial 'Wandering Jew', even if I was at that moment opening my mouth to utter this same phrase in reflexively self-effacing self-description. Not that the phrase 'Wandering Jew' is perforce derogatory, but hadn't it ever occurred to either of us that the phenomena of emigration and migration are as American as acculturation and as contemporary as the computer? Sensing that I might be dealing with another Egbert (burned once, on guard, if not paranoid, forever), playing a game whose rules I've come to understand a lot better but which I did not wish to play, I was anxious to get away before the gentleman, who had AOB (medicalese for alcohol on breath) during the performance, had any more to drink. But there was a big difference between the way I connected with him from the way I had connected with such types in the past. I wasn't really afraid. I was entirely there for the conversation we did have. Just as Arnie had recently confronted the anti-Semitism of a fashion designer who kept trying to reinsinuate himself in Vito's life long after the designer's affairette with Vito had ended and Vito had made it clear that he didn't want to maintain contact, I was self-affirming and articulate about my Jewish identity and experience, and about anti-Semitism. I knew who and what I might be dealing with and made a reasonable assessment that there was little to be gained from further interaction. When we parted, I suspect he was a lot more preoccupied with our discussion of the medical aspects and consequences of alcoholism, about which he knew next to nothing, than I was about the ubiquity of anti-Semitism at the United Nations, about which I already knew enough. As we bade farewell, I reassured him of my good will with a promise to send him my two volume study of homosexuality, sexuality and identity, which I guess I hadn't earlier found the opportunity to mention.

'Wandering Jew' is an expression I'd heard – and used – often enough, but knew nothing about. As with so many of the details of Jewish history and culture, in fact, as long as I could keep my distance from it – as long as it didn't too directly insult me – I didn't care to know more. I might even utilize it, unconsciously and masochistically, as a way of defusing anti-Semitism, the same way the Jewish treasurer of my twelve-step recovery group recently utilized a joke that invoked the stereotype of the Jew as a money-grubbing Shylock (an epithet my financially troubled brother likewise used to characterize a creditor, and a Jewish actress I knew from twelve-step meetings aimed at her landlord). In Dorothy Allison's *Bastard out of Carolina*, reference is made to the plant that is widely known in this country as 'The Wandering Jew'.

In the wake of the worst (yet) of the Farrakhan explosions, a black colleague casually compared herself to the plant – in conscious or unconscious efforts to aggravate or defuse tensions (I'm not sure which). As a florist once explained to me, the plant derives its name from the fact that its new shoots wander away in all directions as the old leaves die out. Although there are many variations, some of which portray the wanderer sympathetically, the basis of the legend – the story of the man who laughed at Christ's sufferings – is in fact profoundly anti-Semitic. For many years, I'd been using this self-deprecating phrase with regard to myself the same way so many Jews characterize themselves as 'JAPS' (Jewish-American Princes or Princesses).

There were other impressions in Montreal. My very generous and genial host there was George Leigh, the partner of my agent and good friend, Norman Laurila, in A Different Light (ADL) bookstores. I stayed at George's office/apartment near Place Saint Henri. In my bedroom, there was an ADL calendar called *Women of ADL*. For May 1991, the featured author was Dawn Levy, who characterizes herself in the little bio underneath her photo as of mostly Welsh and Scottish descent with Buddhist beliefs, and also as a Gemini. Not a word about anything that would suggest where her name comes from. Does she *look* Jewish? I asked myself, the way I've often asked whether so and so looks lesbian or gay. 'If it walks like a duck, talks ...' jokes my preconscious.

How desperate assimilationism can look. Arnie's Jewish friend and colleague, Ruth, has Christian icons (madonnas, saints, crucifixes, etc) covering her living room wall. Similarly, the Jewish owner of a gay guest house in Chelsea, one of the original GMHC volunteers, does paintings and collages dominated by crucifixes. During the period when I was in love with Andy Bullen, I, too, did a number of drawings with crosses, the largest of which is in our living room now, albeit covered over behind a bookcase. In those days, my favorite school of painting was the Italian Gothic, most of whose subjects were madonnas and saints. In this time frame, my politics were like my sister's, which were the politics of the majority of the Jewish leftists I have known: filled with internalized anti-Semitism in having no ethnic pride – even into the new era of multiculturalism – and virtually no awareness of the long history of the failure of assimilation to prevent discrimination and persecutions in socialist as well as in democratic systems; above all, no awareness of the *pain*, the *experience*, of anti-Semitism. In radical-left perspective, Jews are a sector of the privileged white majority. The absence of Jewish pride and consciousness of anti-Semitism as one of the most virulent prejudices ever known is so conspicuous here that the whole mechanism of what's going on is clearly exposed: in so ardently championing the indigent, especially persons of color, *while never giving our own experience of dispossession and persecution its due*, we were actually identifying with the aggressor. We weren't saying we identify with you because we're Jewish and we know what poverty and discrimination are, even if that's what was really motivating us. Notwithstanding that helping the poor and disadvantaged is written into Jewish law and is a principal goal and achievement of Jewish culture, we were saying we're bad and we owe you because we're white and privileged. I espoused my politics for the same reason I did my crucifix drawings. As an armchair Marxist, I was identifying with the disadvantaged for the same reason I simultaneously still wanted to be Christian. I didn't want to be Jewish.

Other bedroom reading in Montreal included some of George's porn, among which is a Boyd McDonald anthology Arnie and I both have our own copies of (*Skin* or *Flesh*) that contains a photo I hadn't noticed or remembered of a long-haired hunk with a swastika tattoo. Rereading my program notes for *La Veuve Joyeuse*, I learned that during the Nazi years, Lehar's works had to be performed omitting the names of his Jewish librettists, Leo Stein and Viktor Leon. It's also noted that Lehar's wife was 'of Jewish origin' (does this mean she converted to Catholicism?) and that she died in 1947 at their home in Switzerland, where they moved from Austrian Bavaria in 1945 (does this mean that she was allowed to stay with him in Nazi-occupied Austria until 1945?). In George's living room, there are about 30 LPs, one of which, *Synchronicity* with The Police (Sting), was sticking up above the others. The only other album cover so visible was Bette Midler's *Songs for the New Depression*. As I surveyed the premises, the preconscious jukebox played the 'Va Pensiero' chorus, the Hebrew prayer of deliverance from bondage, from Verdi's *Nabucco*, a canny (Ned Rorem's word for *Madame Mishima*) selection that may have been as stimulated by my having just read in the *Veuve Joyeuse* program that the Opéra de Montréal will mount *Nabucco* next season as by my paraconscious need at that moment to comment on five thousand years of Jewish history.

Walking around the McGill area I came upon a four-story rowhouse, Maison Khabad, the Lubavitch Youth Organization. In front of it was a large menorah, as high as the building. The windows on the first floor were cracked, and the glass door was half-shattered. Across the street from Sauna 456, where I spent much of my time in Montreal, there was a large graffito: 'Gassenhauer Skinheads' and next to it, in different but equally large script, 'Are Shitheads'. On the stretch of Sainte Catherine Avenue that is known as the gay village, there was another scrawl: 'Skins and Fags Unite'. Was this written by a gay fascist hoping to draw gays into the neo-Nazi movement, the way Ernst Roehm was involved in recruiting for the real thing? Probably. In total, I saw only a few swastikas and anti-Nazi graffiti, much less, overall, than I would have expected in a Catholic city with such visible Jewish and gay communities. On the last day of the trip, walking through the cruisy areas of park Mount Royal with the Italian-American philosophy intellectual, whom I'd met at the sauna, we came upon a large Jewish cemetery adjacent to what must be the wealthiest neighborhood in this very working-class city. We both remarked on the number of Jewish cemeteries that have been desecrated and wondered where it will happen next. Next turned out to be the grave of Ryan White, the youngster the public accepted as an 'innocent victim' of AIDS, but who fought discrimination and died a martyr for all.

Several weeks after returning from Montreal, I had dinner with Arthur, one of the shining lights of ACT UP and Queer Nation, an intellectual of considerable achievement, integrity and charm. We were joined in this conversation by my brother and his girlfriend, who recently edited an acclaimed anthology of Japanese short stories, and whose mother, the Holocaust survivor, lives in Montreal. When I mentioned the broken windows at Maison Khabad, Arthur observed that full Hassidic garb has changed little from the eighteenth-century European fashion it was modeled after. He then informed me that the Hassidic community in Montreal is large and very rich, that the women pay as much as $1,000 each for the multiple wigs many of them own (I didn't even know they shave their heads). Now, I can't help wondering whether the lore about the Hassidism is local or from the folks my friend still occasionally visits in God's country, where he was born and reared.

At a subsequent dinner, Arthur mentioned that his first therapist, like so many therapists twenty years ago, including mine, was homophobic. He also noted that she was 'a Zionist' and that she disliked his Arab boyfriend. Uncomfortable, I did not ask what he meant by 'Zionist' or whether he thought the therapist's dislike of the boyfriend was more homophobic than 'Zionist' or vice versa. (I don't think he considered the possibility that at least some of her discomfort, like that of so many Jews with Arabs, may have been in reaction to the extent and virulence of Arab hatred of Jews and Israelis. Did the boyfriend harbor no ill will toward Jews and Israelis?) Like so many of our brothers and sisters in ACT UP and Queer Nation, my friend's view of the Persian Gulf War was unqualifiedly critical of American participation: 'Bush bombed Iraq back into the Stone Age. Meanwhile, there's no domestic agenda' – i.e., 'Fight AIDS, not Arabs.' More recently Donna Minkowitz criticized the prejudice she says she encounters at ACT UP, fueled in no small measure by the ravings of its Jewish founder, that the Jews were passive victims of the Nazis (i.e., if only they'd had their act together ...).

Taking a while to get back to me to finalize the dinner plans he had claimed to be enthusiastic about, Erick Neher explained he'd been very busy looking for an apartment in Manhattan, how difficult it was, how impossibly expensive. The paranoid in me couldn't help wondering to what extent this communication about the high cost and unavailability of living space in New York was really about Jews and economics, and ultimately about where we stand on Wagner and anti-Semitism, the subject we were both struggling with and writing about from mutually respectful (at that time) by inevitably conflicting perspectives.

At dinner again, this time with a former agent, another Aryan–American, some of whose best friends are Jewish, whose participation in our community has been tremendous, and who complimented me on my tan: 'You Jews get such great tans.' I'd like to think that with his consciousness of my work on these memoirs (which he had declined to represent) and his awareness of Arnie's and my sensitivities about anti-Semitic generalizations and stereotypes, he was proving his affection with the boldness and implicit irony of his humor. Even so, I'm not sure he realized this was a generalization, that in fact many Jews of Eastern European extraction, Arnie for example, are fair-skinned and don't tan well. Just as I don't think he realized what a generalization it was when he likewise observed that Jews have a tendency to grieve – translation: to wail – louder and longer than other groups, He was referring to Arnie's immersion, within months of Vito's death, in a biographical memoir of his friendship with Vito. Meanwhile, the next day there was a *New York Times* story on how Romania is finally beginning to acknowledge that most of the hundreds of thousands of 'Romanian citizens' who were mass-murdered, often with enthusiastic Romanian complicity, were Jews. The point to make about Jews and grieving is not that Jews grieve too much, but that there is altogether too little grieving for Jews in most of the places where they have been most persecuted. I sent a copy of the article to the agent, which he did not acknowledge the next time we saw each other. For his birthday Arnie and I sent him a card that said, 'You people sure do age well', which we signed with love.

When I asked the United Nations gentleman about anti-Semitism in Ireland, he said that there's little because there are so few Jews in Ireland. He then noted that his close Jewish friend likewise found anti-Semitism in that observation. In Barcelona, two years ago, a gay man at one of the saunas said the same thing to me, but with a twist: 'The Jews were expelled from Spain in 1492. Now, we have no Jews. No Jews, no anti-Semitism.' (As in Japan, where there has never been a Jewish minority, where the Nazis found their strongest allies, and where grossly anti-Semitic literature boldly and broadly sells today?) The same gentleman, a

physician, joked about a group of Miami Jewish tourists who
seemed more disturbed by the opulence and cost of the old Gothic
cathedral than by its achievement. At which point I got very angry
and told the sonofabitch off. He hadn't realized I was Jewish and
seemed astounded at the idea of being accused of anti-Semitism. He
couldn't see the gross persistence of anti-Semitism in Poland, in
Austria, from the Vatican and throughout Europe even after most
of its Jews had been exiled and mass-murdered. Earlier that spring,
the Pope had visited Kurt Waldheim. Earlier that day I looked in
vain for some designation of the old Jewish quarter of the city, in
the area of the cathedral. In 1390 the ghetto was razed when the
Jews were blamed for the plague. 'No, there's not even a plaque',
the cathedral guide repeated, 'but there is a Jewish quarter that has
been restored in [the old Roman settlement of] Girona.' I read my
Spanish Tourist Office history guides, which downplay the expul-
sion, when they mention it at all. These are the kinds of things you
question and notice when you finally come to understand, accept
and *feel* that whatever else you are, whatever else you may want to
be, are trying to be, claim to be, however assimilated, you're still
Jewish.

It's anti-Semitism, not Israel or any institutional orthodoxy,
that defines being Jewish for most of the world. Among my dearest
and most assimilated Jewish friends is a very brilliant, humane,
distinguished and politically radical academic who believes, however, like his German–Jewish and Russian–Jewish ancestors, that
his assimilated status and sensibility leave him a little in common
with Jews as a minority, a designation that is appreciated as referring primarily to non-assimilated Jewish fundamentalists. He does
acknowledge his ethnicity in one context: his status as a privileged
white male, a 'JAP', a phrase he seemed to have no understanding
of as anti-Semitic when Arnie and I confronted him with it. His
denial of this ethnicity is such that on the one occasion he's written
about in which he came face to face with overt anti-Semitism, when
he was called a 'dirty Jew' by a closeted gay man, he thought it had
something to do with gay and class politics. As if the closet case
would automatically be free of anti-Semitism if he came to terms
with his gay identity, a fallacy I likewise used to believe in (e.g., if
you're self-accepting and openly gay, you must therefore automati-

cally be non-racist, non-sexist, non-ageist, non-classist, etc.). But what was most interesting about this incident was that the slur didn't hurt. There was no pain because there was no real Jewish identity at any level of consciousness. My friend didn't *feel* Jewish – i.e., it was *them* the closet case was talking about. I'm not one of those people.

In January of 1991, our wanderings brought Arnie and me to Hawaii. In Hana Maui two days into the war in the Persian Gulf, we ran into Hal Offen, Arnie's good friend of many years. Like Arnie, Hal speaks some Yiddish and is extrovertedly Jewish. ('Only an anti-Semite doesn't capitalize the language Yiddish', Arnie commented when he proofread an early version of this chapter.) The evening of our meeting, Hal came to our hotel and brought fruit he had just picked from the trees along the road – guava, papaya, mango and passion fruit, the dark, sticky, threatening but ambrosial core of which he somehow persuaded me to try. As always when Arnie and Hal get together, they told Jewish jokes and laughed loudly. Hal had a copy of the poem, 'The Night Before Christmas' in Yiddish. As their laughter became more raucous, I became very uncomfortable, the way I must have been when my parents and relatives spoke Yiddish within earshot of friends and neighbors in Georgia, the way Jews must have felt when hiding out in Nazi-occupied Europe. 'Sshhhhh!' I hissed. In the mirror on the opposite wall, I caught a glimpse of myself a moment before I realized it was me. The person in the mirror had a scowl on his face. It was the face of fear.

When I took my mother to Yom Kippur services in New York last year, she wished me a good holiday in a Yiddish of such clarity and fullness of tone that I realized this was a large aspect of herself she had suppressed throughout her life, an aspect I never really knew. I do recall her speaking Yiddish (her parents spoke almost no English) in my early childhood. In fact, one of my more vivid memories is of an incident that happened when we were visiting my mother's sister in Chicago. Mom and Aunt Lee were speaking Yiddish with each other, something about the children, when my sister suddenly shrieked at them: 'Quit your crazy Jew talk!' Aunt Lee slapped her and told her she must never say such a thing again.

Today, Masha is married to Bill, a retired electrical engineer from a conservative white middle-class Christian background. Judith, now divorced, was married to a socialist of WASP extraction (Judith says their irreconcilable differences were personal, not political). Masha is a semi-practicing Unitarian and has been involved, with Judith, in WILPF (Women's International League for Peace and Freedom). For many years Judith has worked with the Sister Cities project in Cambridge, Mass., where she lives with her son, Edmund. Cambridge's first sister city was Yerevan (there are now others), and Judith spent a lot of time and energy extolling (Soviet) Armenian culture from a background of knowing little about her own ethnicity, which, as she interpreted it, was Russian rather than Jewish. When Arnie suggested an affirmative comparison between Armenian and Jewish cultures, in view of their shared background of mass 'extermination' (something I never heard Judith discuss), she seemed defensive. Over the years, she and Edmund have observed the Passover Seder in Cambridge at the home of a 'very ethnic' (as we say) cousin who wrote a book on Jewish cooking. Not long ago, she participated in a Holocaust Memorial program at the high school where she teaches. Otherwise, Judith has made little claim to Jewish identity and heritage. When we tried to arrange a gathering for Rosh Hashanah, itself an unprecedented (since childhood) initiative for the family, Judith balked at the idea of asking her department chief if she could take the day off, explicitly for the Jewish holiday, even as I tried to reassure her that school officials everywhere are familiar and comfortable with these requests. 'We don't identify ourselves that way', she said. Judith wanted us to reschedule the Rosh Hashanah gathering for another day; a request she made with the same casualness, incidentally, with which I more recently asked my mother to consider rescheduling the Seder to accommodate my own needs.

It's one thing to be agnostic, socially conscious and socialist, but Judith was (in middle age, she seems to be mellowing) the kind of socialist who could not accede to any criticism of Castro, who had no sympathy for the Refuseniks in Russia and who couldn't acknowledge the seriousness of anti-Semitism there, pre- and post-*perestroika*. It came as no surprise, then, that Judith had no comment on the Soviet practice of generically designating the massacred

victims at Babi Yar, which she visited on the last of her trips to what
was then the Soviet Union with her son, as 'Soviet citizens', with no
acknowledgement that nearly all of them were Jews. It was a trip I
helped pay for with the expectation that Edmund would be able to
appreciate for himself, at a visceral level, regardless of whatever
propaganda he might otherwise see and hear, the extent of Soviet
repression. In all the years I've known her, I've never heard Judith
utter one pro-Israeli word. Conversely, I've never heard her say one
critical word of anyone or anything Arab. Although she has begun to
acknowledge the existence of black anti-Semitism, she attributes it
exclusively to social and economic factors (i.e., to white racism).
Farrakhan is anti-semitic, yes, but it is not his fault. It's ours.

What's so sacred about socialism, I asked my mother one day
when she refused to hear any criticism of Judith. 'Socialism was a
concept the Nazis used too', I explained, 'as in *Nazional Sozialismus*.
My mother looked shocked. As with so much other basic information about the Holocaust, she never knew that that's what the
acronym NAZI stands for – National Socialist German Workers'
Party. ('Nazi', incidentally, is not listed in my new Cassell's German
Dictionary.) Like all socialists, Hitler was fervently committed to the
elimination of *class* – a word that has such resonance when Judith
speaks it you'd think it has six syllables!

Judith did with her Jewishness exactly what Marc Blitzstein,
like other Jewish socialists of his time and today, did with his gayness
as well as his Jewishness. She subordinated it to the greater good of
socialism – i.e., she was able to leave it in the closet. Is it the same
process of subordination that rendered my socialist friend and colleague Eric Gordon unable, in his biography of the composer, to
adequately assess the impact of those closets on Blitzstein's achievements?

On the other hand, I recall the time, pre-Egbert, pre-Arnie
and pre-sobriety, when my own anti-Semitism was still so deeply
internalized, that I inveighed wildly against the Hassidim and orthodox Jews for their truly pernicious hostility toward the gay community and their consistent and major role in preventing passage of
civil rights legislation for sexual orientation in New York City for
more than fifteen years. (Incidentally, their role here was strikingly
parallel to the role of their Israeli counterparts in fighting the Israeli–

PLO negotiations, though I can't recall any instance of their involvement in physical violence against gay people, certainly nothing
comparable to the Baruch Goldstein massacre of Palestine civilians.)
Like Allen Roskoff, who, in a moment of extreme frustration,
responded to Jewish fanaticism at civil rights hearings (on top of
having been ostracized by his ultraconservative Jewish parents) with
the Nazi salute, I said something to Judith about how 'their' obnox-
iousness was the reason we had anti-Semitism and that, as far as I
was concerned, they all 'deserve' whatever has happened or will
happen again to 'them'. Cutting me off with a very serious tone, she
said 'You don't mean that.'

Masha recently marched in the Israel Day parade here in New
York, in the Peace Now contingent. I doubt that Judith would ever
march in a pro-Israel parade under any banner. When she lived in
Israel, where her son was conceived, in the late 1960s, Judith's and
her husband's identity during that time was entirely with the non-
Jewish 'outsiders' and dispossessed – Palestinians, Armenian Christians, and other non-Jews. The psychology of identifying with the
outsiders and dispossessed makes sense and would seem to be an
altogether healthy and constructive adaptation for assimilationist
Jews, if not for one problem: that identification never seems to
extend to Jews. What persons of the left, Jewish and non-Jewish
alike, so often seem oblivious to is that while a subset of Jews may be
militaristic, even fascistic, and another subset may be ostentatiously
privileged, serious anti-Semitic prejudice and discrimination do still
exist, to say the least. Hate slurs and crimes (terrorist murders and
bombings, cemetery desecrations, etc.) directed against Jews remain
common (in fact are rapidly increasing) and are often as virulent as
they come. When they happen, they must be decried, not ignored or
tacitly excused, as they so often are by persons of the left, not treated
as if Jews aggregately deserve anti-Semitism because 'too many' of
them are privileged or otherwise politically incorrect.

Now, of course, 'the new anti-Semitism', as cover stories
from *New York* to *The Nation* have called it, has gotten so bad that
even the most committed socialists at least acknowledge it, whatever their beliefs about its origins or solutions. Meanwhile, the first
comprehensive survey since 1981 of attitudes toward Jews in
America, conducted by the Anti-Defamation League and as re-

ported by Craig Horowitz in the *New York* piece (January 11
1993), shows that anti-Jewish attitudes 'have become more insidi-
ous and now resemble the anti-Semitism that was prevalent in
Europe in the first part of this century. The charges: Jews have too
much power and are more loyal to Israel than America.'

When he visited here last year, I told Edmund – who has
'really blossomed', as Arnie put it, into a young man of character
and sensitivity – how much I admired the historical pieces he'd
written on the black infantry division that was the subject of the
film *Glory*. Like his mother, Edmund is deeply empathic and articulate about racism, among other social issues. Also like his mother,
however, he is reticent and inarticulate about anti-Semitism. In a
good conversation, I explained some of my concerns about the
growth of anti-Semitism among blacks, especially on campuses.
Then I told him something he needed to hear: 'Having one parent
who was born Jewish, you would have been classified as a Jew and
"exterminated" in a concentration camp in World War II. Regardless of how you may identify yourself, regardless of who or what
you want to be, whether you like it or not, you *are* Jewish. Regardless of how hard you try to relegate that fact to the closet, it will
eventually come out.'

Months later Edmund became editor of a campus newsletter
that features two essays he wrote on education and race relations
from a socialist perspective. Here, scapegoating is acknowledged,
albeit perfunctorily, and (implicitly) deplored. Not surprisingly,
however, Jews are likened to the Irish and Italians as peoples who
may have known some discrimination in the past but who must be
regarded, today, as being within the privileged white majority.
Likewise not surprisingly, there isn't a word about his own ethnicity. The newsletter was sent to me by his mother. Several weeks
earlier I had sent Edmund a letter, which concluded as follows:
'The next time you write me I hope you will have seen *Schindler's
List* and will share your thoughts about it with me.' With the
diplomatic evasiveness of a consummate politician (like his
mother), he wrote back several days later that he hadn't yet seen the
film, but hoped to. My experience with Edmund is like a divine
commentary on my own upbringing, when I so resented my parents
and relatives for 'trying to ram their Jewishness down my throat'.

In a recent talk for the Unitarian Church in Cambridge, Judith affirmatively quoted Jewish writers, as well as writers from other ethnic and theological backgrounds, and extolled the pantheism of Walt Whitman. Last year, she briefly dated a Jewish man who is very concerned about resurgent anti-Semitism. Currently, she is out of work and living with an itinerant laborer whose background is New England WASP. With his help, she and Edmund are renovating the second of two three-family houses they now own. People do what they must to survive. Still, it seems a twist of fate that such a hard-line Marxist has become a landlord.

Like my mother and father, and, in fact, like the vast majority of Jews, Arnie did not come from a privileged background. When he was a child, there wasn't enough money to send him to the dentist. Whenever the teacher would ask for verification that he had had his required annual dental examination, he always procrastinated, often inventively. In high school, finally, he went to a dentist on his own. There were twenty-eight cavities. Prematurely, he's now having serious dental problems, Actually, there wasn't even enough money to buy him a new pair of shoes. When Arnie showed his father a hole in his shoe, he was given a wad of paper with which to repair it. 'I guess we were poor', Arnie says, with the same look (and eliciting the same response) as when he told me what a ruggelah was.

Between the ages of thirteen and eighteen, Arnie worked every summer at his uncle's five and dime store, seventy-seven hours a week, seven days a week, for less than a minimum wage. The first summer, his mother took all his money. Several years later a gay friend borrowed all the money Arnie had saved from one summer – several hundred dollars – to buy a car. He never returned any of the money. 'No good deed goes unpunished', as Arnie so often quotes Clare Booth Luce. For his bar mitzvah, his uncle and aunt promised to give him a camera. They never did, and his mother used all the money he was given to pay for the occasion.

Recalling the joy of learning that his autobiography, *Under The Rainbow*, would be published by Morrow, Arnie ran to look at himself in the mirror, 'to see what I looked like when I was happy'. 'I must be happy', Arnie said the other day. 'I have gas.'

254: *Confessions of a Jewish Wagnerite*

The summer of 1990, Arnie was back in New Mexico with a grant from the Wurlitzer Foundation and a tooth abscess, a bigger worry than usual since the diabetes diagnosis two years ago. Now he has nightmares that he will end up like his diabetic father, slowly losing his legs over the course of many operations. The Wurlitzer grant Arnie got was the same one I had to decline, primarily because of the insurmountable reality that I only have a few weeks of vacation a year. Deprivation, if not poverty, comes in all forms.

Which reminds me of another missed opportunity. When I was in my mid-teens, I wrote to John Crosby, Director of the Santa Fe Opera, explaining that I loved opera more than anything else in the world. Was there any possibility, I wrote, of my working there as an apprentice (in stage management, direction, administration)? I was answered very affirmatively and invited for an interview. My parents, however, were uncomfortable. Friends of theirs who lived in Santa Fe warned them that the opera was crawling with homosexuals and that it might be a dangerous place for a teenage boy. My parents didn't force me to decline. Instead, *I* decided to work in my father's X-ray and clinical laboratory, beginning my apprenticeship in medicine. It's a decision I have and haven't regretted ever since, a decision I will and won't regret for the rest of my life.

When Arnie was in Taos three years ago, we celebrated our sixth anniversary at Casa Cordova, the best restaurant in the area. Later, Arnie vomited, probably from the appetizer of grilled chanterelles and porcini. 'Is this God's comment on our relationship?' I asked. 'No', he said. 'It's just the mushrooms. If it were God's comment on our relationship, our relationship would be a bad novel.'

Mom and Bill live in one of the nicer towns in New Jersey – a lot nicer than Newark, where Arnie was born and raised – but adjacent to a German enclave where an old Nazi war criminal was recently found to be hiding out. In the same town lives a former co-worker, a Catholic heterosexual with a large family whose last name is Irish or Scottish. In casual conversation, I was startled when, out of nowhere, he said '*sehr gut*'. Why did he use this phrase? Was it unconscious? Was it German or Yiddish? Another co-worker, a nice Jewish girl, wears a black and gray striped smock. Did it ever occur to her that it looks just like concentration camp garb? When she saw me putting up the Hanukkah decorations in the clinic, she seemed delighted, notwithstanding her longstanding 'democratic' policy, like that of so many Jews (formerly including me) to celebrate neither Hanukkah nor Christmas. A third co-worker, a gay physician from God's country who was active in the gay community's earliest responses to the epidemic, responded to my assessment at an AIDS conference in 1982 that Dr Frederick P. Siegel, the immunologist, was attractive: 'Sure', he said, 'if you like Jewish frizz.' Which reminded me of Dr Jock's term for his own curly hairdo, 'Jewfro', and of the Spanish terms, 'Judios' and 'Jewbeans', for the little white beans with black caps that are common in Mexico.

Throughout Hawaii, where we took helicopter tours of older and active volcanoes, Arnie and I were enamored of the legend of the Menehune, the leprechaun-like little people who were believed to be endowed with supernatural powers and subjugated as slaves. Their existence has never been proven. Were they Jews? we joked. Thereafter, we began to use Menehune as a term of endearment in our love talk. Ironically, what's happened to the Menehune is what seems to be happening to Hawaii generally. The peoples and cultures of Polynesia, what we know of them, are being destroyed and glorified simultaneously by a stronger, more 'advanced' civilization. As the people and their culture disappear, ever greater hotel complexes (e.g., Princess Kaiulani, King Kamehameha) and tourist traps (Polynesian Villages) are erected in their 'honor'. We've done the same thing to our other native Americans on the mainland. They are increasingly enshrined by the very culture that is destroying them. In their vision of the Third Reich, the Nazis planned to have museums of Jewish life, culture and history. Will the epidemic result in the enshrinement of the culture it's destroying, we wondered as we hovered above a town that was buried by still-smoldering flows from Mount Kilauea?

Are Jews dying out? In contrast to the Hassidim, assimilated Jews in America have low birth rates. Certainly that's the case with most of our relatives. Arnie's cousin Cathy Kent has three children, but his brother, married to a woman of Russian Orthodox background who converted to Judaism, has none. My brother has never married and has no children. My sister had one son. Neither of

Cathy's brothers has children. Nor does my first cousin on my father's side, or either of the Segal sisters.

Save the whales. A Nightline episode paired a fifteen-minute segment on King Hussein, the PLO and Israel with a piece on the entrapment of three whales. Were the producers consciously attempting to make an editorial statement with this pairing? And if so, were the whales the Palestinians or the Jews? Or both? Like the Jews, the Palestinians have wandered in search of a homeland. Both peoples have suffered injustice and persecution. I could not answer these questions, but generally rather than comparatively speaking, I do perceive the Jewish peoples to be like the whales. Hunted to the brink of extinction, Jews tenuously entered a period after World War II of finally beginning to be recognized for the gentle, intelligent, industrious and even majestic creatures we (I originally typed 'they') are. Little people. Wandering giants.

When Arnie's beloved Bette Davis died, he cried. I bought lilies and we watched *Now Voyager*. At Reminiscence, the New York clothing store that specializes in nostalgia fashions from the 1940s and 1950s, the latest craze is *Bayern Trachten* (the jacket counterpart of Bavarian *lederhosen*). 'Professor Kantrowitz sucks Jew cock', read a graffito on Arnie's desk at school ... (In a trance-like state, my mind speeds up the basic mechanism of this chapter – of this book and of my life: alternatively flashing loving thoughts of Arnie against free-associated perceptions of anti-Semitism and/or other hatreds, in reality or in dread) ... *Fahrvergnügen*. The new Volkswagen advertisements don't have anything for a paranoid to obsess about, unless you consider the color scheme of the more recent ones – black, white and red. Likewise Mercedes Benz, the full extent of whose collaboration with the Nazis is now documented, has as its current theme an MB researcher explaining in German-accented English to an American researcher that the reason MB has no patent on one of the safety features it invented is that 'some things are too important not to share ...'. Jane Kramer wrote a piece in the *New Yorker* about a German filmmaker who is doing a documentary history of political advertising in the German automobile industry. Why does the new Volkswagen advertisement have Irish music? ... Like Henry Ford, Senator Joseph Kennedy, the patriarch of the Kennedy dynasty, was a Nazi sympathizer ... The

New York Times reported that Arnold Schwarzenegger, whose father was a Nazi and who has married into the Kennedys, got an award from the Simon Wiesenthal Center. Why? Was it like Israel's award to Theodore Blarney? ... Arnie's beard is a New Mexico sunset of burnished reds, the rays of a *goldene neshummah* (the term of endearment my grandfather used for my grandmother), a golden soul that perceives and cares through eyes with a depth and beauty of eternity. His beard is a rainbow but his head is bald – prematurely, Arnie believes, from the hormone injections. Like the nose jobs that were more in vogue in the next generation, hormone injections were the latest fashion among assimilationist Jews ... On the front page of the *New York Times* there was a story about how discrimination barred a Jewish soldier from getting a medal for valor in battle during World War II. A busy and prominent New York theater director – a former Jesuit seminarian whose unreciprocated flirtation distorted his later requests for medical advice – told me he was worried that 'the New York Jewish intellectual critical establishment' would prevent his latest project, a thoroughly generic, disposable entertainment, like everything else he's done, from moving to Broadway. 'Is Frank Rich Jewish?' I asked. 'I don't know, but the *Times* is owned by Jews', he said. (In this instance the play got good reviews, especially from Rich, but audience response wasn't enough to back a major run.) The director, some of whose best friends were Jewish (as he explained when I confronted him with his prejudice), was furious at Larry Kramer for casually mentioning, in a semi-public circumstance, that he, the director, was gay and had AIDS. In the *New York Times* there was a piece called 'Painting a Place in America', about an exhibition of Jewish artists in America from the turn of the century to the end of World War II. Trying to measure what progress this might represent, I wondered how many leading contemporary Jewish artists would be happy to be included in a parallel exhibition entitled something like 'Jewish Artists in America Today'. ... Arnie loves muted colors. Earth tones are his favorites. 'Arniecolors', I call them ... At an exhibit of the black and white photography of Mariette Platty Allen at the Gay and Lesbian Community Services Center, I was startled by a study called 'Transsexual Hookers at the *Déja Vu* [club] in San Francisco'. Between the two hookers in the picture is a Hell's Angel type biker wearing a sweatshirt with a large swastika and an axis of identities: Frisco Choppers, Harley-David-son, San Francisco. The photograph arouses concern about gay life in San Francisco. Should it also arouse concern about the photographer? ... Tim, the lithpy, green and red-haired movie star (there was one photo in one porn mag), wore an SS-looking lightning bolt earring to our lunch ... Arnie's peculiar locution: 'I don't have what to say or what to wear.' Is this manner of speaking Jewish? ... At the gym, a gay WASP told me he saw Larry Kramer on TV. 'You live with him, right?' he said. Translation: 'It's true you live with him or one of those Jews, right?' In a commentary on Herbert von Karajan for *Opera Monthly*, I made what appeared to be the same mistake in confusing Joseph Horowitz and Edward Rothstein ... In a feature in the *New York Times* at the time of the première of *Schindler's List*, Steven Spielberg recalled tales from his mother. One was of a pianist who was playing forbidden music. The Nazis came up on stage and broke every finger on both hands ... 'Happy Barrington'. Arnie said to me. It was the Valentine's Day greeting he learned when he was a little boy ... Knowing of my involvement in issues of Jewish consciouness and having read the 'The House-mates Who Got Nailed', the first installment of these memoirs, Pat Califia sent us yearly Christmas cards, not ones that said 'Season's Greetings' or anything more inclusive, just 'Christmas'. In the last exchange several years ago, we sent her a Happy Hanukkah card ... At the College of Staten Island it takes Arnie nearly two hours to travel to, a notice about student papers was defaced with a swastika sandwiched between the words Nazi and Punks. 'Professor Leibo-witz is a Jew Homo', it also read. In fact, Leibowitz is heterosexual ... Arnie wrote a loving note, attempting to educate a Catholic ex-lover with little gay consciousness who made callous and deeply hurtful remarks about AIDS and the Holocaust, complaining at one point about Elie Weisels's 'incessant whining'. Arnie's letter fol-lowed an earlier response to the lover's anti-Semitism, a telephone response that ended their relationship: 'You complain about the mourning of six million Jews by a few million people for forty years, but not about the mourning of one dead Jew for two thou-sand years by hundreds of millions.' ... In a recent *New York Times* there was an art revue entitled 'Making the Chaotic Manageable'. At first glance, I thought it read 'Making the Catholic Man-ageable'. 'Department Refuses to Fund Holocaust Program' read a headline in Arnie's school newspaper. Under pressure from Phyllis Schlafly and other right-wingers who believe that teaching about the Holocaust must include KKK and Nazi points of view, the Department of Education refused to fund a national Holocaust curriculum for students.

Not a day goes by when Arnie and I don't confront some new anti-Semitic horror like this. In fact, that's how our day usually begins. One of us points out to the other the latest incident being reported in the *New York Times*. The trance continues ... *New York* features a cover story on Lauren Hutton, in which the former swamp girl waxes ecstatic about Ezra Pound and blames 'mono-theism' for the plight of women. Included is a tour of her apart-ment, which displays the complete works of (supreme French anti-Semite) Céline ... Arnie says his feet are starting to tingle, the way his father's did. Meanwhile his 'packratism', as I call it, continues. Was this obsessive collecting of plastic containers, paper bags and other household goods, which he learned from his father, a cardinal feature of the lives of his – or our – ancestors? Reading about the resurgent anti-Semitism under *glasnost*, Arnie said: 'I know about anti-Semitism in Russia. It's real. My mother fled from there. They [Jewish people] couldn't be who they were.' ... Ivana Trump's new clothing line – as modeled by Ivana and her daughter – is domi-nated by what must be the biggest crucifixes yet ... In the early 1970s, Arnie co-hosted a Christmas party that featured Christmas cookies you could decorate yourself with various colored frostings. These are the people the anti-Semites have tortured and murdered in the millions ... At the time of Jerzy Kosinski's suicide, he had been working with a fledgling Jewish culture organization. Did Kosinski and Primo Levi commit suicide from the pain of their pessimism about future prospects for curtailing anti-Semitism? Larry Kramer, Arnie and I shared the same psychiatrist, Norman Levy. Perhaps the main thing he helped me come to grips with, as I slid into the major depression for which I had to be hospitalized, was how tough it is to be Jewish. As an extrovertedly Jewish friend in AA looked me in the eye and reminded me recently, 'It's tough to be a Jew. It always has been and always will be.' ... Breaking the fast with Arnie's relatives in Connecticut, Arnie's Uncle Albert Kent, who calls himself 'Allen', a gifted but 'very ethnic' singing actor and jazz pianist who gave up his hopes for a career in the theater to become a salesman so he could support his family, sang a Yiddish song about a little blossom in the middle of the road that keeps getting trodden upon. In the song, which was Arnie's grandfather's favorite, the blossom is likened to the Jew ... For his fiftieth birthday I gave Arnie what he wanted most, the new Macmillan Encyclopedia of the Holocaust (nearly $500!) ... Sitting with Don Knutsen and Sal Licata at their house, Miramar, in Cherry Grove the summer before they both died of AIDS, other friends were reminiscing about their trip to the Grand Canyon. My heart suddenly ripped open as I recalled Arnie's story of his cousins, newlyweds, who were murdered on their honeymoon there. The murderers were never found. Though robbery appears to have been the motive, I can't help wondering what role anti-Semitism played in their fate. Arnie's family. During the intermission of Herb Gardner's play *Conversations with My Father*, Arnie told me the story of how his mother, who had changed her first name from Jenke to Jean, tried to persuade Morris, Arnie's father, and later Arnie, to change their name to Kent. They both refused. Later, when she divorced Morris and married an Italian, she was ashamed of his name, Macchia, and got him to change it to Michaels. 'Whether dyeing her hair blond or changing her name', Arnie observed, 'she was always trying to hide.' Meanwhile, Gardner's play deals with a Jewish family's experience of anti-Semitism, from being tortured and murdered during the pogroms in Russia and Poland to being Jew-baited in New York in the 1930s. It was the same odyssey traveled by Arnie's mother, her people and mine ... In Cherry Grove on the same July 4 weekend three summers later (the same July 4 weekend with which these memoirs and the AIDS epidemic commenced), I stayed at the Belvedere, which is adjacent to Miramar, the house where Sal and Don stayed. (*Outweek* did a cover story on John Eberhardt, owner of the Belvedere, and Craig, a houseboy and Eberhardt lookalike who became his lover and adopted son.) Next to the Cherry Grove dock, there's a combination clothing and leather store that sells *Bundeswehr* T-shirts in a prominently designated trunk outside the store. The Italian philosophy teacher, my roommate at Belvedere that weekend, who says he was horrified by the recent increase in 'ethnicity scenes' (mostly Nazi/Jew) at The Compound, a leather club in San Francisco, shared my discomfort at the store's connection of the *Bundeswehr* T-shirts and leather paraphernalia. A few feet from the leather store, meanwhile, the ubiquitous New Alliance Party, grossly anti-Semitic (they support Farrakhan) and widely believed to have been backed by the fascist Lyndon LaRouche, was aggressively soliciting passersby. It was their aggression that prompted me to ask who they were. (Because of their bad reputation, they tend to keep their identity closeted.) ... Arnie adopted a new kitten, an orphan he found in Taos. What joy the little one gives him, even the fretting when Taos is 'bad' ... In a piece about the European tour of the New York City Gay Men's Chorus, Craig Sturgis wrote 'In Munich, everyone was prepared to find boys looking silly in *lederhosen* – but there's something about *lederhosen* that makes one want to faint.' ... When I use gel, Arnie says my hair feels like astroturf... For Jim Saslow's costume party, I suggested that we go as Hassids (easy and cheap enough, even at otherwise staggeringly expensive Abracadabra, the Greenwich Village costume shop), but Arnie didn't like the idea – 'too scary' in a world where Jews get attacked every day now, as throughout history, just for being Jews. The Hassidic Jews next door at K & B Photo never smile or say hello. In their faces, I can see that they continuously live with and anticipate anti-Semitism, a little of which I can actually feel as a response to what I interpret as their unfriendliness (even less than the 'average' New Yorker?), but that feeling quickly becomes one of horror as I imagine Arnie and me in costumes that suddenly become real ... There are more and more news stories about skinheads and resurgent neo-Nazism throughout Europe. I recently dreamt that I was confronted by neo-Nazis in Berlin. They demanded I apologize for my negative references to them in this book. I was absolutely terrified and immediately did as they asked ... Driving up Eighth Avenue to Port Authority, the cab passed the Harry Kantrowitz sewing accessories store. In a moment so painful I can't bear to remember it, it suddenly became The Shop on Main Street and Arnie was its proprietor ... One of Arnie's favorite movies is *The Unsinkable Molly Brown*, a corny tale of courage, survival and triumph over snootiness in Denver high society (an oxymoron?) that transcended the sentimental when we watched it again, coincidentally, as Colorado was passing its anti-gay ordinance . . . When I told Arnie how much pain it was costing me to tell the truth I claim to be of such overriding importance in a piece about outing in the music world that outs someone I love and have no wish to hurt, Arnie tells me a little story. At school one of his students was wearing an ugly dress. In those days of likewise believing in the truth as more important than anything else, Arnie took her aside and told her bluntly that the dress was ugly, to which she sheepishly responded, 'Oh, I made it myself.' That's when he learned, he said, that there *was* something more important than truth: kindness . . . In *The Last of the Just*, there's a chapter called 'Lord of the Flies' in which the protagonist has become so profoundly empathic that he can feel the pain of maimed insects . . . At the gym, a person I'm pretty sure is gay has a double lightning bolt tattoo. The bolts have two notches instead of one and aren't right next to each other . . . In Bill Hoffman's play *Riga*, the Hoffman character confronts anti-Semitism in his lover, a black gay man. Reflecting on unlikely opera productions we'd like to see, Bill has the best: a *Capriccio* where half the stage would show scenes of Auschwitz throughout the performance . . . Arnie and I watched a Dutch movie, *The Vanishing*, about a serial killer. For several days following it, I experienced a presentiment of evil, a feeling that I, that Arnie and I, could end up like the gentle, innocent lovers in the film, the victims of something demonic. Is *this* what my interest in Gacy was *really* all about – trying to understand a level of evil that is in fact pursuing me, that I may actually have to face someday? The possibility of that happening seems no more likely than the possibility of Germany taking over Europe and wiping out the Jewish race seemed to pre-Holocaust Jews . . . In the early draft of *Riga*, the Hoffman character (Bill is also known as 'Wolf', and the animal is a symbol for Bill in the play, as it is in life) says he can smell 'it'. He has 'the scent'. 'It' is happening again. More than half of the few thousand Jews who survived the Holocaust in Latvia, where most of Bill's relatives were murdered by the Germans and their enthusiastic Latvian collaborators – who took snapshots (as the play reveals) of each other killing the women – have already fled for their lives. This news story is not from Bill's play but from a feature in a special Christmas issue of *Life* magazine. The date of the issue is not 1942, but 1992. Bill believes that to truly understand the Holocaust, you have to understand where the anti-Semites are coming from. 'You have to see things with Nazi eyes', he says. He's the only Jew I know who has read *Mein Kampf* (twice!) and who has copies of the two most notorious Nazi propaganda films, *Jud Süss* and *Ewige Jude*, which even Arnie has never seen, and which Bill is planning to screen for Arnie, Michael G. (my co-sponsor) and me. Incidentally, it was the comparisons of Jews to vermin in *Ewige Jude* that was the inspiration for the villains 'rat aria' in *The Ghosts of Versailles*. 'It' *is* happening again. In *Riga*, the Hoffman character literally becomes a wolf, howling the call to remember, and to awaken ... At the conclusion of this year's classes, one of Arnie's students – among the many students and colleagues at the College of Staten Island who, over his thirty years there, have sent him letters of praise and thanks for his shining example – told him something another teacher had said to him years ago: 'You wear your jewels on the inside.' ... On the subway there was a man with an SS tattoo – two lightning bolts – over his right jugular vein ... For several years now, black zealots (Muslims? though they dress in Arabic garb and their symbol is the Star of David, they don't clearly identify themselves as such) in Times Square, mostly on 42nd Street opposite Port Authority, have been loud-speakering their hatred of 'the so-called white man', of 'faggots' and of 'those rats in Brooklyn with the skullcaps' ... When Arnie arrived for this semester's last class at CSI, there was a Christmas gift from his students, a miniature plaque on an easel that read: 'To Teach Is to Touch a Life Forever' ... In the most recent revival of the harrowing John Dexter production of *Dialogues of the Carmelites* at the Met, the tribunal who announces to the imprisoned nuns that the Revolution has found them guilty of treason, and that they are condemned to death, is black. At a substance abuse recovery program meeting in Palm Springs, a low-life's short sleeve shirt casually revealed a swastika tattoo ... Hotsy totsy.

Arnie brought home a pictorial with essays called *Tattooing* he found prominently displayed at B. Dalton. The first issue of a

264: Confessions of a Jewish Wagnerite

series, this one was devoted to 'The New Tribalism' and featured a discussion of 'The Swastika'. As with *Big Daddy and the Muscle Academy*, the film documentary on Tom of Finland, what's being discussed is art, not politics, so the swastika's ability to profoundly upset people for whom it still has ethical and moral significance is not even mentioned, though it is hinted at in the essay's final paragraph:

> The unfortunate usage of the swastika in the last fifty years has occasioned much prejudice and misunderstanding. Since the Second World War, the symbol has purposely been omitted from numerous books on Oriental and American Indian art! But strictly from a graphic standpoint, the bold powerful strokes of the swastika continue to fascinate all those interested in the geometry of art and life.

The news has returned. Its newspeak is precisely as Orwell foresaw. Did Israel become Orwell's Goldstein? . . . More exploding volcanoes, this time in Japan and the Philippines . . . On another channel there's an interview with George Friedman and Meredith Lebard, co-authors of *The Coming War with Japan*, who waxed ecstatic about their association with their editor, Michael Denneny.

Following the Crown Heights confrontations, which occurred in the wake of the grossly anti-Semitic tirades of Leonard Jeffries, which occurred in the wake of the grossly anti-Semitic tirades of Louis Farrakhan, there were a number of pieces about the new anti-Semitism, including some from writers who have been consistently identified with the radical left – e.g., Richard Goldstein. But there was only one demonstration, which was well-attended considering how poorly it was advertised. Over the years, I'd made special efforts to hear the Reverends Dr Martin Luther King Jr and Jesse Jackson in person, and I'd marched for racial equality and against apartheid in South Africa on a number of occasions, but I had never participated in a demonstration against anti-Semitism, for Israel, for Soviet Jewry or anything else Jewish. This time I was determined to be there, but so primally terrifying was the idea of publicly identifying myself as Jewish that my subconscious managed to botch it. Just as in my recurrent dreams of being late in my travels to destinations that are usually unclear, I arrived late, and wasn't able to find Arnie, who had gotten there on time. But I did get there.

Over dinner with Erick Neher just prior to the publication of the Gottfried Wagner interview, my self-possession was such that I was able to speak sincerely and comfortably of my concerns. I pulled no punches in stating the belief I share with Dr Wagner that Bayreuth has failed to come to grips with its past and my belief that Wagner, like but much more so than Ezra Pound and T. S. Eliot, will always be a beacon for anti-Semitism. In fact, there's no other artist of even remotely comparable stature whose legacy of prejudice has done more damage. There is no final solution to the Wagner problem. Certainly censorship isn't the answer. But as long as Wagner remains political, which will be as long as anti-Semitism endures, there must be discussion. I know Erick shares this conclusion, notwithstanding his unwillingness to respond to the Gottfried Wagner interview when it was published, even when Dr Wagner himself specifically asked – through me – for his reaction; a situation that will be rectified, however, when the two meet, as they are now set to do, in my home.

At the corner market, they were out of clementines, the seedless tangerines that are so easy to peel. They're in season only a few months a year. In their place are mineolas, tangelos, honey tangerines and blood oranges. The first time I saw blood oranges, a relatively recent hybrid of oranges and ruby grapefruits, I experienced a moment of absolute terror. It was during the Anita Bryant period, when oranges became symbols of 'pro-family', anti-gay (and anti-Semitic?) hatred. So strong were these associations that I wouldn't eat any kinds of oranges throughout that whole period. That was more than a decade ago. When I saw blood oranges again the other day, I didn't even wince, though I did remember. This time I decided to try them. I wasn't bothered by the old thoughts, but the association with blood – they really look like oranges that have been injected with blood – turned me off. I ate one and gave the other to Arnie, a more adventurous eater.

Back in Orlando, I did my daily meditations during my daily walk around Lake Eola Park, with its Fantasy-Land fountain, oriental pagoda, neon bandshell and rich bird life. On this occasion

I finally remembered to do something I had often wanted to do, but kept resisting, perhaps because it was something I associated with older folk. I brought pretzel and cookie bits for the animals. Mostly I wanted to feed the turtles, giant carp, ducks, geese and cranes, not the more ordinary starlings and sea gulls. Actually, I hadn't previously noticed the sea gulls in Orlando, which is about fifty miles from the ocean. What are they doing so far inland, I wondered. Perhaps they're fleeing a storm or other catastrophe – the way my relatives, the Segals, ended up in Chicago? When I fed them I was rewarded. Their cries changed from the wails of deprivation I'd heard on the beach in Miami to squeals of joy, as they caught the pretzel pieces in mid-air. Are any other species this adept at in-flight feeding?

Around the time of my hospitalization for depression, following the period of my affairette with Egbert and bottoming-out on alcohol, marijuana and cigarettes, I experienced an attack of acute paranoia at the substance abuse clinic where I worked. It was Easter and one of the patients took it upon herself to place a crucifix above my name on my office door. Taking this as an insult, I exploded with anger. The patient claimed she did not realize she had done anything insensitive. She didn't even know I was Jewish, she said. This Easter, one of the counselors placed an Easter egg on the door to my office, which I share with my non-Jewish physician's assistant, just as she placed eggs on all the other doors in the clinic. I remembered the earlier episode, but there was no pain or fear. In their place were consciousness, acceptance and serenity. Leaving the clinic, a co-worker wished me a Happy Easter. With genuine good will I wished her the same 'and a Happy Passover'. 'To you too', with a smile, was what came back.

I celebrated my forty-fifth birthday with Percy and a new sponsee. Arnie sent me a 'Birthday Fish' (play on wish) card. The face of the card is a photo of a multi-colored reef fish. It elicited mixed feelings of sweetness and sadness. Sadness in that the diving and sea life and coral reefs and opera and chocolate desserts are pleasures and fantasies my workaday, overweight and hypertensive reality can no longer sustain or share with Arnie, who dislikes opera, who isn't a diver, who's fair-skinned and can't take much sun, who's diabetic and with whom sexual intimacy has faded.

Sweetness in that Arnie is nonetheless so much like me, and with me. Still my little Jewish pastry. My partner on the solitary voyages that are our lives.

Glowing memories of the evening Arnie and I watched *Million Dollar Mermaid* on television. There we were looking out at ourselves from the large portrait I had commissioned from my close friend, David Alexander, with whose lover, Richard Howard, Arnie and I went to see Visconti's *Ludwig* when it was re-released in its original (uncut) version, and with whom I've sparred about Wagner over the years. The portrait was completed in time to become the centerpiece for the fiftieth birthday party I gave for Arnie in our home. Surrounding us in the portrait are morsels of our lives, individually and together. There are pansies, cats, fish, orchids, books (a book entitled *Richard Wagner* emerges from the head of a ceramic cat, who stares at us and our three cats with an equivocal expression – a face from Art Spiegelman's *Maus*) and videotapes, pieces of coral, opera recordings, monkeys, a small Buddha, skulls and shells. Interconnecting them are floating symbols: a yellow Star of David, Silence = Death, an AA (Alcoholics Anonymous) triangle, GMHC (Gay Men's Health Crisis), GAA (Gay Activists Alliance). The Star of David reproduces the cloth star from a Dutch concentration camp Arnie was given by Neil Alan Marks, who later sold me the 1930s postcard of the allegorical painting of Einstein confronting Hitler. Arnie had the badge framed and placed it in a central position in the collage he's been working on throughout the twelve years of our marriage, not so unlike the collage Anne Frank was starting to make on her wall. Touching the star in the painting is a recreated snapshot of Vito Russo and Jim Owles. Other recreated photos, in black and white, are of Arnie and me at Yad Vashem, at Niagara Falls, and of us marching together with other gay friends and writers – Nathan Fain, Robert Ferro, Brandon Judell and Jim Saslow, at the 1987 March on Washington. And there are pictures of us by ourselves: Arnie with his shaved head and mutton-chop mustache from the early days of the movement, when Arnie, Jim and Vito led GAA; and me in full scuba gear, my hair much thicker and longer than today's astroturf. The little portrait of Arnie the GAA activist is painted more intensely than the other black-and-white photo recreations and is positioned in such a way that it is possible to see the entire conception as Arnie's dream and achievement. At the top of the painting, in a place that clicks the viewer in, is a pair of ruby slippers with red sequins that seem to draw their sparkle from the sanguineous, plum-colored background that flows through the painting and gives it such life.

Watching the Esther Williams/Busby Berkeley spectacular in Arnie's embrace brought me back to so much that I loved and wanted. I was a champion swimmer in grammar school, the first to earn an athletic letter in high school and, several years ago, I was certified in scuba. Swimming and diving are still great pleasures for me and they will always beckon, but today my sport is paddle ball. Since I began writing this installment, my game has improved to the point that I now get to play with the better players. I finally joined the Men's Health and Fitness Club, and the middle-aged players are now just the guys. When Mel, one of the older, Jewish and better players, sings 'Ooo-rah-cheem!' – as he does whenever he slams home a killer – my laughter is less inhibited than it used to be. Meanwhile, as I patted myself on the back the other day for my dearly earned self-awareness and assertiveness about being gay and Jewish, I caught myself thinking about lying, for the first time, about my age. I was speaking to a younger man, a paddle ball player, as we left the gym and walked down Seventh Avenue. I was on my way home.